HUMAN UNDERSTANDING
AN ENGINEER'S ANALYSIS OF LIFE

GETTING TO THE BASICS

HUMAN UNDERSTANDING
AN ENGINEER'S ANALYSIS OF LIFE

GETTING TO THE BASICS

Robert J. Brust, PE, SE

Henschel
H A U S
publishing, inc.
Milwaukee, Wisconsin

HenschelHAUS Publishing, Inc.
2625 S. Greeley St. Suite 201
Milwaukee, WI 53207
www.henschelHAUSbooks.com

Ordering Information:
Quantity sales. Special discounts are available on quantity purchases by corporations, associa-
tions, and others. For details, contact the "Special Sales Department" at the address above.

ISBN: 978159598-538-5
E-ISBN: 978159598-539-2
LCCN: 2017948153

Publisher's Cataloging-In-Publication Data
(Prepared by The Donohue Group, Inc.)

Names: Brust, Robert J.
Title: Human understanding : an engineer's analysis of life : getting to the basics / Robert J. Brust,
PE, SE.
Description: Milwaukee, Wisconsin : HenschelHAUS Publishing, Inc., [2017] | Includes bibli-
ographical references.
Identifiers: ISBN 9781595985385 | ISBN 9781595985392 (ebook)
Subjects: LCSH: Life. | Thought and thinking. | Reality. | Psychology. | Religion.
Classification: LCC BD431 .B78 2017 (print) | LCC BD431 (ebook) | DDC 113.8--dc23

DEDICATION

This book is dedicated to all the people in my life who have directly or indirectly brought about this book. This includes the people who have brought sorrow, as well as joy, into my heart. All these people and experiences have helped me to understand that pain and effort, as well as acceptance and giving, are very important parts of coming to understand life itself.

TABLE OF CONTENTS

PREFACE

uman Understanding is an analysis of life from an engineering perspective. It looks to develop some simple basics from which other related life issues are more easily understood. Typically, fields of thought in philosophy, psychology, archeology, astronomy, and even religion rely on information and evidence that fits the conventionally accepted paradigm and ignore information and evidence that does not fit. Engineers deal with fixed numbers and facts and overlooking any information or evidence that may affect a project brings the risk of failures and lawsuits.

In this book, we look at information and evidence that is overlooked by conventional thought and see how it could affect conventional thought. Perhaps the biggest oversight looked at is that of consciousness independent of the physical body. Evaluation of the evidence is not based upon any religious consideration. It should be realized that the existence of an independent consciousness would indicate a purpose for life beyond physical existence. It would likely also mean there are consequences for how life is led.

The book also looks at such things as growth in knowledge and other aspects of life in ways not generally considered. In the end, the biggest universal simplification that can be made in life is that it is virtue that is responsible for order and joy and culminates in the highest reality—love. Conversely, vice is responsible for chaos and eventual despair. This simplification holds for all dimensions and levels of conscious reality.

—Robert J. Brust

INTRODUCTION

What is life about? There are more than an adequate number of ministers, psychologists, philosophers, and friends who will tell you what they think. They might even they tell you what you should think. But it is what you actually think and believe that really matters. You need, for yourself, to come to an understanding of what will actually lead to a feeling of self-worth and personal happiness. If you don't, life may hold some unpleasant surprises, even when you follow some supposedly good advice. This book is intended to help people develop a personal understanding of what is important for happiness in life.

I grew up like so many other people, living in my own thoughts of what is important, which I learned from my upbringing. I adopted a personal view of reality based upon my experiences and how I perceived their importance. I never questioned the accuracy of my thoughts. Tragedies have a way of awakening people to new thoughts of what is important in life.

Unfortunately, the process is not normally pleasant. In my case, it was the death of a son and subsequent divorce. I'm sure other people have faced worse than I did and held it together. But it destroyed my personal view of what is required for happiness in life and caused me to question my personal beliefs. What is the purpose of living? How do I really know what is important and of value? What was it I was doing wrong? After a time of self-pity and counseling, I came to realize that I needed a better understanding of what is important in life. At that point, I decided to search for an understanding of life that would make sense in this world—past, present, and future. I have put 27 years of work into the understanding I have arrived at.

In engineering it is most important to have a good understanding of basic concepts. With the understanding of basic concepts, in any field of engineering, the secondary and peripheral issues are more easily understood. Likewise, a good functional understanding of life comes from an in-depth understanding of the basics of life upon which the rest of life makes sense. I realized that I needed, as do most people, a simple, logical, and basic understanding of life upon which to make informed decisions, rather than having my thinking controlled by the world around me. I believe there is a reason for living that, if properly understood, can lead anyone to a rewarding and fruitful life regardless of personal circumstances. But without some simplified way to understanding life, life is anything but simple.

This book also looks at many of the controversial issues of life to open the minds of the reader. It does so not to confuse, but rather to point out two things. The first thing is that, as humans, we do not know as much as we would like to think we know. The other point being made is that no matter how controversial or complicated life seems to be, what is important in life always goes back to the basics, which provide the clarity needed when facing these issues. Understanding the basics removes the need to be worried about numerous controversial and irrelevant issues that people fight over. It also makes those things, which are important, more easily understood. In understanding the basics, the path to self-worth and personal inner happiness becomes clearer.

There are many books written on mental health and wellness from which to learn. However, many of these books, in my opinion, address specific areas of wellness in such length and technical language that the average person is sometimes lost or turned off. This book focuses on the basics needed for understanding how we think and function, as well as how these things can affect our lives. It employs simple language in usages that should be easy to understand. The book does not take any specific psychological perspective about life, of which there are many. Please realize that although this book focuses on some philosophic issues, it is not meant to say that people should not enjoy life. When properly understood, life should actually be more enjoyable and feel more worthwhile.

As an engineer, I learned that I always have to be open to many different possibilities. If all possibilities are not accounted for, no accurate evaluation can be made. With that in mind, it should be realized that although various fields of philosophy, science, and religious knowledge express definitive positions on specific issues, in many cases these positions not only overlook, but also conveniently ignore conflicting information. Pointing out the controversies, as this book does, is meant to show how conventional thinking can close the mind to other possibilities, including a better understanding of life. It is in opening the mind to new possibilities that a new, and possibly better, understanding of life can be found.

Conventional thinking itself is a controversial subject. As will be pointed out, people tend to think as they were induced to think by their upbringing and education which, in modern society, teaches conventional ideas. Science, religion, governments, educators, political parties, and other groups try to educate as many people as they can with what they have decided is important. The result is the minds of many people are closed to new ideas and even to good, creative, old ideas that have never been accepted.

I try to address various subjects and controversies from perspectives that may not have been previously considered. I also include facts, some of which are not well known or much thought about. I do not try to arrive at definitive opinions. To do so would be contrary to the idea of opening the mind. I would hope that after reading this book, people will realize how blindly accepting what they have been taught could lead them away from truth and happiness.

This book points out basic realities that I have come to accept as applicable to all life throughout the universe and which do not change regardless of all the scientific, religious, educational, or even political opinions that can come about. An understanding of these basics can bring a worthy purpose and direction to life. The actual message of this book is a message of hope. The best is yet to come—if we so choose.

The book is divided into four main sections. Part I in simple language, presents a basic understanding of how we mentally function and how that affects what we think, feel, say, and do. Part II is more intellectually interesting and addresses the fleeting nature of reality, both personally and in general. It also addresses the reality of independent consciousness. Part III addresses various topics that are directly and indirectly related to the overall purpose of this book. They help develop an understanding of how the basics apply to various topics and to various aspects of life. It includes a philosophic look at religion and also imparts some new and even controversial thoughts about prayer, nutrition, and exercise. Part IV addresses steps required to make changes in thought reality which are needed to make changes in life. The last chapter summarizes the basic realities of life.

Since I am an engineer, not an historian, philosopher, psychiatrist, or theologian, this book should not be considered a scientific study. This book is based on personal observation of people, on personal experiences (some learned the hard way), on research, on a logical progression of thought, and on discussions with people in the fields of healthcare, psychology, and medicine. It is also based upon independent study of the major religions and study of the history of metaphysics.

There is a section on engineering to begin the book. This section provides some insight as to how an engineer thinks and why an understanding of the basics and an open mind are important to overall understanding of any subject. Only with a good understanding of the basics and with an open mind, in any field of endeavor, can advancement be made.

Before going any further, I will mention that my thinking has been affected by being witness to a specific event—the last moments in the life of our son Andrew. He had no strength left and the priest had given him the Last Rites. We expected him to just quietly die very shortly. But then Andrew suddenly sat up and reached up higher as he said; "They're coming to get me." At that point, he died.

AN ENGINEERING PERSPECTIVE

Engineering is described in the *New World Dictionary* as "the science concerned with putting scientific knowledge to practical uses, divided into branches such as civil, electrical, mechanical, and chemical engineering." The branches can be further subdivided. I am a structural engineer, which is a division of civil engineering.

To utilize something properly, it is important to understand how that something functions. Before there were any basic engineering principles to rely on, there was no understanding of how things worked. Steps to utilization began with observation, guess work, and testing to establish some basic principles. Once some basic principles were established, they were utilized and improved upon. Sometime in history, people observed repeated patterns, and they began to utilize these patterns as basic principles.

For example, they realized that water always ran downhill and that some plants produced edible food. That basic understanding developed into farming and irrigation. People recognized that understanding how things worked could be advantageous. They realized they could sharpen certain stones into spearheads. And, possibly, after being hit in the face with branches while walking too close together in the woods, they realized there is spring energy in branches. That realization eventually led to the bow, which would make small spears fly further. The basic principle of the lever—that a small force moved a long distance could move a large load a short distance—eventually brought about the pulley and the building of the ancient world wonders.

The understanding of basic principles is important. But every bit as important is developing applications of the basic principles. Take the pulley or the arrow for instance. Just because the lever was understood, creating the turn block and rope pulley was not a simple next step. The arrow may seem a simple step from the spear, but until someone thought to add feathers to the back of the arrows, they did not fly straight.

Engineers, in the various engineering fields, develop new and better ways to utilize basic principles that help improve the world we live in. Figuratively speaking, the world has been lit up by developments in electrical engineering; structural engineering has built up the world.

My field of structural engineering deals with the understanding of forces and how to resist or to utilize those forces so as to be able to build buildings, dams, bridges, towers, highways, and other structures. Through experience and research, maximum forces from gravity, wind, and earthquakes are estimated for specific areas of the country and form the basic loads likely to be exerted on structures. There are also basic loads for superimposed loading for different usages such as school rooms, libraries, gymnasiums, and storage areas. Dynamic loading and impact loading also have to be taken into account. The structural engineer calculates all the maximum forces that may be exerted on all structural members and with that knowledge, is able to design structures. In large buildings, that can be complicated. Fortunately, there was another basic engineering principle discovered—loads distribute to supporting members proportional to the stiffness of the supporting members. Knowing basic principles, basic forces, and by calculating the stiffness of members, the engineer can begin to design a structure.

But beyond forces, the structural engineer must also understand the engineering properties of the building materials used on various projects, such as concrete, steel, aluminum, various types of stone, and even plastics. An understanding of basic engineering principles and an understanding of the capacities of the various building materials are all required to build the new wonders of the world. No matter how complicated a structure may seem, the design always goes back to known basics. If an engineer does not understand the basics, he/she can easily get lost or make some major mistakes.

There is also a lot of sophistication in the engineering of structures and other engineered products today. Advancements in engineered materials and how they are used grow with each passing day. The new sophisticated usages come with imagination, analysis, common sense, and perseverance in new ways the basics can be implemented. Surprisingly, many of the big advancements have been made in engineering and in other fields of endeavor not by highly educated people. They were made by less educated people who understood the basics of what they were working on and who were not restricted to conventional thinking. They had minds open to new ways to apply the basics.

Ben Franklin had two years of formal education before dropping out of school at the age of ten. Edison had no formal education. Bell dropped out of school at the age of 15. Michael Faraday had no formal education. Einstein dropped out of school at the age of 15 because the teaching was to rigid and left no room for questioning. Later he did go back to school. Leonardo da Vinci was only home educated in elementary reading, writing, and math. Most people would also be surprised to know that Winston Churchill had limited education due to the fact he did poorly in school or that William Shakespeare and Mark Twain had little formal education. Andrew Carnegie, only formally educated to age 13, became the world's richest person in his day.

When the basics of what a person is trying to achieve are well understood, the advancement a person can make in any field of endeavor is related to that person's imagination, analysis, common sense, perseverance, and sometimes enough guts to challenge conventional thinking. The person who stays within the limits of accepted knowledge and understanding will never amount to more than average. A mind open to all possibilities, including what seems impossible, is required to move beyond average or at least beyond conventional.

Engineers can hypothesize on many issues. But when it comes to implementation, they cannot afford to make mistakes. Engineering mistakes can be costly and catastrophic. For that reason, applied engineering is not based upon just hypotheses. Good engineering requires that if there are any potential anomalies and other reasons to suspect there may be a problem, such issues must be fully resolved before the engineering project moves forward. That is different than science, which can make suppositions based upon interpretation of the majority of scientific evidence and then hold many of these suppositions to be fact, even when there is evidence that does not correlate with, or even contradicts, the suppositions.

As Thomas Kuhn, an American physicist, historian, and philosopher, most noted for introducing the concept of "paradigm shift," points out in *The Structure of Scientific Revolutions*, scientists work within a paradigm of what is considered legitimate to scientifically question. If something is questioned that does not fall within the accepted paradigm, it is not considered acceptable and is dismissed. When something is discovered that does not fit the paradigm, it simply fails to be something the paradigm recognizes. The assumption is there has been an error made somewhere in any conflicting discovery.

Whether it is because of pride, out of the embarrassment of being wrong, or fear of other possibilities, scientists, and even educators, tend to discard conflicting evidence to accepted suppositions until such evidence proves overwhelming. For an engineer, it is not acceptable to regard any scientific supposition as fact when there is conflicting evidence. The next few paragraphs provide an example of an accepted scientific paradigm for which there is significant conflicting scientific information that has been ignored.

The example is intended to get people thinking rather than as any commentary on the accuracy of the paradigm.

Until the middle of the 19th century, there were only guesses on the age of the earth. In 1862, Lord Kelvin, based upon earth's cooling, calculated its age as 98 million years. But in 1897, he revised its age to 20 to 40 million years. The first real scientific dating arrived with the advent of radiographic testing in the early 20th century. That testing put the earth's age about 4.5 billion years, which is now an accepted scientific paradigm. What most people, educators, and even some scientists are not aware of is that age determination by radiographic testing is based upon specific assumptions that there is no way to validate and which are now coming into serious question. (1)

New research has raised serious questions as to the accuracy of all the various methods used for radiographic age testing. Science has also failed to account for conflicting radiometric test information—the small radiohalos that exist around various minerals in rock. Small radiohalos indicate that there was a very quick hardening of the rock, which is not consistent with assumptions made for the age of earth arrived at by radiographic analysis. Instantaneous petrification of wood is now known to be possible. (2) Yongsoon Shin and colleagues at the Department of Energy lab converted wood to mineral in days. Also in the July issue of *Sedimentary Geology* five Japanese scientists reported their experiments on the rapid petrification of wood as an indication that silicified wood (fossilized with silica) found in ancient strata likewise have been rapidly petrified. However, conflicting evidence to the accepted paradigm, is disregarded and the paradigm remains in place.

An engineering analysis of research, based upon assumptions about which there is conflicting evidence, will say that no definitive conclusions are possible, only opinions. Science can be most useful for developing understanding, opinion, and even fact. But if science is going to proclaim something as fact, all conflicts must be accounted for. Perhaps the scientific paradigm of the earth's age is correct. At this time, however, there are too many loose ends to accept such figures as actual fact.

If you want even further controversy and conflict on the age of rock and how it was formed, look up articles like Impossible Stuff found in Coal and Rock or the London Hammer (3), on the Internet. There is no scientific explanation for these things. Things are not always what they appear to be.

There is not much history about Christopher Columbus or any about his schooling. But there is a story (most likely fictitious) that after discovering the New World and getting back to Spain, he was told by some other ship captains they could have done the same. At that point, he called his detractors together and challenged them to set an egg on end. After hours of trying, they gave up and challenged Christopher to do it. He took an egg and brought it down hard enough on the table that it flattened the end slightly and the egg stood. At first the detractors said he broke the egg. He replied that he never said anything about the egg not being cracked.

The detractors then said they could have done the same if they had known that fact. To which Christopher replied that they had their chance, but he was the only one smart enough to do it. True story or not, this is what would be referred to as creative thinking. (Please note that there are various versions of this story.) Although engineering involves the understanding of basic principles, more important to progress is the understanding of how they can be creatively applied.

From my engineering perspective, in many ways, I see the proper approach to life as similar to the proper way to approach engineering. In both, it is important to have basic fundamentals from which to make good life decisions. Without these basics, there is no fixed reference upon which to accurately evaluate what life is about. Without some basis for evaluation, people, and even some engineers, will typically conform to what is considered most acceptable, even when conforming may not be the best thing to do. Also, as in engineering, with an understanding of the basics and a mind open to new thoughts, we can discover the potential happiness of virtue and love. And we can come to understand those things which can lead us away from real happiness.

PART I

HOW WE FUNCTION MENTALLY

THOUGHT REALITY

Our physical nature is based upon how the brain, through the nerves, signals the body to react to what is encountered. The brain functions like a computer. Physical reactions, and likely some mental reactions, appear to be the result of how the brain is programmed.

However, how the mind thinks goes beyond inborn programming. It incorporates what it learns into what we call "personal knowledge." What we mentally come to know, to believe, to value, and to expect is typically based upon what we learn from our early experiences and environment, although additional changes in knowledge, beliefs, and values occur later in life. Because of the differences in such things as religion, class, wealth, education, nationality, and other differences in our formative years, each of us has a somewhat different view of what is important in life and what to expect from life.

The result is vast differences of beliefs, values, purpose, mental notions, and thought habits, as well as different expectations. These form what I refer to herein as "thought reality." Although the brain acts as a computer, the human mind can do what a computer cannot do. It can ask how and why. It can also decide to reject the present beliefs and values of thought reality and find new values and beliefs. But the biggest difference between human minds and computers is that human beings can look beyond their own wants to forgive and to love. We might want to look at our lives to see if we are acting more like humans or computers.

"Thought reality" should be considered the personal thought reference each of us uses to evaluate what we encounter and upon which we base our decisions in life. It is also used to establish our expectations. It includes our conscious and subconscious beliefs, mental notions, sense of values, and perceived purpose for which we are living. It presents us with our personal image of what we believe life is all about.

The mind uses what knowledge it possesses, and the mental notions of thought reality, like a computer uses input information to arrive at an answer. Therefore, it is important to realize the correctness of our beliefs and values is limited by the knowledge, understanding, and even the misconceptions that form of our thought realities. Regardless of the limitations and the correctness of our thought reality, we use it as a reference to evaluate what we think is right and wrong, to decide what is important to us and what is to be avoided, to decide if hard work is necessary, to determine what is pleasurable, to decide what constitutes happiness, to reason if a Higher Power or even UFOs exist, and so on.

Right or wrong, we typically accept the correctness of our thought reality because we can only evaluate something new based upon what we already have come to believe and value. What thought reality accepts as basic truth becomes the reality upon which personal decisions and beliefs are determined. The problem is that if what is considered basic truth is not correct, all the evaluations of the mind, based upon that incorrect truth, will be incorrect. It is critical to properly understand the basic realities of life.

There is a cute story about different thought realities and how different their choices can be. Three men were adrift on the ocean in a raft. When their ship had gone down, they had managed to only rescue two cases of beer. The three men consisted of a German, an Irishman, and a person who had been isolated from other people all his life. The German and Irishman, not expecting to be saved, decided they might as well end it all with a good time. So they drank, told jokes and laughed and got the third man to join in. For the first time in his life the third man was having a good time with other people.

They had just finished the last beer when they spotted a bottle floating near the raft. When they picked it out of the ocean, a genie inside the bottle said that he would grant them three wishes if they let him out. They agreed and the German wished first. "I vish I was back in de taverne mit my friends." And instantly, he was there. The Irishman was next and he said, "I wish I be back at the pub with me friends." And instantly, he was there. The third man was reluctant to wish until the genie demanded he do so. At which time he said, "I wish my friends were back here with me."

Thought realities are considered actual reality and as such tend to remain relatively constant. But they can and do change with the perception of new values. New values can be new thoughts, actions, or things perceive as desirable. Not many people initially thought they needed car air conditioning or microwave ovens. However, once people realized how beneficial they were, these items became of value to thought reality and desired. Thought reality changes when it perceives new values or new truths.

Because people typically spend most of their days involved with material things, the values of their thought realities are mostly based upon material things. That makes logical sense. Few people spend any significant amount of time thinking about the values of the intangible beliefs in life and how important those beliefs are related to happiness. As the pace of life increases, people are more involved with keeping abreast of what is important to physical well-being and spend less time trying to understand the purpose for life itself.

For that reason, most people, in an attempt to understand life, opt to listen to supposed experts, such as ministers and psychologists or even scientists, to find something that is reasonable and valuable to what they already have come to believe is purpose for life. People generally look for what fits into their present thought reality, rather than anything that would challenge it. Thus, without new values, thought reality tends not to change.

In *Human Understanding*, we come to understand that people need a fixed basis on which thought reality can correctly and logically operate and evaluate. If there is to be any true reality, the fixed basics need to be universally true. This book looks to establish fixed basics for understanding life that make logical sense, yet which do not depend upon religion, science, or politics.

LEARNING—THOUGHT REALITY
DEVELOPMENT

W̲e begin life knowing nothing. But our brains are geared to learn very quickly. There are many factors that influence how we learn. Though not critical to how we live, understanding how humans learn is very important to the future of humanity. Therefore, this chapter presents some issues that affect human learning and intelligence. You might want to visualize how these issues were possibly a factor in your learning.

In 1989, Dr. Hallam Hurt, then chair of the neonatology at Albert Einstein Medical Center in Philadelphia, began a study to assess the intelligence of cocaine babies compared to that of other babies. To her surprise, her research showed that the biggest factor in the intelligence differences was not cocaine exposure; it was a byproduct of poverty.

Over the last thirty years, there has been a significant amount of research on learning and on things that affect intelligence. That research is telling us that nurturing is extremely important in learning and that those things that affect nurturing significantly impact learning. Research also shows that poverty has a significant negative effect on nurturing and indirectly affects intelligence.

The January 2015 issue of *National Geographic* had a very interesting article on learning in the first few years of life. Sources and information used in the article are listed as: tests at Robert-Debre hospital in Paris; research at the Max Plank Institute for Cognitive and Brain Science in Leipzig; study by psychologists Todd Risley and Betty Hart at the University of Kansas in Lawrence; research by Patricia Kuhl at the University of Washington in Seattle; and research of Charles Zeanah, a child psychiatrist at Tulane University, Nathan Fox, a developmental psychologist and neuroscientist at the University of Maryland, and Charles Nelson, a neuroscientist at Harvard.

This article points out a number of factors important to learning, especially the critical importance of the first few years of life. It also points out the importance of face-to-face interaction with adults for brain development in babies. In some tests, children watching strictly videos showed little to no learning compared to children given the same information face to face. Personal interaction with children is critical to their mental development. And the earlier this interaction begins, the better the baby's brain development. That is because, as the article points out, a baby's ability to learn actually peaks around the first year of life. The amount of social interaction in the first few years of a baby's life will have a very large influence on the baby's cognitive development and eventual intelligence and socioeconomic status.

Risley and Hart also established a link between the number of spoken words heard by young children and their IQ level. The more words heard in the first two years, the higher the eventual IQ. That link is not surprising, since children who hear more have more information on which to evaluate, while at the age they learn the most.

It should also be realized that children with almost no social interaction in early years develop more feral behavior. Although the importance of social interaction and nurturing is mentioned in the article, it does not address the effect of emotional bonding and of giving children a feeling of self-worth through acts of recognition and love. It must be important if children learn when personally taught and learn little with the same teaching on video. Perhaps teaching by videos may not be the best way to educate. That fact is important to realize in the modern texting world.

These articles not only point out important aspects of learning, they also highlight the fact that parents have a greater influence on the lives of their children than they might have realized, especially in the first few years of life. Good parenting takes much effort. Parenting has consequences, both good and bad. Parents need to understand the importance of teaching and social interaction if they want their children to be average or above in intelligence, as well as to feel good about themselves. They also need to be aware of the adverse consequences of poor nurturing and bad parenting.

It is easy to blame social issues on poverty. But when the importance of good parenting is understood, it should be realized that intelligence and even possible future poverty of children is greatly dependent upon their parents, regardless of socioeconomic status. Poor parenting and the results of poor parenting can easily be passed down from one generation to the next. Poor parenting is a very significant aspect of poverty.

Without considering different physical and mental abilities, the two biggest factors associated with learning are desire and repetition. (Natural curiosity is considered desire.) Without the desire to gain new values, thought reality will not make an effort to change. Natural desire to learn is the front door to initial thought reality. But because there is no initial thought reality on which to evaluate what is desirable, an infant's initial learning comes through observation of repeated words and actions of others. Children use observation to learn how to act and what is of value. Consequently, children's thought reality and reasoning tend to initially develop along the lines of what they are exposed to. This includes morality and respect or disrespect for authority.

Although repetition is important for initial learning, after the evaluation process begins, the biggest factor in what children learn is what they perceive is the most valuable to learn. Their desire for happiness requires it. Even as adults, what we perceive as valuable and desirable is often based upon what we perceive as valuable to others. We like to think we teach and children learn because of what we tell them.

However, children learn mostly from what they perceive as valuable to others. We don't have to tell them to walk and to talk. For children, what adults seem to want the most and what generates the most enthusiasm in adults and teachers is what children will want the most. This holds not only for children; it is true for anyone who perceives there is some new value they would like to acquire. Teachers need to realize that if there is no enthusiasm, what is being observed may be of no perceived value.

Understanding the importance of enthusiasm is also important for parents, business leaders, politicians and even ministers. Perhaps one of the reasons videos are not successful in teaching young children is the lack of actual physical human enthusiasm. Good or bad, when something or some attitude is perceived as valuable, it can spark a desire to understand and attain. Love your work and your children will want to follow in your footsteps. Present a negative attitude as important and your children will develop a negative attitude. Present your work and/or your attitude in a way perceived as important and you can effectively teach or deceive a multitude.

A problem with thought reality is that it develops habits of evaluation based upon whatever it has come to believe will result in the most value. That makes change difficult without some major change in life values, and even then, it can be difficult. Entering new thoughts and concepts into thought reality means it is often necessary to bring them through the back door. As repetition is important to initial thought reality, it is also the back door to an already developed thought reality. Repeat something often enough and it will be remembered, even when the desire is to forget it. I would never have learned math skills without repetition. I may be good a math now, but I never liked it. As motivational speaker Zig Ziglar said: "Repetition is the mother of learning, the father of action, which makes it the architect of accomplishment."

It is the repetitive thinking about new concepts that allow them to enter thought reality and permits people to expand their thinking and accomplish so much more than they would otherwise. The need to repetitively focus on new ideas and new concepts will be stressed often in this book. As we grow older, thought reality tends to become more opinionated and new ideas are harder to accept. If we want to amend present thought reality, in some way, it is necessary to repeatedly focus on what changes are desired and why.

That said, be careful with what is learned by repetition. Repetition can also introduce harmful images and desires into thought reality. Even specific undesirable words, repeated often enough, can become part an undesirable part of a vocabulary.

Another influence on learning is emotions. Emotional problems can back people into corners where they do not know how to relate to situations or to others. This has led to the introduction of Social and Emotional Learning programs, referred to as SEL. Although SEL programs use the same basic tools of repetition and desire to implement, it is important to realize that how things in life are implemented can also have an effect on learning. These programs focus more intensely on such things as self-awareness, self-management, empathy, perspective, and cooperation. These tactics are very useful in any learning atmosphere.

A major factor affecting thought reality is conformity. Children's thought reality about what is important can be significantly influenced by the intensity and means by which their parents and others teach them to conform. One of the more important points in this book is the need to open one's mind to see other perspectives. Unfortunately, being taught to conform can have a detrimental effect on children's ability to think for themselves. Conventional thinking has its place, but when it interferes with the ability to evaluate the pros and cons of what is being taught, it is detrimental.

Research, as well as observation, tell us that teachers and parents like children to conform. Life is much easier when children conform to behavioral standards. But it is not only behavior conformity that takes place in the education system. There is also conformity of curriculum. Sir Ken Robinson, who has published a number of books on creativity, (4) said, "We are educating people out of their creativity." Schools take children from entirely different backgrounds with different skills and different cognitive abilities and make them all conform to whatever standards of education the school wants ingrained into them. The more children are required to conform, the more likely they will eventually expect that everything should conform to conventional thinking, even when conventional thinking is flawed.

An interesting test of the effect of requiring conformity was administered by Dr. George Land to 1,600 people in each of four age groups. (5) The test was meant to determine the amount of creativity in each age group. It was the same test that NASA used to determine innovative engineers for the space program. The test results indicated that at five years of age, 98 percent of individuals were considered creative. The number dropped to 30 percent by 10 years of age and went down to 12 percent by the age of 15. At 25 years, the number was only 2 percent.

A most important aspect of personal happiness is the ability to think and act independently. That is probably the reason that some children rebel against conformity. Not too surprisingly, a 40-year study, published in *Developmental Psychology* of 745 children-to-adulthood conducted in Luxembourg found that the breaking of rules and defiance of authority were the best predictors of students ending up with the highest income. The brain that is not geared to conform is more creative and is more valuable, as well as more personally satisfied.

School systems generally push children to conform. Tests are standardized even for children of different aptitudes and talents. Many educators realize that it is not healthy to ignore creativity. But being able to control students and control what they learn seems to be more important in many education systems. Because of potential violence in schools and the potential cost of education addressing children's particular aptitudes, I can understand why the education systems want conformity. But there are still ways of encouraging creativity.

With children, some amount of misbehavior should be expected. It is their way of being creative and learning at the same time. Although significant misbehaving should not be tolerated, there should be way to encourage some amount of creativity. There can be creative ways to encourage and control at the same time.

When I was teaching a religious education class to high schoolers, I told the students that I was very intolerant of class disruptions. However, I told them that as long as they paid attention and learned their lessons quickly, I would make time to discuss some other things they would like to discuss. I also told them that if one of the students said something or did something so clever that it made me laugh, he or she would get away with it. It took them a few poor tries to realize it had to be really funny or clever to make me laugh. But after that, both the class and I had some good laughs and some good discussions. They realized I respected them and they respected me. They actually spent time outside of class thinking of ways to get me to laugh, as well as thinking of some challenging questions to ask me, including questions concerning the topic for discussion in the class. The classes went well and we all enjoyed them.

Although this approach or something similar would be difficult with children who have already learned there are few consequences for class disruptions, it could work if started with young children. Giving children the ability to discuss stimulates their creative thinking. Create a constructive challenge to children's creativity and everyone wins and learns.

Conformity is so prevalent in society that many of us will typically think negatively about any person who does not conform to what is considered acceptable conventional behavior or belief. Such people are criticized, ridiculed, and even persecuted when what they do or say is not even harmful. Conformity teaches bias. Learning is about opening the mind to new ideas.

The proof of how close-minded even educated adults are, including scientists, is the fact that more than ten Nobel Prize-winning ideas were originally ridiculed by other supposed expert scientists. Where would science be if it were not for some scientists willing to challenge contemporary scientific beliefs?

Conformity also encourages viewing specific ideologies as either right or wrong, rather than simply as opinions. A good example is the polarization of politics. Polarization is caused by people seeing only their own ideology as the only correct way to view issues, rather than trying to understand the legitimate points of all sides. I believe that the modern education system, in which children need to conform to specific ways of thinking, is a significant factor in the increase in political polarization. And the polarization is perpetuated by reporters who subtly put their polarized thinking into what they write. I wish they would just give us, as Jack Webb of the old *Dragnet* TV series used to say: "The facts, Ma'am, just the facts."

In the building business, it is very apparent that governmental boards will typically hire big-name firms for the design of government buildings, even though they have the least amount of leverage over such firms. What they overlook is the fact that unless a project is very prominent, it is not likely the best designers will be assigned to the project. It might be a better idea to hire a very good smaller firm over which they have much leverage. But it seldom happens. Why? Because that is the way it is almost always done, so if something goes wrong, they can say they hired the best firm and consider themselves free of blame.

The research of Polish psychologist Solomon Asch (6) found that although people prefer to act independently of others, they normally conformed even when they knew what they were doing was counter to their own values. Whether it was a question of their judgment or fear of being different is not certain. However, he also found that when one person dissented from conformity, others would follow. They then have a different opinion to conform to. It is important for each person to realize that they all too often let others dictate what they say, do, and sometimes think. Adolf Eichmann (7) considered himself a normal person who was just following orders. The need to conform can even overcome concern about right and wrong.

As previously mentioned, we tend to be slow to change our thought reality without a new value to be gained. That is because significant change to thought reality would mess with our present ability to evaluate what we encounter. Significant change in thought reality would mean that much of our present thought realty is not reality at all. That is difficult for many people to accept. Significant change can only come about when we are able to accept that much of what we think is only personal opinion and that we still have much to learn.

Also important to understand about how humans function is that specific thoughts themselves can become addictive. The more children, or even adults, are exposed to a specific thought, without any reason to question it, the more likely it is to become an established thought or even belief. If the mind does not question a specific thought or belief, after a while, it becomes a thought habit and potentially a thought addiction.

In the learning process, we are presented with many different images of happiness and self-worth—money, friendship, religion, pleasure, recognition, revenge, love, things selfish or unselfish, things smart or foolish. We choose what we believe is most valuable for us, based upon our thought reality's perceived values. It is therefore important to understand what values will lead to a sense of self-worth and personal happiness.

While wealth and intelligence may bring moments of personal satisfaction, they do not bring inner peace or fulfillment. Cognitive thinking and a high IQ are actually not needed for happiness and a sense of fulfillment in this life. For babies, happiness comes from being given love and good nurturing. But once we begin to think for ourselves, happiness comes from within—how happy we are with ourselves. This is a very important lesson to learn.

Our present thought reality has been greatly influenced by different socioeconomic conditions and varying upbringing. Whether these things have hindered us or blessed us have been beyond our control. But it is how we live in the present and choices we now make that control our lives. Learning is not confined to what we have been taught. It is only confined to what we allow ourselves to think. Learning does not stop until we give up trying to learn more.

There is much to learn about happiness and what brings it about. As with any subject, the more we study a subject, the more likely we are to understand it. Happiness is no different. We can choose to be satisfied with where we are in life or we can choose to learn a new way of living that could bring more happiness. We get to choose what is important to us. And then we get to live with the consequences of our choices. Therefore, much care must be taken in deciding what is important to our thought reality.

The most basic choice we make in life is the choice between virtue and vice (good and evil), although most of us choose some of each. The existence of virtue and vice is a basic fixed reality of the universe. It is virtue that creates order and happiness in life and opens us to self-worth, to joy, and to love. It is vice that open us to selfishness, disorder, and chaos.

In *Human Understanding*, we realize that what we initially learned, and even our ability to learn more, has been greatly influenced by how we were raised. Similarly, we influence our children by how we raise them. We need to understand the importance of early nurturing and teaching. We also need to understand that the desire to learn comes mostly from observation of what other people are enjoying.

Desire and repetition are the keys to learning. We must be careful in how we teach because too much conformity can kill creativity. Another aspect of modern education is that most all of it focuses on physical reality. The brain is physical. But feelings themselves are not physical. Feelings are intangibles that are the result of thought reality perception.

As happiness is related to how we think, it is the intangibles which can lead to inner happiness and self-worth—or the opposite. There is more to consider about life than just the physical aspects of life. We all need to spend time learning those things that promote inner happiness and self-worth, as well as to learn the consequences of life choices before they are made. As in engineering, knowing the basics is most important. But also, as in engineering, it is important to know how to apply the basics to life.

Means and Methods

"Means and Methods" is actually a construction term. In the construction business, there are a number of ways to actually build something. Each contractor bidding on a project will have different equipment, different experience, different skill sets, and different ideas of how things can be integrated for construction speed, profit, and so on. Therefore, the procedures of building a project are left up to the contractors involved. The contractors can use the "means and methods" they are familiar with to accomplish the project goal. In life, each of us develops our own means and methods of accomplishing what we want to accomplish, which is uniquely our own.

As children are building their thought reality of what is important to them, they are also building their mental concept of what is the most effective way to accomplish what they perceive is valuable to them. Due to different genetics, environmental issues, and any inborn personality traits this will be different for each child. Individuals each develop their own means and methods for getting what they want.

We all like to think that we are open-minded and flexible. But the truth is that we are more creatures of habit than we like to think. When we find something that seems to work well for us, we tend to stick with it. Even as babies, each of us quickly developed methods to get the attention of the people around us. The first instinctive method was crying. Soon after, we observed methods of interaction used by our parents, siblings, and others used to get what they wanted, and we imitated those we sensed worked best, as well as other methods we found successful.

My wife once got into the back of a car in which a four-year-old girl was sitting. She sat there without fastening her seatbelt. The little girl looked at her and said, "Ass——." It was as much a shock to her mother as it was to my wife. It turned out her parents occasionally referred to people, in other cars, who did not wear seatbelts in that terminology.

We initially learn by imitation. A mother who gets her way by pouting can be a big influence on a child, as can a demanding, drunken father. We may have learned to imitate the words and actions of a pouting or demanding parent and found it successful for us. Crying or demanding are just a few of the methods we might have learned to get what we wanted. Maybe smiling worked wonders for us or maybe being persistent helped. Submission, deviousness, and even rebellion are some of the methods of interaction we might have developed in response to dominating parents.

Some of us learned to act weak to get what we wanted through sympathy. Some found that tantrums got a positive response. Some of us found different methods of interaction worked on different people. We all developed methods or combinations of methods to try to get attention and the results we wanted or to avoid punishment. These methods often reflected the interaction methods of one or both parents or even siblings, especially when those methods worked for them.

The influence of a parent was addressed in the book *My Mother / My Self: The Daughter's Search for Identity* by Nancy Friday. But it should be realized that a father will also have an influence on his daughter, as will both mother and father on a son. However, the biggest influence will generally be the parent who is the same sex as the child, as that is the parent the child can most easily relate to.

Whatever the circumstance associated with learning, children learn what actions or inactions best result in their getting what they want or perhaps result in the least amount of inflicted pain. The methods that work best are used again and again, to the point that they become habits. And when the habits of interaction are successful, children, and even young adults, tend to refine these habits as they grow older, rather than developing other ways to relate to others. Why throw away what has already proven successful, especially if it is going to take time and effort to change and we are unsure about the result?

The nuances of the interaction habits may change somewhat with new relationships and other responses to us, but the initial underlying habits of getting attention and what we want most often remains, at least to various degrees, as we age. Those of us who refine the habit of acting weak are often referred to as "low self-esteemers." Without realizing it, we develop a thought reality habit in which acting weak or helpless to influence others is important to our ability to get what we want. When such a thought habit is well developed, we may actually perceive ourselves as helpless victims. And indeed, we are victims, but mostly of an addictive thought habit.

There are many methods of interaction that can become habitual or even addictive. There are those of us who develop the art of pushing others around physically or even verbally. We are referred to as "bullies." Some of us develop an ability to be deceptive or argumentative to get what we want. Still others of us learn to get what we want by lying, cheating, and stealing. There are some of us who find that honesty and kindness works best. And some become submissive or even devious. How ingrained in us these various methods become depends somewhat upon how successful they are in getting us what we want, and how open we are to developing new tactics. The majority of us developed combinations of ways to get what we think we need, and these become the primary way we relate with other people. We need to realize this fact about ourselves.

Our "means and methods" not only determine to how we relate to others, they also determine how we approach other things in life, such as how we approach problems or face difficulties. I see the influence of my mother on the way I perceive and approach problems. She was a down-to-earth, smart, woman who, when faced with a problem, rather than get upset, would say "Now what do we do to solve the problem?" That underlying thought process eventually led me to try to solve my personal problems by attempting to understand life. I also see that same influence of our mother on most of my siblings, where there is logic and little sympathy. Our father helped in that as well. His normal response to what he considered unnecessary crying was typically "louder and funnier." The result was a more rational and unemotional approach to life for us children, especially the older children.

I'm sure that most everyone can see their parents reflected in themselves in some ways. But whether the methods of interaction were generated by our genes, our upbringing, our inborn personality traits, or from our own creativeness, we use them for whatever purpose we have in our minds. Unfortunately, the "means and methods" we use can become such a habit that we do not even think about the ramifications. We just do as we always do. The result can be the low self-esteemer, the perpetual martyr, or perpetual bully, the arrogant person, the rationalist, the aggressor, the overly affectionate person, the person who worries about everything, and so on.

We need to consider what the way we relate to other people, and how we approach problems, tells us about ourselves. We might be surprised. Problems with relationships could be the result of our habits of interaction. Maybe we are our own worst enemy. We need to open our minds to see how our thought habits, whether copied from those who raise us or from some other source, could be affecting our lives and influencing others we communicate with. It should be important to know what other people think about how we relate to them. We all have the opportunity to choose and to change how we relate to others. But before we become willing to change, we must first understand how we are controlled by our habits of interaction.

In *Human Understanding,* we realize that to get what we desire, we typically rely on interaction habits of our thought reality. We realize how we think and act is most often related to habits developed during youth, which may not serve us well later in life. Therefore, we need to look at what our habits of interaction tell us about ourselves. We need to open our minds to be as critical of ourselves as we are of others. We need to realize that the habits of our present thought reality can keep us from moving forward to a happier life. We can choose to open our minds to new and better ways to relate to others and to problems in life or we can choose to stay where we are. We get to choose.

Purpose, Values, Habits, and Change

What is the purpose for living? What is life all about? Am I just a combination of cells that have evolved to think and run? Is my purpose just to be an insignificant step in the evolutionary process? Do I have my own real purpose? Why do I bother doing what I do each day?

We need to understand the importance of purpose in life for it to have meaning. Although we do not normally realize it, purpose is present in all that we do. Extending a helping hand or even taking revenge has a purpose of some kind. Because we are creatures of habit, we often act without conscious consideration of how we are going to act. We just do it. We often fail to realize there is a conscious or subconscious purpose for all that we do and that purpose(s) plays an important part in our happiness or unhappiness.

We learn words to develop a thought image of what is trying to be communicated. In a similar way, the different values we learn help us form a thought reality image of what we believe will most fulfill. The desire to attain the perceived reality of happiness, of self-worth, of being loved, or even of satisfaction, normally becomes the main purpose(s) in life. This is true whether what we value is influenced by a perception of an afterlife or not.

Purpose and value are sometimes confused. They are different. Survival is a value. Surviving itself is a purpose. Survival is our initial purpose. After survival, the next important purpose we normally seek is to attain a sense of happiness or fulfillment. In that quest, what we perceive as valuable to happiness, mental satisfaction, and/or sense of fulfillment becomes our purpose(s).

Purpose follows personal beliefs. Some of us may visualize the highest value as an eternal paradise and live for that purpose. Some of us may see the highest value as simply being kind and helpful. And some of us may see it as having the great material existence. The human mind can think of many purposes to live for. The stronger the sense of purpose, the greater will be the resolve to overcome obstacles to attain what is desired.

When we picture a man without a specific purpose in life, we see a man who doesn't know what to do with his life. He goes from one thing to another looking for some form of happiness or satisfaction. He may be happy when he is occupied with something enjoyable, but otherwise he is easily bored or even mentally lost. When we picture a man with a purpose, we see a man who knows what he wants out of life and works at it. He is not bored. He may not have the best purpose, but at least he has a direction for his efforts and can feel good about himself when a goal is achieved. Purpose is the fuel upon which the inner fire of life depends. Without purpose, there is no reason to keep the fire burning.

Is there a focused purpose in your everyday life? Is there even a specific reason or purpose to get up each morning? Or do you just get up because it is time to get up? We all need focused value and purpose for life to have meaning. We need a reason to get up, especially when we experience grief, suffering, disillusionment, or depression, and when there is no one to encourage us. Each of us needs a positive purpose for which we act. When no positive overall purpose comes to mind, we may eventually have no reason to get up, or even a reason to live.

Purpose can be a factor in our health and happiness. A 2009 study of 73,000 Japanese men and women over ten years found that those with a strong sense of purpose lived longer. (8) Also in 2009, Richard Leider, founder of Inventure, The Purpose Company, teamed up with MetLife to assess purpose in the lives of over 1000 adults. They found that those with a high sense of purpose spent more time and attention on loved ones and their communities. They also enjoyed more satisfying relationships as a result. A 2013 report by UCLA, in collaboration with the University of North Carolina, found that "happiness derived from purpose in life has a healthier genetic effect than pleasure seeking." (http://ucla.in/13UG3gI)

Richard Leider states that "Purpose is fundamental. It is not a luxury."

Purpose is also very important to families, communities, and governments, as well as individuals. Groups function well when there is a strong common purpose. At the beginning of the Second World War, the United States was not even in the top five military powers. But with a common purpose, within a few years, it quickly became the strongest military in the world.

With a strong, meaningful purpose, there are fewer dissenters. Where purpose is weak or unclear, discord grows, values change, and families, societies, and governments begin to lose effectiveness. This is especially true when the original moral purpose and values, upon which those groups were founded, is no longer considered that important. Maintaining purpose and values is important to the health of families, communities, and governments.

As purpose is focused on attaining a value, it would be wise to have healthy values. Unfortunately, many of us have some unhealthy values and resulting purpose that have been imposed upon us. For real inner happiness, each of us needs to search for the values and purpose that will lead to inner happiness and self-worth. Inheriting the purpose(s) of the people who have influenced us may not lead to happiness, especially if the influential people are not people of inner happiness and self-worth. The following can provide an insight into what values might and might not provide the most happiness.

The *Huffington Post* published an interesting article, dated January 6th 2016, entitled "The Psychology of Materialism and Why It's Making Us Unhappy." According to the American

Psychological Association; American well-being has declined since the 1950s, while our consumption has increased.

David G. Myers, author of *The American Paradox: Spiritual Hunger in the Age of Plenty*, states "Our becoming much better off over the last four decades has not been accomplished by one iota of increased well-being."

The value required for real happiness is not physical. Material things only satisfy the body. To have a sense of happiness, the mind needs to be satisfied. Material things and physical pleasure only provide moments of personal satisfaction, but they do not provide an overall sense of happiness and fulfillment, which are derived from mental satisfaction and self-worth.

In looking for values that actually increase the sense of happiness and self-worth, on a purely sectarian basis; we can look at the value of helping other people. Mark Snyder, a psychologist and head of the Center for the Study of the Individual and Society at the University of Minnesota, stated, "People who volunteer tend to have higher self-esteem, psychological well-being, and happiness...All these things go up as their feeling of social consciousness goes up, which in reality, it does. It also improves their health and longevity," from *Live the Good Life: Why Helping Others Makes Us Happy*

Spirituality can also provide purpose. A study at the University of British Columbia, published in the online edition of *Springer Journal of Happiness Studies*, according to researcher Mark Holder, shows that children who feel their lives have a meaning and value and who develop deep, quality relationships—both measures of spirituality—are happier. Researchers Dr. Michael Yi and Sian Cotton at the University of Cincinnati, in a study of 155 teens, found that higher levels of spiritual well-being were associated with fewer depressive symptoms and better emotional well-being. And the benefits of spirituality extend even where we might not expect it to, in an article entitled "Spirituality Equals Happiness in Kids," in the 10th Anniversary issue of *Aspire Magazine*.

The *International Journal of Management and Sustainability* published an article entitled "The Relationship between Spirituality and Meaning at Work and Job Happiness and Psychological Well-Being: A Spiritual Affective Approach the Psychological Well-Being." The study showed that spirituality and meaning at work have a positive and significant relationship with job happiness and psychological well-being.

When we look for an overall fulfilling value on which to form a purpose in life, it cannot be something selfish, for selfishness does not satisfy the mind. It only gives a temporary illusion of fulfillment. It is interesting that there are monks all over the world who, with the concept that life is for a higher purpose, can willing give up the good things and pleasures of the world and feel a more permanent sense of fulfillment in so doing.

Purpose provides a meaning that forms the direction of our lives. Without meaning, there is no direction. And direction in life will be dependent upon what is understood about life. A poor understanding of life can lead people to do irrational things and result in a bad feeling about self. Again, purpose will follow belief. It is therefore very important to develop a belief base upon what is actually important for a happy and personally fulfilling life.

Although we develop values and purpose for what we do, most of what we actually do, we do without thinking. Seldom do we take the time to evaluate our words and actions or even the correctness of what we are thinking. Most of how we act or respond is habit. We previously looked at how we develop "means and methods" of interaction and how they develop into habitual ways of relating or even thinking. Unless we encounter something unfamiliar, we normally react out of habit. And unless we are aware of that fact and are open to learn new ways to get along with others, what we do, say, and how we act will not change. When people are not willing to open their thought reality to new values or new ways of understanding, their thought habits can actually become addictions. We all need to occasionally evaluate why we think, speak, and act the way we do.

Changing minor habits is difficult. Major changes in life are even more difficult. It is most difficult because it means changing what we have considered reality. We must realize that where there is unhappiness in life, it is our thought reality telling us we are unhappy. What is needed for significant change is to establish a new thought reality that will bring self-worth and inner happiness to thought reality. But this is most difficult, because changing thought reality often requires us to admit that a lot of the unhappiness in our lives has been the result of our own closed-mindedness. Change will likely require letting go of some of the security of present thought reality and some of the perceived value of worldly pleasures we may not want to give up.

To some people, changing life values would be like leaving solid land to cross a lake filled with imaginary monsters when there is no assurance there is another side. Another great deterrent to change is fear of ridicule or the loss of personal relationships. Some people may be just too proud to change. Some people may feel comfortable with present values, no matter how selfish those values are, especially if life seems to be good. Others will not care to make the effort.

Then there are the tactics people employ as an excuse to avoid responsibility for the problems their choices create. The most obvious one is to blame others for difficult situations or problems. People pass themselves off as victims and do not look at how they often create their own problems. Another tactic is to change some habits (those that are not important to thought reality) without changing the basic thought reality values. Changing values may be difficult, but happiness may require real changes in the understanding of what life is about.

We all too often play mind games with ourselves to assure that our present thought reality values remain in control while we tell ourselves that we are changing. However, if the underlying value for a habit remains important, no habit can be broken indefinitely. To believe otherwise is a delusion. Should we decide to give up smoking or alcoholic drink, we may be able to quit smoking or drinking, but it will not be possible to eliminate the desire unless the mental and physical value of the habit is overpowered by something of more value or the habit's value is lessened. If we abstain from smoking or drinking long enough, the physical value of the habit can be reduced. But unless the value, mental as well as physical, is replaced by something more valuable, the old desires will not go away and the habit will return as soon as the old desire overpowers the alternative value. Should we find a new beliefs or new values, those new beliefs or new values must remain or the old habits will return.

When trying to make significant changes in life, it is often necessary to look at purpose for which life is being led. This is because purpose affects what is perceived as value and values affect habits. Where purpose is selfish, values are selfish, and habits are selfish. Where purpose is loving, values are loving, and habits are loving. Where purpose is not strong, values and habits are often a mixture of selfish and loving. What we value in life goes back to that which gives meaning to what we do. It goes back to purpose.

What has been indirectly said is that free will is not deeply associated with the words, thoughts, and actions of our everyday lives. Most thoughts and actions are controlled by habit of a somewhat rigid thought reality. Free will, on the other hand, is mostly associated with choices that affect beliefs, purpose, and sense of values of our thought reality, especially those that challenge our basic thought reality as to purpose for life. We all have the free-will ability to evaluate our present thought reality and resulting purpose and values. And we all have the free-will ability to change purpose and values if we really want to.

We may not all have had a good education or good environment to grow up in, but if we want to claim we have free will, we also have to admit that, as adults, we make the decisions that affect our beliefs and our lives. Sometimes we will make bad decisions. And maybe some bad decisions are necessary to learn what is important in life. But good or bad decisions, it is in those moments of mental contemplation between the fixed realities of good and evil, of contemplation of purpose for living, and of contemplation of what is necessary to live a worthy life, that we actually use our free will. Those are the free-will decisions that have the biggest effect on our self-worth and inner happiness.

Do you use your free will to question your habits, values, and purpose for living, or do you allow your thoughts and actions to be controlled by worldly wants and physical cravings? The latter has little to do with free will. Free will requires that the mind be open to thoughts and ideas about the reality of virtue and vice, as well as the physical values and purpose for which we are living. It is with free will we choose between virtue, which brings order and love, and vice, which brings selfishness and chaos.

There is a short story about a young man sent to get something in a cabinet. Unfortunately, the cabinet door had a combination lock. The young man summoned the minister who had asked him to get the object. But the minister also had no idea what the combination was. The young man was ready to give up, but the minister explained that prayer and fortitude open many doors and that he would not give up. So the minister prayed and looked upward to heaven. Almost immediately after that, he spun the lock dial and opened the lock. The young man was astounded and asked the minister how the numbers came to him. The minister replied that someone had written the numbers on the ceiling.

When we look for new ways to solve problems, new doors can open for us, often in surprising ways. When we decide that we cannot open new doors, or decide not to make an effort to open them, they will never be opened.

As people get old and realize the end is near, the reduced ability to accomplish worldly desires can have a significant effect on thought reality. For many people, it can lead to depression. In some instances, people see no purpose in remaining alive. However, for those who open their minds to an afterlife, purpose and the value of life do not end with physical death. Whether an afterlife exists or not, where there is purpose, there is hope and satisfaction.

In *Human Understanding*, we realize that those purposes and values in life, which we choose for ourselves, will determine our eventual feeling of fulfillment of happiness and love. We realize that we operate mostly based upon habits that reflect the purpose and values for which we are living. Should there be any dissatisfaction with life itself; it is most likely associated with what thought reality considers purpose(s). If there is no fixed purpose for living, or if purpose is based upon that which will not actually fulfill, life will feel empty. A happy life is one that is based upon the intangible feeling of accomplishment for the good of others and society. It is based upon the fixed basic of virtue, which leads to order and love

In *Human Understanding*, we also realize that what really counts in life is not that we totally succeed at all we desire, but the realization that we are making the effort to succeed at some purpose. It is in making the effort to do the best we can that we feel good about what we are doing. But that will not come without having a meaningful purpose for living. We have the free will to search for and live for such purpose. However, such purpose will often require a change in thought reality. The question we have to ask ourselves is: Are we willing to do what it takes to change our lives as is needed to find real happiness? The real use of free will is in choosing the purpose for which we live.

LEVELS OF THE MIND

Most people acknowledge there is some type of subconscious level to the mind. Some of us believe there is even a spiritual subconscious level. Scientists admit there is much which is not understood about matter, energy, or even time. But, unless something can be proven, it is just a hypothesis. Science has measured brain waves in an unconscious person, so it has established that there is something beyond the conscious mind. But exactly what transpires beyond the conscious level is not really known. Is there a spiritual level of consciousness, as many people believe, or are subconscious levels just a function of how the physical brain works? Modern science has a major limitation in evaluating the subconscious

Modern science deals with measurable, physical reality. It also assumes that the various levels of the mind, whether conscious or subconscious, are all a function of the physical brain. To explain the freedom of the brain to make choices that do not necessarily follow logical sequences, science has proposed that the brain is a quantum computer that does not have to follow logical sequences.

Actually, the concept of the brain as a computer is very logical. I do not doubt that the brain itself functions as a sophisticated computer. But I contend that the brain is only part of the human mind. The conclusion that the mind only consists of a physical brain ignores much pertinent non-physical evidence, information, and statistical improbabilities that conflict with the accepted scientific hypothesis.

From an engineering standpoint, if there is a significant amount of conflicting information and evidence, only opinion is possible.

With regard to the mind, there is anecdotal evidence and there have been mental feats that are unexplainable in physical reality. It should also be noted that not all scientists, philosophers, and other educated people agree with the hypothesis of the evolution of consciousness. Even artificial intelligence expert Piero Scaruffi, author of *Thinking about Thought* and *The Nature of Consciousness*, said, "I am conscious. I am made of cells. Cells are made of atoms. Atoms are elementary particles. If elementary particles are not conscious, how is it they can yield a conscious being like me?"

The case for the existence of an independent consciousness is presented in the chapter "The Reality of an Independent Consciousness." Probabilities are addressed in the chapter "The Concept of a Higher Power." It should be noted that it is in more modern Western philosophy that the non-existence of an independent consciousness has arisen. In Eastern philosophy, the concept of an independent conscious is manifested in the concept of reincarnation. Even some early Christians accepted the preexistence of souls, as will be further discussed. Ancient philosophers Aristotle and Plato accepted the concept of an independent soul.

For actual research into the mind itself, we turn to psychologists and psychiatrists, not philosophers. Based upon observation, tests, and how well observations align with different hypothesizes, they try to come to an understanding of how the mind works. Although the basics of how the brain functions are beginning to be understood, it is way too early to assume that the brain is the source of all human consciousness. But what is understood is still important for utilization and for further evaluation.

In the past few hundred years, psychology and psychiatry have vastly expanded the understanding of how humans function mentally. Recently there has been significant neurological investigation of how the brain functions. But it has done nothing to explain consciousness.

History and the writings of psychologists and psychiatrists show us that humans are very complex beings. We may not know it all, but thanks to thinking and analyzation of some devoted researchers, we can make some educated hypotheses on how the mind works. The writings of the psychoanalyst Carl Jung have had a profound influence on modern psychology. Jung, founder of the school of Analytical Psychiatry, provided humanity with a good hypothesis on how the mind works, which is accepted by many, but far from all, people in the field of psychology. It involves various levels of the mind.

Jung took Sigmund Freud's original concept of Ego, Id, and Super-ego and looked at them in a different way. Although Jung's hypothesis is no longer be the prevailing concept in psychology, the concept of separate levels of consciousness is too profound to disregard. A separate level of consciousness could actually include an independent consciousness.

Jung's ego consciousness is the level of consciousness we use to make decisions affecting our everyday life. Beyond the ego, Jung's levels of consciousness also include the "personal subconscious" and the "collective subconscious." Personal subconsciousness can be thought of as the origin of subconscious urges that affect our thoughts, feelings, and attitudes. They are based upon personal lifetime experiences, including those we do not remember.

For Jung, the collective consciousness is considered a matrix of all conscious occasions of humankind. This can include intelligence, dreams, phobias, aggressiveness, the ability to sense things, fuzzy memories of ancestors, and other things that in some way are passed on genetically. Research has shown that genetics can play a part in how we consciously think.

I accept the concept of the ego and personal subconscious, mostly because they make sense. With the collective unconscious being totally the result of genetics, I have a problem and I see another possibility. To me, it makes more sense that Jung's collective unconscious is an independent consciousness. It could be that the mental perception of such intangibles as virtue and vice comes from an independent inner consciousness, and it could be that this inner consciousness connects humans to a higher level of reality than physical reality.

It should also be realized that what Jung considered the collective unconscious being an independent consciousness actually makes good sense if reincarnation of inner consciousness exists or if souls preexist physical life. Whether these things exist or not, it is a concept that should not be dismissed without examining all the evidence, of which there is a significant amount, as is pointed out in the chapter "The Reality of an Independent Consciousness."

The ego mind can close itself off to the existence of an independent consciousness, and to any confirming evidence, simply by denying its existence. In engineering, simply denying the existence of whatever cannot be explained would be considered incompetence. Either all information is considered, including conflicting information, or no reliable conclusion can be reached. The possibility of an independent consciousness must be considered in any hypothesis about consciousness and the mind.

The term I often use in this book for the independent consciousness is "inner consciousness." I believe it is this inner consciousness that makes us human and allows us to possess the intangibles of faith, hope, and love, as well as evil. Others, including the Greek philosophers, label this consciousness "the soul." The problem for humans is that inner consciousness is of the subconscious and functions through the physically conscious mind. It can be effectively shut down by the ego or by problems with the brain.

In separating consciousness into a physically conscious and independent inner consciousness, it would make sense that each level of consciousness would each have its own thought reality as to what is important and what is perceived to be most fulfilling. It should also be realized that inner consciousness, which is not of physical reality and therefore not necessarily controlled by the physical brain, can, like ego consciousness, possess vice as well as virtue and can desire either.

As virtue and vice are also options for inner consciousness, inner consciousness, like ego consciousness, can also lead a person to make choices that can enhance inner happiness or be detrimental to it. The traditional image of inner consciousness and the ego is that of an angel on the right shoulder holding us back from what the imp on the left shoulder is suggesting. But the angel on the right shoulder may not always be objecting to what the imp on the left is suggesting. Inner consciousness, in the desire to be fulfilled, can choose the dark side of virtue, which is vice. Inner consciousness can mistakenly accept worldly power, pleasure, and grandeur as what is the most fulfilling. However, these things only mask the inner desire to be loved and to feel self-worth. Only virtues, culminating in love, will bring a true sense of fulfillment to inner consciousness.

When we want to do something we sense is something we shouldn't do, there is conflict between levels of consciousness. We typically refer to the conflict as "conscience." Conscience has been described cleverly by American journalist and satirist Henry Mencken: "Conscience is the inner voice that warns us somebody might be looking."

Even if both ego and inner consciousness realize the importance of virtue, it does not mean the ego and inner consciousness will follow the same thought reality. The imp and the angel may be constantly fighting for dominance. When they do not desire the same thing, personal disharmony can result. For inner happiness and personal peace, we need to work on understanding how to coordinate what is important to our egos with what is important to the inner consciousness. If we do not take the time to understand the importance of virtue to inner consciousness, as well as to the ego consciousness, we may never find inner happiness and self-worth.

In *Human Understanding*, we realize that there is a level of inner consciousness that functions independent of the brain, and is concerned with the intangibles of virtue and vice to human feelings and happiness. Thought reality, focused on virtue, brings self-worth and the feeling of inner happiness. Thought reality focused on vice leads away from the self-worth that inner consciousness desires. The end game for all consciousness is to be united with the oneness of unconditional love, regardless of religious belief or even unbelief, and regardless of reincarnation or one physical life.

Self-Worth

One of the most important things for satisfaction in life is a feeling that we are worth something, that we know we have value, and especially that we are lovable. If we feel an interior self-worth, we will feel good about ourselves, even through difficult times. Where there is self-worth, there is optimism.

On the other hand, if we do not have self-worth, we will not be happy or even feel worthy to be loved. Without self-worth, we are not only unhappy with ourselves; we tend to blame the world around us for our unhappiness. This often leads to jealously, anger, stress, and addiction. Without self-worth, we also tend to become dependent upon others and material pleasures for feeling good as well as for our individual needs.

We must understand that without self-worth or an effort to attain it, things will not get better. Worse yet, people who do not feel any self-worth may ask themselves if there is any reason to live. If there is no reason or no hope, suicide is a consideration. Some experts consider low self-esteem the cause of virtually every psychological problem. I believe a better term than self-esteem is "self-worth."

For personal happiness, it is critical that we know what will cause us, and those we love, to feel a sense of self-worth. If we look at life on purely physical bases, one way to consider self-worth is monetarily. The blog Data Genetics broke down a normal human body into its various chemicals. Based upon the value of the different chemicals, it put human worth at just over $160. IFL Science looked at the value of a human body based on parts and came up with a value of over $22,500. The Science Degree Center, in *How*

Much is Your Body Worth on the Black Market, came up with a number of $45,000,000. The range is very interesting, but for that self-worth, we must be dead. There are a number of ways living people can try to value themselves. But the important question is what will actually result in personal self-worth for the living?

The lowest form of measurement of personal value is based on what we accumulate. It is nice to have many things. But the satisfaction with things most often has more to do with patting ourselves on the back or impressing other people by our power, control, and intelligence in getting them, than it does with things themselves. Accumulation may bring some amount of status. But status is nothing more than a security blanket for the insecure. Where accumulation is important, there is never enough. This can eventually lead to the vice called greed. Accumulation of things may bring temporary self-importance, but it will not bring inner self-worth—a sense of inner peace which can exist even without "things."

Another way to value ourselves is to rely entirely on how well we measure up to our own goals. This may seem good at first, but then we need to be careful about how we set goals. We may accomplish something easy and over-value ourselves. Or, we may fail at unrealistic goals and feel depressed.

If we think hard about it, there is a problem with the concept of measuring our own value. We can only measure against a fixed base, but everyone has different gifts and opportunities. Also, what does accomplishing a goal really mean? It may mean we have value when we accomplish a goal, but can that value be assumed to last forever? What we did has already been accomplished. Wouldn't that mean we are capable of even more?

Looking carefully at self-evaluation, we find that it is unreliable and not a good method of determining self-worth. If not controlled, it can lead anywhere from pride to depression. And yet it is the way many people evaluate their self-worth.

We can also rely on other people to tell us our worth. There are a number of ways other people elevate or deflate our personal value. They can praise us verbally or criticize us. People can also reward us materially or monetarily and they can punish us. One way people let us know that we are worthwhile is to appreciate and love us. But they can also express dislike. What people tell us can have different effects on self-worth—even those comments intended to make us feel good. As babies have not been influenced by the world, what is important to them should give a good perspective on what is important in life—what brings the feeling of worth.

Earlier, we looked at the importance of interaction of adults with children in the first few years of life as most important for learning and for cognitive thinking. There is something even more important to babies than just learning. Babies need to feel they are worth something. They need to be nurtured. They need to feel loved.

There is a story about infant orphan children in London during the Second World War that is important in understanding a child's need for love. The exact facts in this story, heard at a workshop on healing, may not be exactly correct but the gist of the story, as told by Dr. Margarett Schlientz. (9) During WWII, there were many infant orphans in London. Although the orphanages were under-staffed, it did not account for the fact that many of the relatively new born orphans were dying for no apparent reason, except at one orphanage. When that orphanage was investigated to find out what was being done differently, only one thing surfaced. At that orphanage, one nurse would hold and hug and talk to each baby each day. After this approach was used at the other orphanages, the death rate dropped. The need to feel personal acceptance and love is as important to a baby as life itself. Words alone do not give babies the feeling of self-worth.

Initial self-worth comes with a feeling of being loved. The importance of personal nurturing on the feeling of worth may be one of the reasons that face-to-face interaction with young children is critical to learning. As the extent of nurturing has an effect on learning and cognitive thinking, it will likely have the same effect on self-worth. It should be realized that until a person has matured enough to be secure with his or her personal self-worth, that person will still be at least partially dependent upon the evaluation of others for self-worth.

As children develop cognitive thinking, they, consciously or subconsciously, evaluate the praise they are given, or even the lack of praise. Think back to when you heard people tell you; "good job" or "good game" or something similar. You appreciated the praise when you felt you did well. But, if you didn't think you did well, you did not really believe what you were being told. Although praise can make people feel better, typically cognitive people already have their own opinion of what they have accomplished. Unfortunately, the opposite is not always true. When you believed you did something well and received no praise or were criticized, you might question your self-evaluation unless you are already secure in your self-worth.

What makes each individual feel self-worth will vary greatly, and so will the recognition for personal accomplishments and how recognition is accepted. But without some amount of praise or recognition for personal effort and accomplishment, how people think of themselves can be compromised. Personal recognition is important. However, even more important than verbal recognition is how it is given. Personal recognition and praise must be given sincerely to be effective.

Sometimes, people reveal our value to them with rewards. When it comes to material or monetary appreciation or even a promotion, we generally feel good because it can be measured against a fixed base or against someone else. However, material and monetary remuneration are really not much different than accumulation of material things. They provide more access to worldly "things" and more pride. They do promote a temporary feeling of self-importance, but it quickly fades.

Appreciation that is expressed in the form of physical contact is similar to verbal appreciation, but more intimate and personal. It can warm the cold heart if it is accepted as sincere. As we reviewed, it can be critical to initial self-worth. However, I'm sure many of us have been hugged by people we felt were only doing it for show or just formality. If the physically expressed appreciation is accepted as true appreciation, it will warm the heart in a way that no material reward can. If it is given for any other reason than true appreciation, it may only be may be outwardly accepted.

The problem with evaluating our worth on the praise we receive or do not receive is that we still evaluate our worth based upon what we think of ourselves and of what we believe is the sincerity of others who try to encourage us or discourage us. Praise is a factor in self-worth, but it can also be misleading. Praise for worldly accomplishments can increase also self-confidence and self-importance. But these do not of themselves increase self-worth. Self-worth is not based upon what we have done in the past but rather upon how well we see ourselves accomplishing what we consider to be our purpose in living. It is only in doing what we know that we should be doing that produces self-worth.

It is important to understand the difference between self-worth and both self-importance and self-confidence. Self-importance and self-confidence are both of ego consciousness. The value of each is measured in terms of worldly comparisons. Self-worth is of inner consciousness and comes from an inner innate knowledge that what a person is doing is virtuous and caring of others. It does not come from being bolder and more confident or even the smartest. People who are smart, self-confident, self-important, and other people that seem to have the world in their hands, are not necessarily people happy with themselves.

A few of many famous and worldly successful people, from many different walks of life, who were unhappy enough with themselves to end their own lives are: Vincent van Gogh, painter; Alfred of Edinburgh, prince; Ernest Hemingway, writer; Kurt Cobain, singer; George Eastman, inventor; Dick Trickle,

NASCAR driver; Junior Seau, football player; Brian Keith, actor; Capucine, model; Rene Favalora, heart surgeon; Gilles Deleuze, philosopher, Vince Fister, White House counsel; Lester Hunt, U.S. senator; Finn M. W. Caspersen, financier. There are literally hundreds of important, popular, and very successful people in all professions who did not consider life worth living. (Wikipedia has a long list of just those in the 21st century for those interested.)

We know there was a lack of self-worth involved because suicide is an act concerned with feeling about self. Intelligence, self-importance, and self-confidence can help in having a successful and good life. But they can also produce an illusion of self-worth. However, illusions are momentary. When everything else is gone, it is the belief in personal self-worth that will provide the stable thought reality necessary to carry on.

What we normally know we should be doing comes from having an overall purpose in life. We feel good when fulfilling a purpose. However, even without a specific purpose, we instinctively know when we are doing something worthwhile. When we contribute to a just cause or just to lend a helping hand, we feel a sense of worthiness and purpose. When we see the smile on the face of someone we just helped, we feel good in a way that worldly success cannot make us feel. It is something which we don't even have to evaluate to know we are doing the right thing, even if our efforts did not get the results we hoped for. Self-worth comes from what we give rather than from what we receive. That is because purpose for life is beyond self. If we do not give of ourselves to others, is there any reason others should respect or even like us? If we do not give of ourselves, are we really worth anything to the rest of the world? It is very important to understand what will bring about the feeling of self-worth and a reason to exist.

While there can be an understanding of the need for self-worth, what seems to be missing is an understanding of ways to help people of little self-worth to understand they are important and have worth. We need to realize that simply using words of praise to help adults and older children of little self-worth is of little use unless our words are honest and expressed lovingly. Words and praise given without love or sincerity may increase boldness and some amount of self-importance but not self-worth. It is only words of praise and appreciation given honestly and lovingly that will help self-worth.

It would also help if more importance and notoriety was paid to loving and kind people rather than people who attain notoriety in unloving ways. We all need examples of acceptance and love to be given the recognition. It is only through such recognition that acceptance and love will be seen as a value to be desired. It is most important to learn to express to others how important they are to us, before we learn the negative effects of not sincerely expressing their importance. Success in school sports or academics may help some students feel good. But the best way to foster real self-worth in schools is to have programs that focus on the benefits of effort, respect, acceptance, and love, which foster the feeling of self-worth. As the lack of self-worth is considered one of the most critical issues in psychological disorders, why is it not a priority in education? The importance of the virtues that lead to self-worth seems to be ignored in most public schools, possibly because they can be associated with religion.

The truth is that virtue and self-worth are independent of religion, though important to religion. Modern education provides meals for physically underprivileged children and teaches them what they need to function on the physical level. But they do not provide lessons in the importance of self-worth for the emotionally underprivileged nor provide lessons in what is required to achieve it. So many children and adults learn the importance the hard way, while others never learn.

If you want to build your self-worth, you have to work for it by giving of yourself. All this may seem unfair to those born into unloving life situations. However, it is often harder for the more well-to-do to gain real self-worth because it requires that they give of themselves rather than of their affluence.

One way to increase self-worth or even initiate self-worth is to accept the spiritual basic of the existence of a Higher Power of love. Accepting that humans are unconditionally loved by the Higher Power can provide the self-worth the material world cannot provide. The concept that all people are worthy of being loved and that life has a higher purpose than worldly pleasure and success seems to be missing in modern society.

In *Human Understanding*, we realize that self-worth is not about the physical world of self-confidence and self-importance. Self-worth is an intangible that results from doing what we know in our hearts is right and loving, as well as appreciating the positive and loving feelings that result. This springs from inner consciousness rather than the ego. The thought reality of a person with self-worth is one that is concerned with the welfare of others and provides them with hope and love. And in giving hope and love to others, Thought reality can come to sense and understand hope and love.

FEELINGS AND EMOTIONS

This chapter only addresses some overall concepts about feelings and emotions. For a more in-depth understanding of these subjects, there are many books available. I hope this overview will be helpful for understanding some basics of feelings and emotions.

The first thing to take into account is that although feelings and emotions are often considered the same, and are similar, they are actually different as to origin. Feelings originate in the consciousness mind whereas the origin of emotions is biological. The difference is best summarized in the words of Dr. Sarah McKay, neuroscientist, science communicator, and founder of The Neuroscience Academy, "Emotions play out in the theater of the body. Feelings play out in the theater of the mind." http://www.jolsid.com/emotions-vs-feelings-dawn-of-justice).

It may not seem to be important to know the difference between the two. However, if a problem arises with either, understanding them can be helpful in addressing the problem.

Humans are aware of things that go on around them though the senses. The senses send messages to the brain. Therefore, the body is actually responding biologically to what it senses, even before the mind has the information it needs to react.

Also important in the biological response are subconscious ideas, beliefs, and biases. Because they exist and can affect biological reactions prior to any conscious mental evaluation, they contribute to emotional reactions. Instantaneous biological emotional reactions are a blessing that humans possess that allows them to react to dangerous situations, for which there is little or no time to evaluate.

Positron Emission Tomography (PET) scans of the brain show that as little as five percent of the time, people's initial reactions are based on conscious thinking. Initial reaction is normally emotional, based upon biological body reaction. We jump when we are startled. When what the body senses gets through to the brain, further reactions should conform to how the brain tells the body to react.

The mind is then supposed to combine the mental perceptions of what is encountered with conscious and subconscious preconceived ideas, beliefs, and biases of thought reality (labeled "preconceived notions" in this book) to evaluate what the senses encounter and how to react. Although we are not normally aware of it, this process goes on with everything we encounter, including what we hear, see, and touch. It is this process by which we add to our thought reality and learn. However, not every new mental evaluation creates a sensed feeling, because most are incidental or not rationally considered important enough to have feelings about.

When resulting mental evaluations are important to perceived security or happiness, of mind or body, they are manifested as what are called "feelings." The more important the mental evaluation is to perceived joy, happiness, danger, anger, fear, and similar, the greater the intensity of the resulting feeling.

The accuracy of resulting feelings relies upon the accuracy of both preconceived notions and of the mental perception of what the body senses. The more limited the development of thought reality, or the greater the belief that existing notions are true reality, the greater the chance that what is sensed may not be correctly preconceived by the mind.

When preconceived notions of thought reality are confused by what is perceived, people do not know how to rationally evaluate what is perceived.

An extreme example would be the perception of something never imagined. People in that situation often freeze rather than immediately react because they have no idea how to react. In the chapter on Perceptions, we will see that the mind does not always perceive correctly what the body senses. Thought reality can—and often does—filter out things the body senses, which do not agree with preconceived notions. Sometimes it happens just because of how the mind works. When preconceived notions or perceptions are limited or inaccurate, it can lead to improper evaluation. Alcohol and drugs can also increase the probability of inaccurate or even illusionary perceptions.

With proper knowledge, and assuming the brain is functioning perfectly, thought reality should evaluate what the senses encounter and cause the body to act in an appropriately rational way. However, when thought reality encounters what it does not understand or what is very upsetting, it can react without any rational evaluation. It can omit evaluation and continue the initial emotional reaction instead.

Thought reality notions of control, anger, vengeance, elation, or even physical desire, as well as fear, can overpower rational evaluation. The intensity of reactions resulting from mental evaluation, or lack thereof, depends upon how thought reality perceives what is encountered, as well as upon the level of desire for personal self-control, which may exist in thought reality.

Emotional reactions are also affected by those things that affect body chemistry. Physical injuries and traumas can affect body chemistry. Genetic make-up affects body chemistry and can affect emotional reactions. So different people can have different emotional or rational reactions to what is sensed. Drugs and drinking can also change body chemistry.

Change in body chemistry can affect how what the body senses is transmitted to the brain and also how the brain interprets what is sensed. We can observe how people under stress often react more emotionally and intensely when disturbed. No surprise there since stress is known to cause chemical changes in the brain. Therefore, differences in initial reactions for different people and for people in difficult, or even happy, situations are natural and should actually be expected. But regardless of the cause of emotional reactions, it is up to thought reality, including the importance of self-control to thought reality, to get them under control. If they are not quickly controlled by rational thought reality, uncontrolled feelings can lead to problematic mental and physical reactions.

Although the mind does not normally control initial emotional responses, thought reality has the ability to control any additional reaction. Additional reactions depend upon understanding of what is encountered and upon the importance of self-control to thought reality. Where self-control is important, even normal emotional biological reactions can be brought under control.

Buddhist monks have shown that self-control has the ability to control what would normally be considered biological reactions. Unfortunately, few of us have been trained in self-control thinking like Buddhist monks and detrimental mental notions can overpower rational thinking. But if we open our minds to introducing the importance of self control into our predconditioned thought notions, we have the ability to alter initial emotional responses and our resulting feelings

Besides professional help in dealing with emotional and feeling problems, there has been a significant amount of research on these topics, which has resulted in written information helpful to know. In his book, *Cause and Consequences of Feelings*, Dr. Leonard Berkowitz, noted American psychologist, says that we can change the way we feel by changing the way we think.

Another interesting research study is *Rethinking Feelings: An MRI Study of the Cognitive Regulation of Emotions*. The study by Kevin N. Ochsner, Silvia A Bunge, James J Gross, and John D.E. Gabireli begins with a quote from Shakespeare's Hamlet. "There is neither good nor bad, but what we think makes it so." The study showed that reappraising an adverse event in an unemotional state reduces feeling problems. The point they make is that if people can be brought into an environment where they can look at things objectively and rationally, rather than react emotionally, the cause of their adverse feelings can be reduced.

In effect, these methods open thought reality to understanding how people are be controlled by their thought notions. This knowledge allows them to make better, rational evaluations. This procedure is intended to change the values and habits of thought reality that lead to problems with emotions and feelings. Essentially, such research basically says what I have just presented: we can change the way we think by changing what is of value to thought reality.

Another method of influencing a lessening of adverse feelings is talking about them as presented in *Putting Feelings into Words Produces Therapeutic Effects in the Brain*. This information is based upon a UCLA neuroimaging study, as reported in the *UCLA News Room Science and Technologies* (June 21, 2007). The concept is to let out the feelings. Although this article may seem to renew the concept of a person on a couch talking to a psychiatrist, it actually tells us to talk about our feelings more freely. Talking with others about feelings and emotions and listening to the way they have dealt with feelings can also present new ideas and new values to thought reality.

It is interesting to be aware that regressive hypnosis into past lives, that seem to have initiated the phobias, has been successfully used to relieve the phobias, as will be noted in the chapter Reality of an Independent Conciousness. It is time to investigate all possibilities.

A perspective that can be helpful in managing feelings is the concept of Higher Power and ultimate justice. Obviously, not everyone will accept that reality. However, that acceptance could bring new values and reduce feelings of injustice and relieve stress for those who do accept that reality. If the acceptance of a Higher Power can help addicts recover, such as with Alcoholics Anonymous (AA), it is something that should also be considered.

Essential to control of emotions and feelings is personal self-control. If we do not have self-control, we are less likely to respond rationally to the things that upset us. Unfortunately, not everyone is raised with the thought notion that self-control is important to mental health and safety. Where self-control is lacking, it can be gained through self-discipline in both thoughts and deeds. When it comes to having some control over emotions and feelings, self-control is something we all need to work on.

Something else that can help control feelings is the practice of meditation. Meditation requires learning self-control of conscious thought. The objective is to get in touch with inner consciousness, which is blocked by conscious thought. Meditation allows a person to gain the inner peace and insight of inner consciousness. However, it takes much self-discipline and much practice to be undertaken properly. In that meditation requires learning control of self, it is not surprising that it is helpful in controlling feelings.

When we practice effective self-discipline, we can pause to think of consequences before reacting. We can learn to control our feelings even when emotionally excited. To change values of thought reality, we must have enough self-control to say "no" to old, uncontrolled thought habits. That will only come with focus and effort.

We normally visualize personal problems with feelings as being manifested in fear, anxiety, and anger. But these can manifest themselves in other ways. The lack of control over feelings has many secondary, negative consequences. It can also be detrimental to something as innocent as the ease of falling asleep. Dr. James J Gross and Hooria Jazaieri, in an article in *Clinical Psychological Science* entitled "Emotion, Emotional Regulating, Psychopathology: An Effective Science Perspective," indicate that the inability to regulate emotions and feelings is at the heart of psychological disorders such as depression and borderline personality disorder.

Problems with feelings need to be addressed before they adversely affect health, as well as happiness in life.

Because our emotions and feelings incorporate—consciously and subconsciously—all our life experiences, they also indirectly tell us where we have been, where we are, and where we think life will go. Maybe we like what they tell us about ourselves and our lives and maybe we don't. But for good or for bad, our long-term happiness is dependent upon a better understanding of our emotions and feelings, of what they are telling us about ourselves, and of what we need to do to change them for the better.

As our ability to deal with feelings matures, we will find feelings actually exist to help us to learn, as well as to protect us. This will happen when we accept and understand our feelings for what they tell us about ourselves, as much as they tell us about what we encounter.

In *Human Understanding*, we come to better understand our emotions and feelings. Emotions are a natural biological response of the body to what the senses encounter. Emotional responses are also affected by subconcious preconditioned thought notions. Feelings result when the brain incorporates emotional responses, along with perceptions and all conscious and subconscious notions to arrive at an evaluation of what is encountered.

When rational thinking does not take over biological reactions, emotional reactions can escalate into something unfortunate. When emotions and/or feelings are a problem, it is important to understand how limited understanding and incorrect notions of thought reality can play havoc with proper perceptions, proper evaluations, and with happiness. Opening thought reality to new values and to new notions can provide new reasons and new ways to control emotional reactions and feelings.

This chapter was difficult for me to write about. In many respects, I have had a very difficult time dealing with feelings and emotions. For many years, I considered feelings a detriment to reason. I learned to stifle my feelings and suppress my emotions at a young age. Logic and common sense were what were important.

Feelings were not important to me, so why should they be important to others? In so thinking, I hindered both them and myself and, among other things, hurt others. I have learned that people are all different in how they handle feelings and emotions, including myself, and that I have to respect that fact.

I have learned that life is a process of learning and we all need to open ourselves to change, even in how we experience what we feel. I also realize how difficult change can be. Even today, though I now recognize my problems with not fully respecting emotions and feelings of others, I still have difficulty discussing issues with emotional people. At least I do a better job at it now. But it would also help if emotional reactionary people would depend less on feeling and more on trying to be rational.

PERCEPTIONS

What we learn and understand begins with what the senses impart to the brain. In the *New World Dictionary*, perception has two basic definitions, shortened herein to: 1) a mental grasp through the senses, and 2) awareness or understanding. But those definitions overlook something important. The mind will not always, or cannot always, accurately comprehend all the senses observe. Therefore, a more accurate way to define perception is: that which is registered in the mind from what the senses observe. Because our minds are not always open to accept all that the senses observe, perception is not always reality. Therefore, perceptions can be accurate, inaccurate, or anywhere between.

What we perceive with our senses, together with thought notions, form the basis for mental evaluation. If the mind does not properly perceive what is encountered, the resulting evaluation will not likely be correct. Therefore, it is important to understand the limitations of our perception.

IQ tests provide a general idea of a person's ability to perceive things and correctly relate them to the conscious mind. If we realize how far the average IQ—about 100—is below the highest recorded at 230, we should realize just how limited normal perceptions and evaluations are, especially when we consider that even the person with a 230 IQ is still quite fallible. Although intelligence is required for an IQ test, mental perception is the first step to understanding the questions on a test or for whatever is encountered, even for the people with the highest IQs.

An example of a variation in perception is contained in a short, humorous story about a thin, hungry beggar who approaches a plump, well-to-do lady and says, "I haven't eaten in a week." To which the amazed lady replies, "Gosh, I wish I had your will power!"

What is important to understand about this story is more than the unexpected perception of the plump woman that brings about her response. Also important to understand is the difference between our mental perceptions of what the lady would likely say and her actual response. The humor in jokes is caused by misleading, preconditioned thought reality expectations. It is the change from what is expected that creates humor. Humor is most effective when the punchline in something totally unexpected. Magicians set up the audience to expect something different than what is actually happening, so observers will not perceive what is actually happening. Perceptions can be very different than actual reality because we mostly perceive what we expect the reality of the situation to be.

It is important to realize our perceptions can fool us.

In the process of learning, people will not or cannot process all of what is observed. Consider how people learn to process information. What children first hear is nothing more than mumblings to them. They perceive which mumblings are important to adults and work on understanding them. Even though adults do not pause between words, children associate repeated sounds with specific things and actions until they learn their significance. This is the beginning of thought reality, by which further understanding of additional words is possible.

Children also have to let go of many spoken things that do not make any sense to them. To young children, for whom so much is new, the process of discarding what seems unimportant is necessary to concentrate on what does make sense. Children concentrate most on those things that seem valuable to the people they are learning from. And they filter out words and events they do not perceive as significant.

Filtering is important in initial learning, but it generally carries on beyond childhood. As we grow in knowledge, the amount of filtering we need to do should diminish. Unfortunately, many of us continue to filter out whatever does not fit our existing thought reality. Even scientists have a similar problem when they disregard facts that do not fit into the accepted scientific paradigm.

A good way to think about how perception works is the process of putting together a puzzle. We generally start with the edges and with similar colors and we initially ignore pieces that do not seem to fit anywhere. As we get the easier pieces together, we can more easily visualize the whole picture and determine where the more difficult pieces should fit. However, sometimes the pieces do not seem to make sense and the puzzle is not correctly completed.

Perception is similar. The mind initially scans the pieces of information the senses provide for what is familiar so it can put together a mental picture of what is encountered. The mental picture depends upon the knowledge and the notions of thought reality. The pieces of information that cannot be understood in relation to what makes sense to the mind are initially ignored. After the easy-to-understand information begins to form a mental picture, the other pieces of information are added. However, if the remaining pieces do not fit the mental picture, they will be filtered out. Otherwise, uncertainty will remain. As a result, the picture the mind puts together can be different than what actually has taken place, even though the observer can swear he or she knows what actually occurred.

People perceive issues important in life in the same way. When people do not fully understand specific or even general issues, they perceive the issues based upon the limited amount of understanding they have of the issues. When people rely entirely on what they already know and do not try to expand their knowledge and understanding, they often do not see the big picture, and their evaluations are often incorrect. Yet they will continue to believe they have the pieces of knowledge they need to understand life.

Perceptions are influenced by what people understand. Proper perception of information, even on specific issues, is dependent upon previous information and knowledge. The more that is understood about an issue, the more likely the resulting perceptions will be correct. It is important to realize how the lack of knowledge can lead to incorrect perceptions.

One of my favorite perception stories is about little Johnny, who is at a cemetery with his mother on Veteran's Day. Johnny asked why there are little flags at many of the grave sites. When his mother responded that they mark the graves of people who died in service, Johnny said: "Boy, I'm glad we don't go to that church."

On subjects they do not understand, most people rely on friends, societies, religions, cultures, the media, and even the scientific information, for understanding. The problem is that if the knowledge provided by others is not correct, any perception that relies on such knowledge will likely be incorrect, regardless of what is observed. Also, as people try to make sense of what they encounter or hear, their perception will be biased toward an understanding they have already come to accept as correct.

People are also biased to toward conventional thinking. We see this in the research of Polish psychologist Solomon Asch, which we reviewed above in the chapter "Learning—Thought Reality Development."

The perception of the need to conform can overpower actual perception and personal belief. Conforming to the accepted perception of a group or society provides a form of personal security, especially for people who have learned non-conformity has bad consequences. Conforming to the perception of others leads to such things as popularity of specific individuals, accepted manners, mass mobs, the spread of rumors, runs on banks, and even mass hysteria.

When people let themselves be controlled by their limited knowledge or the limited knowledge of others, they are also open to incorrect perceptions and supposed knowledge. As a result, the biased person remains biased. The bully remains the bully. People who consider themselves victims will continue to think of themselves as victims. Ultra-liberals and ultra-conservatives remain too addicted to their specific perceptions to consider solutions outside of their biases, and nothing constructive gets done. It is most important to realize that what we like to think we know is only personal opinion, and therefore open to other opinions.

Perceptions are also influenced by personal wants. When we looked at the story of the beggar and the plump lady, we saw that the perception of what each was saying and hearing was very different and based upon what was important to each of them. Even in the building business, the perception of what people want is important. The developer tries to perceive what building design, function, and location will have the biggest return on investment. However, when prospective users or tenants perceive something else, the investment in the building is in trouble. It is important to also be aware of how other people perceive things.

The great adventurers and inventors were people who allowed themselves to think beyond normally accepted limits. They were not limited by what other people perceived and even what they were taught. I'm sure that if someone in the 16th century had said that matter was function of energy and speed, that person would have been laughed at or possibly burned as a heretic. That concept did not exist until Einstein thought beyond the conventional perception of matter.

A person's ability to break away from conventional perceptions allows him or her to be creative and find new ways to solve real problems. In the engineering field, the good engineers are those who perceive problems in new ways so as to understand new ways to solve problems. That is why, when I was interviewing prospective employees, an important part of an interview was determining how open-minded a person was. Accepting even the remote possibility of such things as ghosts, sasquatches, UFOs, and other unexplained phenomena, improved the chances of being hired by me.

The more open the thought reality to other possibilities, the greater the potential for new ideas and creative solutions.

To differing degrees, we all let our conventional perception of such things as environment, social class, race, or even religion influence our thought processing. But if we want to truly perceive what the senses observe, we must let go of mental bias and assess things with an open mind, including things our minds may have previously filtered out as not possible. We need to accept that our knowledge is limited and that we have much to learn.

Maybe Bigfoot and UFOs exist and maybe they don't. Whether or not they do exist changes nothing of actual reality. But in opening up our thought reality to new possibilities, we can realize that our rigid ideas and beliefs restrict perception and potentially limit our growth in knowledge, including knowledge that could increase our self-worth and happiness. Regardless of background, unhappy minds will not change to happy without being open to new ways of perceiving what really produces self-worth and inner happiness.

Perceptions are also affected by what the brain is capable of correctly comprehending. The dress that created a color controversy on the Internet in early 2015 was perceived differently as gold and white or black and blue. The difference in perception was explained in Current Biology, based upon research at Giesson and Bradford Universities. Color perception varies because of differences in how people perceive light. The mind can filter out yellows and blues in different light conditions.

The Brain Games television show is great in pointing out that how the mind functions can alter our perceptions. The show basically tells us that the mind keeps us unaware of just how limited our perception is, because if we realized our limitations, we would lose our self-confidence. We need to recognize that perceptions are only as good as the effectiveness of our brains and the notions of our thought reality, both of which are very fallible.

As we reviewed in the chapter "Learning—Thought Reality Development," children's values tend to become like those of the people who raise them. Present a rewarding image of life, and the children's perception of life will tend to be uplifting. Present a poor image of life to children and their perception of life will tend to be bleak. Parents need to realize how their children grow up is greatly affected by how they are raised. Regardless of economic background, it is important that children are raised in a way that they will perceive that life is precious and that they are loved.

The most important perception we can have is a perception of what constitutes a sense of fulfillment and what it takes to achieve it. The biggest difference in human perception is the perception of happiness being related to worldly wants, as compared to the perception of happiness being related to self-worth and love. The perception that worldly things bring happiness leads to selfishness, eventual unhappiness, and often to addiction. The perception that giving of self is most important in life can lead to self-worth and love.

Almost all of what we encounter is subject to many dissenting views and many different perceptions. Everyone has his or her own personal perspective on things. But we need to realize that our perspective is almost all just opinion. Until the perception of what is important in life is based upon a fixed basis, the perception of what is important will continue to be opinion. It is important to search for fixed basics upon which thought reality can go beyond opinion to fixed reality.

In *Human Understanding*, we realize that what the body senses is not always correctly perceived by the mind. How our mind perceives what the body senses is influenced by knowledge, or lack of knowledge, of what the body senses, and even by the limitations of brain itself. The problem with perception is that our knowledge and understanding of what we encounter is generally limited and incomplete. The result is that perceptions are often incorrect even when we think they are correct.

New perceptions to correct false perceptions are only possible when we admit that what we think and believe is only personal opinion and may not be correct. In opening our minds to new ways of thinking, our perception will better correlate with what our senses observe. We will also have a better chance to find happiness in life. There are many perceptions of what is most fulfilling. But the only perceptions that are true are those based upon fixed reality of virtue.

SPIRITUALITY

Spirituality has been defined as activity in which a person searches for the sacred. Most people think of spirituality as related to religion or a higher level of reality. However, for those people who do not believe in a higher level of existence, spirituality can be thought as the realm of those things affecting the inner self, such as purity of motivation, affection, intention, disposition, and so on. Happiness can be associated with purity and goodness of mind, even without a belief in a Higher Power.

Buddhists do not believe in a God as such, but often lead more spiritual lives than many people who believe in a Higher Power. However, Buddhists do believe that there is a higher purpose to leading a spiritually healthy life. For those people who do not believe in a Higher Power, spirituality in this book should be thought of as living a good life for a higher purpose than one's own self wants. For those who believe in a Higher Power, spirituality is normally thought of as doing that which is pleasing to the Higher Power and which also keeps them in touch with the Higher Power.

One of the basics of life defined in this book is the fixed realty of virtue and vice existing through all levels of reality. What is important for any and all spirituality is that people accept that virtue is the path to personal happiness and fulfillment. I believe that in accepting the path of virtue, people are directly or indirectly accepting the path to oneness with supreme consciousness or divinity of love, whether or not they accept that notion.

In recent years, many psychology and personal growth programs have turned to spirituality to help correct problems of the mind and body. Treatment of the entire person, including the inner spirit, is becoming more acceptable and often recommended. It is being recommended because it has had positive results. Psychologists, psychiatrists and others are writing books about the importance of spirituality in our lives.

Doctors today are also writing about many non-physical aspects of life based on research into things that affect people's feelings and well-being. Some of these writings include spirituality, which incorporates a belief in a higher level of reality, and that spirituality can have a positive effect on people. There are also studies that show a positive relationship between prayer and physical health.

Dr. Herbert Benson, a cardiovascular specialist at Harvard Medical School and a pioneer in the field of mind/body medicine, discovered what he calls the relaxation response in relationship to prayer. On www.thelearningmind.com, he states, "Magnetic resonance imaging showed that there was a decrease in metabolism, heart rate, blood pressure, breathing rate, and brain activity. Thus, we have a scientific proof that prayer affects body function and fights stress."

The later chapter on Prayer mentions studies that show that prayer positively affects the health of people who do not know they were being prayed for. That is not a normal physical reality occurrence.

Another interesting fact to consider is that the success of Alcoholics Anonymous (AA), in which the acceptance of a Higher Power is a key step to recovery. This indicates the acceptance of spirituality of some nature can be, or is, important to humanity. In the chapter on Purpose, Value, Habits, and Change, references note that spirituality can help our well-being while all the advancement of modern living has not made any difference in mental well-being.

The more we take time to learn about ourselves and about improving our mental state, the more we find there can be a benefit to spirituality in our lives. The question the engineer might ask is: Why would spirituality affect personal well-being if humans are only physical beings?

Whether spirituality is a function of human physical nature or of a nature beyond the physical is not something that can be proved either way in physical reality. But there is a way an engineer can better evaluate the answer to the question—by checking all the information and the potential evidence available. Even when there is no absolute evidence, there are almost always related circumstances, as well as anecdotal evidence, to evaluate. These can be checked to see if people have a spiritual nature, as well as a physical nature.

In engineering, "Murphy's Law"—if something can go wrong, it will go wrong—is a consideration that should be taken into account. Accounting for "Murphy's Law" was important enough to be an answer on one of my college engineering final examinations. Although "Murphy's Law" is a concept, rather than a reality, it is often stressed so engineers make every effort to know as much as possible about whatever they are working on, especially if what can go wrong can have bad consequences. If there is circumstantial evidence that supports the existence of a level or Higher Power or of an independent consciousness, it would be wise to consider "Murphy's Law" before discarding the possibility.

If humans have an independent consciousness, this would indicate that spirituality originates from a reality beyond the physical. Many books have been written about near-death experiences and other unexplained phenomena that are suggestive of independent consciousness. Although subjective, these books indirectly require that humans have an independent consciousness.

Independent consciousness is a subject that many people in science seem to want to overlook or outright debunk. Fortunately, there are some non-conforming doctors and scientists who are willing to go beyond conventional thinking. Dr. Ian Stevenson (10) has conducted extensive research on reincarnation that quite convincingly indicates that some type of physical and mental entanglement (11) between living and deceased people exists, and would indicate the likelihood of reincarnation.

Dr. Helen Wambach, in her book *Reliving Past Lives—The Evidence under Hypnosis,* also presents some interesting facts, obtained through hypnosis, from ordinary people that coincide with historical facts. (12) Before disregarding the idea of reincarnation or the preexistence of souls, there is much to read and consider. These subjects are looked at more closely in the chapter "Reality of an Independent Consciousness."

Investigations into near-death experiences (NDEs) can also be considered an extension of psychological research. One of the more profound books on the subject is *Proof of Heaven; A Neurosurgeon's Journey to the Afterlife* by Eben Alexander, MD. (13) This book is about his personal NDE. Dr. Alexander did not believe life beyond death prior to his experience. After the experience, he also realized that the detail, clarity, the duration of the experience, as well as his ability to recall what he experienced, could not have come from the brain, which could not have been functioning properly due to meningitis.

What is most interesting about NDEs is how they fit existing religious and historical concepts about an existence after death. Also of interest is how near-death experiences affected the people involved. What follows are just some of the major after effects of near death experiences listed by Dr. P.M.H. Atwater LHD, PhD (Hon). (14) Eighty percent of people going through a near death experience say it changed their lives forever. The changes included: less fear of death, more spiritual, less religious, less competitiveness, less stress, lower blood pressure, more generous and charitable, more detailed and objective, more convinced of a purpose for life, more philosophical, unusual sensitivity to light and sound.

However, not all NDEs are uplifting. Statistically, about 15 percent are depressing to outright hellish. What NDE books point out is that consciousness appears to exist beyond physical death. I do not mean to judge the reality of near-death experiences. But the information provided on the subject indicates a basis for, and points toward, the existence of consciousness beyond the physical brain.

While none of these things prove that humans have an independent spiritual nature, they do present significant reason to believe there is more to existence than this physical life. And then there are happenings that exist in this physical world that science cannot explain. Paranormal and other scientifically impossible events have been recorded. Among many sources for such events, *Reader's Digest* has recorded many in its "Mysteries of the Unexplained" series. There are also many recorded events attributed to saints and other holy people that are not possible by our physical laws.

Physically impossible events have been recorded throughout history and in all areas of the world, and where different religions have flourished. Among other impossibilities are people who have lived for extensive periods of time without eating or drinking. (15)

Another interesting fact is that most physical impossibilities, which appear to have been initiated by humankind, have been instigated by people considered holy or spiritual. Such anomalies are looked at in the chapters "Concept of a Higher Power" and "The Reality of an Independent Consciousness." The existence of miracles and other occurrences, which appear to be beyond the realm of the physical possibility, should open our minds to consider the possibility of a spiritual level of reality. It is possible to say that all such happenings are coincidences or figments of imagination. However, as an analytical engineer, I believe there are too many such incidences to say they are all coincidences.

Spirituality is important to humanity even if there is no Higher Power. When humans turn from spirituality to worldly wants, bad things happen. They happen because without spirituality, there is no good reason to think about anyone but self. As we will see later, when there is no belief in something beyond physical reality, life can end up being very depressing, especially when life is difficult or not turning out the way we would like. The lack of spirituality can easily be replaced with selfishness and the desire for control, which brings about anger, stress, and even wars.

We previously looked at the necessity of self-worth to be happy in life and the fact that it is achieved through acting unselfishly. It is the love of spirituality that causes humans to act unselfishly and lifts humanity above the level of animals.

As previously stated, the engineer must review all the information and evidence and be able to provide reasons that explain issues of reasonable doubt before offering an opinion. Although there is no accepted positive proof that humans have a spiritual nature, no proof exists otherwise. And although there is yet no scientific proof for near death experiences (NDEs), thousands of people have experienced them. Such experiences and other unexplainable events provide a reason to accept a spiritual level of reality beyond the physical. For that reason, "Murphy's Law" predicts that for those who do not accept the existence of a higher level of existence, something will go wrong.

The most important aspect of spirituality is that life is to be directed beyond self. It is interesting that the first book of the Bible, Genesis, tells us a story of how happiness was lost by selfish desire, rather than living for a purpose beyond self. By judging that "they wanted to be like God but apart from God," Adam and Eve lost their paradise. (16) This story presents a basic lesson we need to understand. When we judge others or ourselves, with our limited knowledge; when we try to control others; when we have personal expectations of ourselves and others based upon our limited personal wants and perceptions, we are ignoring spirituality and acting for self, or as the religious would say; acting like God but without God.

As such, we have decided that we have the knowledge of good and evil. We judge others, we judge ourselves, we judge goodness, and we even judge love. And in trying to find happiness on our own terms and by our conditional and limited judgments, we choose to turn our backs on true spirituality and love. We thus condemn ourselves to a world of judgment, dissatisfaction, and unhappiness. We make our own conditional hell.

The Hebrew Bible also has many stories about a people that, at times, turned away from their God. On their own, they continually met with disaster. Humanity needs to heed this lesson. As humanity decides that it can find peace and order on its own terms rather than through love and prayer, humanity should not be surprised to meet with disaster.

Real spirituality cannot exist where ego-wants, judgments, perceptions, controls, security, and other worldly desires dwell. So please realize that if you choose the path of spirituality, judgment and desire for control of the ego will not give up without a fight. Wanting to change is not enough. Effective change in life requires the adoption of new values and habits that reflect a new purpose. Spiritual purpose and values must be included every day in our work, in our thoughts, in our prayers, and in our play if we are to overcome the addiction to selfishness thinking.

Changing worldly material purpose, values, and habits to spiritual purpose, values, and habits will almost always be more than we can do by ourselves. We typically need help and examples. That is the reason that people seeking spirituality often gather together in churches, in prayer groups, or even in volunteer work.

For those of you who believe in the existence of a paradise, you can tell much about your spirituality and personal values by your visualization of a paradise. What is it you expect of paradise? Is it a place of rewards for deeds done? Is it a place where desires come true? Worldly desires are not logical for a true paradise. Such an existence would be one of perpetual selfishness. People who want or who think in terms of rewards will never be satisfied. Even the greatest physical pleasure would get boring after say 10,000 years, or more likely less than 10 years. Then what? We need to understand that it is not paradise that fulfills. It is only in giving up wants and control that we open ourselves to the love of spirituality that will fulfill.

In *Human Understanding*, we realize that spirituality is based the virtue of love. Although the importance of spirituality and any afterlife cannot be confirmed, there are reasons to believe spirituality is important, if merely for the civility of human existence. The best reason to be spiritual is that it provides a purpose for life, which can result in self-worth and personal inner happiness. The spirituality of all people, who live for the higher purpose of love, connects them to the Higher Power of love. Love transcends all levels of reality.

PERSONALITY

Each person has specific traits, mannerisms, sensitivities, inhibitions, intuitions, desires, talents, and needs that set that individual apart from all other people. The sum of these physical habits and mental traits is normally referred to as "personality." Based upon what has been previously written about environmental learning, it would be expected that each person raised in the same environment would have the same general personality. But it doesn't work that way. Although there are usually many similar personality traits within a family, there can be, and usually are, many different personalities in the same family. I had four sons and they all had very different personalities. Why the difference?

Environmentalists will say that even children in the same family are subject to different environments. Based upon the immediate differences in my children and other infants I have been exposed to, I believe differences start before environment takes over. Tell the mother of a baby who cries all the time that the cause is the environment and see if she will believe you. Actually, there are already many different personality traits at birth. Personality traits can be manifested in infants before they are exposed to altering conditions.

With our second son, on the second day of his life, the doctor warned that he would be challenge and could be a problem if not controlled early. And why, in the first few years of my life, did I scream if any woman other than my mother tried to pick me up? For answers to why inborn personality traits differ, there are many theories.

Carl Jung proposed that inborn "temperaments" are part of a person's genetically inherited collective unconscious. Research on identical twins, separated at birth, shows they often have the same habits and similar personalities. This is one of the reasons that many people say personality traits result from genetics. A neuroscientist may suggest that personality traits, from shyness to impulsiveness, are produced by particular brain modules acting on specific brain structure.

But because significant differences exist in children, even with the same genetic parents, there are obviously other factors affecting personalities. It may be that factors affecting a child's personality are related to constantly changing physical or mental conditions of the parents and the specific conditions present at the moment of conception. Behavior theorists may even attribute the differences to the environmental conditions during pregnancy. The religious might likely say that our personalities are predetermined by a Higher Power and are appropriate for the future situation of our lives. The reincarnation believer will say that personalities are a product of past lives. Perhaps there is validity to some or all of these theories. But, whatever the cause, worrying about the cause will not change inborn personality traits.

Since we do not control our inborn and environmental personalities, fretting about inborn personality does nothing but develop a negative personality. One of the biggest differences in personalities is the positive or negative nature of personality. What counts in life is how we use the gifts of personality we do have, not those we are upset we don't have.

There is no need to worry about having the perfect personality. There is none. Thank goodness there are many differences. Life would be a dull place if everyone had the same personality. To grasp what really matters about personality, you only need to ask for words to describe personalities. Words often used are: friendly, caring, fun loving, social, sexy, happy, ambitious, kind, thoughtful, sweet, quiet, loner, selfish, cold, lazy, wise guy, mean, and so on. That is because personalities only matter when we are with other people.

An interesting statement by much-quoted; industrialist Charles Michael Schwab is "Personality is to a person what perfume is to a flower." Positive, loving, and accepting personalities are like pleasant perfume. Good personalities can invade the senses of others and attract them. But then there are also flowers that have little perfume or even a repulsive odor. Controlling or judgmental personalities do not relate well to others, are not liked, and are not sought out. If we want to relate better with other people, we should work on improving those personality traits that help us to do so—being cheerful, patient, willing to listen, faithful, respectful, and willing to think of others first.

Though not always true, how other people treat us is often a reflection of how we treat others. A short quip of comedian Terry Fader, in his comedy routine with the puppet called the annoying neighbor, is: "Everybody has an annoying neighbor, and that if you don't have one, you are the annoying neighbor."

If we feel we are not being treated well by others, we may need to look at how caring, courteous, and accepting we are of others. However, when we are not accepted because of appearance, education, or physical or cultural differences due to some type of bias, it doesn't mean there is anything wrong with our personalities. But even in those situations, we still need to learn how to relate with the people with whom we have to communicate. If we think of ourselves as superior or as victims, we will not improve the way we relate with others or what they think of us. It is most important to realize that the acceptability of our personalities is somewhat inversely proportionate to how important we think we are as compared to others. It would be wise to pay attention to a wise old saying of Judith Martin (known as "Miss Manners"): "It is far more impressive when others discover your good qualities without your help."

Our personalities identify us and make us unique. But the negative or positive nature of our personalities is something we develop. Environment has an effect on how positive a personality we have. But the biggest factor affecting our personalities is the mental decisions we make between learning to appreciating what we encounter in life or being dissatisfied. The decision to act in a positive way and learn more about life will help us laugh at ourselves and kid each other in friendly ways, which makes life and even places of work more enjoyable. Negative personalities can make life and workplaces miserable. As already mentioned, the most attractive or unattractive aspect of personality is how we relate to others. We need to recognize our weakness.

Most of us would probably like to improve our personalities. If you want, you can spend time reading up on improving personality, or even take classes. A greater understanding of personalities could help in dealing with other people. But understand that in all cases, improving personality involves working on changing or improving the habits of how we relate to other people, the most important of which is being positive and accepting. Knowing a problem by itself will do nothing. For that reason, the best thing we can do is to work on those traits that most all people respect: being caring, being positive, listening, accepting, and responding in ways that show others they matter.

In working on improving our personality, we will not only relate better but also gain the admiration of others for our effort. Even those people with severe handicaps or personality disorders can, by their efforts, give inspiration to others. But it should be realized that although some changes in personality are possible, the personality habits we develop in our youth will, to some degree, always be with us. For that reason, it is important that people in relationships learn accept each other the way they are and not expect significant personality changes.

Our personalities, like feelings, tell us much about ourselves. Like we do with feelings, we may use our personality limitations as an excuse for not doing what we should. Like feelings, our personalities—how we relate to others—can improve and mature. Our personalities mature when we learn to use our gifts to be more courteous and caring, rather than using those gifts to manipulate others to get what we want.

In *Human Understanding*, we realize that personality is tied to how we relate to other people. There are many ways we can relate to others. We may not have been born with the personality we would like to have, but we can choose to be positive, kind, and helpful in what we do in life. It will make life much more enjoyable for us and for others.

REASONS FOR PAIN

I looked for references on why pain is important to life. Although I did find some books and articles that talked about the positive aspects of pain, I found no defined reason for pain. But there is a good reason for pain. You may not feel that way when you are suffering. Pain can be horrendous, but that is a result of the human condition that exists so that we may have and better appreciate physical life. Mental pain can be difficult, especially for those who are suffering a loss or have suffered because of violence. The pain of separation is very difficult.

To understand the reason pain is necessary, pain needs to be looked at objectively, like a classroom subject. When people are in pain, they are not normally objective. When people are in pain, they do not realize that it is pain that makes things in life dearer to us and brings about changes that make life better for all. Summer is more appreciated after a difficult winter. Pain is a necessary counterpart to joy and happiness that gives us a basis by which we can appreciate them. It is just that pain seems so unfair at times, and perhaps it is unfair. But then again, we judge based upon our limited view of reality.

This section is intended to present some positive thoughts about pain. Pain is important to the betterment of humanity. Pain lets us know that something is not right. Pain lets us know when changes must be made. Without pain, physical or mental, there would be little or no evolution to something better. Pain and suffering give us a reason to bring about change. Even this book, which is intended to help advance understanding of life, resulted from personal pain.

It would be nice if positive human evolution resulted solely from humans trying to improve their situation for the betterment of all. But the world we live in is not a place where people normally look out for others out of love. Therefore, there needs to be another cause for change to the better. And the main cause for change in today's world is pain. Anyone who accepts the concept of evolution should realize that pain is important for evolution into something better.

I lump fear, humiliation, guilt, and shame with pain because they involve mental pain, whether in the past or future. It is mostly the desire to ease pain that brings about changes and improves humankind's situation. I do not credit the desire to improve things as a significant reason for change because if there was no pain of any type, there would little or no desire to improve things. It is pain that brings about change, or at least the desire to change.

The amount of money and research devoted to reducing physical pain is astounding. We even look to technology to reduce the pain of exercise. We seem to want to eliminate the phrase, "no pain, no gain." But that phrase has a good basis. We are more careful of the hot iron once we are burned. Without pain, would anyone actually mature? Look what happens to children whose parents do not let them feel the painful consequences of poor decisions. Many never learn to take responsibility. Most often, it is the experience of pain that causes us to mature and take responsibility for our actions. It seems humans need painful situations to help us grow up.

The fear of pain can also be a deterrent. In Russia, a bridge engineer must stand below a bridge he designed while it is being load tested. There can be painful consequences for not doing things correctly in the engineering profession. That is a big reason engineers consider all possible conditions. But getting back to pain, this book is mostly meant to address the mental pain we bring about in ourselves by the way we think. It is not meant to address the specifics of physical pain related to illness or tragedy, although physical pain can influence or be influenced by our thought habits.

Even though it may seem very unfair at times, in many ways, pain is actually a gift to humankind. It may seem that I have lost my sanity to suggest that pain is in some way a gift. I personally know the pain of losing two children, a stepson, and other deep hurts. But I have learned that when people suffer the pain of loss, they make the choices that affect how to they will deal with it.

You might want to read Stephen Davey's book, *Pain, A Perfect Gift from God*. We can let the pain hurt and linger and feel sorry for ourselves, or we can accept the pain and then use the knowledge gained by that hurt to help us do something positive. Those people who, as a result of personal pain, help others avoid pain do something positive not only for themselves, but for all of humankind. By doing something positive, they give a positive meaning to all the people and events that have caused them to move forward in life, including those that brought about pain.

When we are sick or injured, the pain in our body is telling us something is physically wrong. If we follow the message of the pain and ease up on that part of the body that is hurting, we can avoid worse injury or sickness and work on healing. As an analytical engineer, it only makes sense to me that if the body has a warning system, the mind also has a warning system when the mind is not healthy in its functioning. That warning system is mental pain.

Most often, mental pain lets us know our thought processing is not functioning properly. (Some mental pain can be the result of biological problems.) Since most people do not realize much of personal mental pain results from worry and stress, caused by negative habits of thought processing, they let the habits continue until they become mentally and physically disabling. Stress is known to negatively affect brain chemical balance. Physical healing in the body can occur by just resting the body. But when unhealthy thought processing is causing mental and physical pain, the unhealthy thinking needs to change to relieve the pain. Medicine and therapy can help relieve the pain of unhealthy thought habits, but unless there is a change in thought reality and resulting thought processing, the problem and pain will never fully go away.

Athlena Staik, PhD, LMFT, in her blog *Neuroscience and Relationships*, tells us that toxic thinking is self-perpetuating. (17) It not only stimulates the body's reward or learning center with pseudo feel-good feelings, but it also activates the body's fear response and the brain responds negatively. How we think--positively or negatively—will have corresponding neurological effects on the brain. Unless there is a conscious intention to make changes in toxic thinking patterns, things will not get better.

There are many paradoxes in life. One of them is that the pain of failure, disillusionment, overwhelming fear, and even depression can sometimes indirectly bring about beneficial change in thought reality and even spiritual growth. With enough mental pain, poor or addictive thought habits can be given up at least for a while, and new thought processing patterns can begin. Pain can bring the opportunity to change if we allow ourselves to recognize the opportunity.

When we feel mentally down, it is not a time to feel sorry for ourselves. Rather, it is a time to reconsider what is important in life. Certainly, suffering is not so important that its cause must be held on to. It is time to introduce new notions into thought reality that will actually make us feel good about ourselves. It is time to consider that happiness is not found in worldly things or worldly concerns. It is time to consider that the degree of mental happiness and peace is mostly associated with our ability to appreciate and to love what we encounter, even when we are not treated well.

As will be explained in a future chapter, happiness, in this book, is related to the acceptance of *what is*.

For those who suffer from stress or worry, my father's words come to mind. "Why take life so seriously; you're never going to get out of it alive." I didn't want to listen when he kept reminding me (I thought he was hounding me.) However, he was right. No matter how much I worry, I will not get out of life alive and the world will get along without me when I leave. But I let my mind think I should be in control. I needed to feel real pain to understand pain, rather than trying to control it and feeling sorry for myself. When in mental anguish, it would be helpful for all of us to reevaluate what the pain is telling us and what is really important in life.

Although not related to severe anguish, my daughter recently told me how she deals with adversity. She said that when things are not going right, she thinks to herself how fortunate she was to be born in America or how fortunate she is to have a job. In looking at positives in life rather than negatives, we are better mentally equipped to face adversity. Not everyone is fortunate enough to have a job or to live in America. However, there is only one person in the entire world for whom things could not be worse. And the odds are you are not that person. Even in pain, happiness is still related to the notions of thought reality. So it is important to think about the bright side of things as often as possible.

Fundamental evidence that the pain of stress and worry most often result from thought processing is the fact that there are many people in similar situations do not exhibit the same amount of stress and fear, if any at all. People in poverty can be very happy people when they decide to appreciate the blessings they do have, although that does not mean they should not work to make things better. It is important to realize mental pain and unhappiness are often brought about by a thought reality that focuses on fear and on worldly values. As previously mentioned, it is the notions of thought reality that determine our happiness. The thought reality that accepts and appreciates *what is*—is happy. The opposite is also true.

Mental pain from worry and fear is a feeling that will not just disappear by wishing it gone. As we reviewed in the chapter on Emotions and Feelings, unwanted feelings will remain unless they are overcome with the introduction of new, positive mental notions into thought reality. When we are mentally suffering, it is important to focus on love and acceptance. And it is also important to have the help of other people to remind us of the need to be positive in our thinking, as well as to focus on new mental concepts.

For those of us who accept the concept of a Higher Power and an afterlife, we might think about the concept that this life is just a short blip in eternity and that our worldly problems are not that important. The story of the Prodigal Son could apply to all of us, but in a somewhat different way. When we are in mental pain, we just need to come to our senses, swallow our pride, turn to the Higher Power of love, and allow ourselves to be embraced by the feeling of love. (18)

Pain also presents an opportunity for the more fortunate to show their concern for people who are suffering due to circumstances beyond their control. In helping those who are in pain, we can come to realize the inner happiness and joy comes with helping others. In the needs of others, we are being given an opportunity to learn what creates real happiness. This will not only help relieve the pain of others; it can also help us to realize how good we actually have it.

In *Human Understanding*, we realize that everything in life has a purpose, including pain. Pain is something that can bring about change to something better. How the notions and habits of our thought reality react to pain will determine the degree of pain we feel and how long we will let pain adversely affect our lives.

To reduce mental, and even some physical pain, we need to realize that such pain is telling us that negative thought notions are adversely affecting our lives. It is the negative notions of thought reality that create an imbalance, which is manifested in feelings of unhappiness and worse. The way to deal with mental pain is to open our minds to new positive values and ways of thinking, and living in ways that increase our self-worth and acceptance of the world around us. The question for each of us is: are we going to respond positively to pain or create even more.

Summary of Part I

Part I presents, in a condensed form, a description of how people function. Understanding how we function is important to making the choices in life that result in self-worth and personal happiness. In many ways, we function like computers. We make evaluations based upon the information available. The brain receives input though the senses. The information of the senses is then processed by the brain, along with how that information relates to thought reality.

Thought reality consists of all conscious and subconscious ideas, beliefs, values, and purposes called mental notions. Thought processing of information relies on existing mental notions as a reference for evaluation of anything new. Like a computer, the accuracy of the evaluation is dependent upon correct information, both existing and new information. Incorrect thought reality notions lead to incorrect evaluations, but so can incorrect perceptions, as the *Mind Games* TV show points out. Because people do not realize the limitations of their thought reality, they tend to accept what they believe is reality, rather than realize it is just a personal opinion.

The brain appears to be programmed to perceive and learn most efficiently at an early age. But unlike a computer, the mind is not satisfied with just information. The mind does not seem to be interested in absorbing the information available without nurturing. To the youngest minds, life is not worth living without the feeling of being loved. Would a computer unplug itself if not loved? Babies not already influenced by the physical world seem to understand that the ultimate goal in life is love, not just physical existence.

Although the brain may be a computer, the mind is more than the brain. The mind can love and forgive, as well as choose evil.

Because the human brain is programed to absorb all that it can, especially when very young, the more information a child is exposed to very early in life, the more information will be available for proper evaluations throughout life. Children learn mostly from what appears to be most valuable to the people influential in their lives, although they also learn from other things perceived as valuable. To get what they perceive as valuable, children develop means and methods of interfacing with others. This will most often have an effect, to a substantial degree, on how they communicate with other people the rest of their lives.

A key factor in learning is repetition. It is important to realize that words and ideas repeated often enough can become part of thought reality. Repetition of words and ideas is a good way to learn. But a problem occurs if what is repeated learned is not correct. Another problem with repetition is that, repetitively conforming to specific rules of behavior without challenging them, at least mentally, can lead to losing mental creativity. The result is that people get hung up on norms of behavior, even to the point they ridicule others who do not conform to the norms. Too much conformity is a detriment to creativity.

When the body reacts to what the senses perceive without a rational evaluation, it is said to be reacting emotionally. The mind is meant to rationally evaluate what the body senses and then to react rationally. But that does not always happen and emotional reactions may continue. Although we have opinions about everything we evaluate, they do not normally create feelings unless they are important to us. Feelings can be manifested as anxiety, fear, happiness, or in other ways. The more important evaluation is thought to be, the more intense the resulting feeling. Intense negative feelings, such as fear and anxiety, can only be overcome by new thought reality information, which allows for better mental evaluation and understanding.

As conscious beings, we seek being fulfilled in some way. What we come to believe will be most fulfilling and most valuable becomes what we desire. Attaining specific values becomes the purpose(s) for doing the things we do. Without purpose, there is no practical reason to exist. To shortcut the process of thinking in depth of how achieve the values we desire, most all we do, we do out of habit. Our habits reflect our values. And what we value reflects what we value in life, including purpose.

What allows people to rise above the level of computers and animals is free will. We can turn our backs on something or on everything we have previously learned if we so choose. We can rise above merely physical wants and learn virtue. Regardless of our environment, each one of us is free to search for what actually brings personal self-worth and real happiness. And if we decide to look beyond our selfishness, we can come to understand that it is in going beyond our own selfishness-wants that we can find self-worth and inner happiness. We are free to choose and in so doing, we choose our degree of happiness in life.

In this book, spirituality is considered living for a purpose beyond self. It does not require a God. However, it does require the acceptance of a higher-level reality of virtue and vice (love and evil). Spirituality can provide hope and a feeling of being loved that the world cannot provide. It is in spirituality that people can come to understand that real inner happiness and joy come with giving of self rather than taking for self.

Thought reality does not always understand that happiness and joy, as well as unhappiness and even depression, result from our thought habits. When thought habits lead away from inner peace and happiness, mental pain is there to tell us to find new purpose and values that will reduce the pain.

Something that should be well understood by reading Part I is that people operate consciously or subconsciously based upon purpose(s) they perceive as of value, whether that value be selfish or totally unselfish. For that reason, people will not change their habits unless there is a perceived change in thought reality values. No amount of words, rewards, or punishment will bring about a change in purpose unless they result in new values or in discrediting old values. New values can change some habits, but without new values that bring new purpose in life, real changes in behavior will be few. If purpose remains selfish, behavior will remain selfish. It is only when new purpose, which is not selfish, is perceived as valuable to thought reality that significant changes can be made in how life is lived. For real changes in human behavior living for a higher value than worldly reality is most important to humanity. But that will not happen until people open their minds to that reality and incorporate that reality into their lives.

PART II

CONCEPTS IN REALITY

REFERENCE FOR REALITY

All human knowledge is based upon some reference. A map is of no use if you do not know where you are on the map. You need a reference point. Human knowledge and understanding are based upon references that have been perceived as being correct. Logic has its basic premise. Science has its tests, which are gauged against some reference.

Languages are references for verbal thought. Since different languages have different words for the same object, language must be only a reference for communication and thinking. We learn a language one word at a time. If we can put enough words together, we learn a language. But if we cannot learn the basic words to make sense of other words, we will not learn a language. Also, if we are exposed to only one language, our reference for learning will be limited to that one language.

In the same way that we learn a language, we learn basic references for our perceptions and beliefs that form our thought reality. If we are exposed to only limited perceptions and beliefs, those limited perceptions and beliefs, right or wrong, form our limited thought reality, which we use to evaluate everything we experience in life.

Thought processing requires that we accept what we are initially taught, so we have a basis for further evaluation. Our initial thought reality of beliefs and values is from our parents, teachers, and other influences. As we grow and are exposed to more things in life, we tend to modify our thought reality when we perceive new values and/or new mental notions. The more we are exposed to, with an open mind, the greater the range of information in thought reality for future evaluation. However, we need to remind ourselves that most of the thought references we use to evaluate things in life are still only references. They do not necessarily represent actual reality.

Reality of intangible beliefs can be vastly different between various people. If we believe we are unfortunate and the world is out to get us, we will be unhappy. If, in the same circumstances, we believe we are fortunate and see the goodness of other people, we will be happy. When we are young, time seems to go so slowly. When we are old, time seems to pass ever so quickly. Even the perception of time can change. As people grow older, or as their knowledge grows, the value of what they have and what they want can change as well.

With time and with our life experiences, thought reality, by which we evaluate right or wrong, good or bad, and truth or fiction, will likely change if life values change. The amount it will change will depend upon how much our minds are open to new values and new thoughts. As we open our minds to new thoughts and experiences and incorporate these into thought reality, we have even more knowledge for additional evaluation and for finding new concepts that could be valuable to us. The net effect is that the reality of what we consider valuable today can change and expand when we open our minds to new ideas and new values. We can even discover ways to improve our happiness if we are willing to make the effort to search for that which truly brings self-worth and personal happiness. It is interesting to see how just time and experience can decrease the value of worldly things and increase the value of friendship.

A good example is the major focus of high school class reunions. For the first 15 years, much of the talk centers on what people have accomplished. Much bragging is heard. Over the next 15 years, the conversation at the reunions slowly mellows. The focus is not so much on self but on how others are doing. By the 40th reunion, those of us who are still alive are mostly just happy to see each other. The reality of what is important in life will likely change with time. It may take a few moments or many years. The change will normally come with the changes in values that come with life experiences. But even after 40 years, some alumni may still be full of themselves. Change still requires a mind open to seek new values.

Although change in what is important to us normally happens over a period of time, it can also change quickly. It can change in as short a time as it takes to truly regret something we have just done that seemed acceptable moments earlier. It will also likely change quickly if you are told you only have weeks to live. Change is directly related to how important new values or even old values are to us. If we are not happy in life, it is important to open the mind and search for new values that will increase happiness. The question for all of us is: Will we let our initial thought realities control our lives, or will we open our minds to challenging our initial thought realities?

If we were taught that the world is flat, and all the people around us believe it to be flat, we would likely believe it to be true. Should we believe the world is flat, we would probably also believe that the sun revolves around the Earth, since we would otherwise fall off. When one thing in our thought reality is misleading, it can lead to many incorrect conclusions. The concept of a flat world was acceptable to many European people only 600 years ago. Some people today still insist it is flat. What is, or has been, considered fact in science can change, even if it has been the perceived center of the universe.

Change requires thought reality to be open to new values. Although many people will amend thought realities with new knowledge, other people will hold onto their old beliefs until holding onto them becomes be detrimental to them, or until they finalize realize there is something new to be gained by changing. This is true for institutions as well. There may be nothing that slows growth in understanding and progress more than so called "established facts" that are not correct.

Reality for each of us is what we accept it to be, based upon our limited knowledge and understanding. These days, most of us realize there is a growth in general knowledge, although few of us keep track of all the advances. Almost every year, there are new discoveries in science, astronomy, and archeology. But we do not normally input those discoveries into our thought reality unless we are familiar with the fields of study in which the discoveries are being made.

When I went to school, electrons were described as particles that revolved around a center of protons and neutrons. Now electrons are considered wave energy surrounding protons and neutrons, which are of themselves almost entirely kinetic energy, (and possibly it is all kinetic energy of some type). Yet those of us who took science classes 60 years ago still have a thought reality image of electron particles on orbits around protons. If we do not work hard to change that thought reality, what we originally learned is what we still image. Correct or incorrect, reality to each of us is what our thought reality images it to be.

Reality of scientific belief can change, even at the level of matter itself. Einstein's concept of relativity tells us that matter is but a time-related form of energy. Scientific testing has shown Einstein's theory of relativity to be correct. Not even time, as we measure it, is constant. We really do not understand the universe we live in.

To further the problem of understanding matter is that at the sub-atomic level, Einstein's relativity does not apply. Quantum mechanics applies at that level. What is most interesting about matter in quantum mechanics is not that matter is some form of energy, but how it supposedly becomes matter. The current simplified explanation of the quantum level is that everything at a sub-atomic level consists of wavelength, frequency, and kinetic energy which when combined with electromagnetism gives us quantum electrical dynasmics. Conscious observation of wave energy causes it to be bottled up and appear as matter. What causes things to feel solid is believed to be the kinetic energy, resulting from the forces of electromagnetism.

In the last few decades, time (speed), miniaturization, energy, and computer processing have combined to give us virtual reality. Because people relate through their conscious perceptions, artificial reality can be created using electronics. With the rate of development in electronics increasing at a geometric pace, it is possible that in the future, completely new, and believable forms of virtual reality will be developed. We may be able to place people in incredibly real, but still hypothetical, life situations. These systems could be used for testing, rewarding, punishing, or rehabilitating people. If we look with open minds, we could imagine that our universe may actually be an interactive virtual reality, of a higher level, designed to test our higher-level consciousness in some way.

Many followers of Taoism (19), an old Chinese religion, believe that our existence is what could be equated to an interactive quantum hologram into which consciousness is placed. The concept of a quantum holographic universe is actually gaining popularity in theoretical physics.

Even if life is a quantum hologram, physical life is real to those who experience physical existence. What is important in life is not what it consists of, but why it exists. I mention this possibility of holographic reality to open the minds of people whose thought reality is fixed solely on physical reality or what they have been told. Physical laws do control the physical level of life. But they do not control the sub-atomic level. Something else controls that. There is definitely something beyond the physical reality we live in.

The reality of what we really know about the universe and our existence is only beginning to be tapped. In a study by Jeanne Achterberg et al, (20) eleven healers chose unhealthy people with whom they felt an empathic connection. From a distance, each healer then sent mental energy, prayer, and good intentions at random intervals to the person they felt connected to, who was placed in a MRI scanner. The MRI scanner found significant differences in the activity of various parts of the brain that coincided with the send periods. Something telepathic occurred. We need to keep our minds open to the fact that what occurs in physical reality may not be simple physical reality.

Human knowledge is limited to that which can be observed and tested. For science, testing is limited to physical reality, so scientific theories are also limited to physical reality. As science works within physical reality and physical tests, most scientists do not recognize anything beyond physical reality. Things that are suggestive of something beyond physical reality are most often ignored, as they are not physically provable. Thus, the accepted hypothesis in science is that humanity is just an evolved physical creature, in spite of happenings that indicate people are connected in some way to something beyond their physical nature. When there are happenings that cannot be explained at the physical level, a person has to be concerned about reasonable doubt with any physical based hypothesis made to explain them.

An open mind would want to investigate the recorded phenomena that science cannot explain, rather than downplaying or ignoring it. What about ghosts, possession, poltergeists, exorcisms, clairvoyance, or miracles? Not all of these are purely anecdotal. How is it that the very early memories of some children are of people who have died, as noted in the next chapter? How is it that some holy people and prayer groups, who believe in a higher level of reality, can initiate healing, as noted in the chapter on Prayer?

Science's explanation of what it cannot explain is that things happen that we do not yet understand, but someday we will. While science's explanation could be the case in some instances, there are many different unexplained phenomena that appear to be well beyond physical reality. For that reason, my engineering instincts tell me that science is missing something. By keeping science theories confined to the physical dimension, science is basically going back to the days it said the world was flat. It is no wonder than the ideas of at least ten Nobel Prize winners were ridiculed initially by other scientists. I choose to accept the likelihood of a hypothesis that has an explanation for the physically unexplainable rather than hypothesis that contains no explanation.

Science must consider the possibility of going beyond the limitations of the physical reality. It is similar to how going beyond the concept of a flat world expanded the knowledge of the universe. The next chapter, Reality of an Independent Consciousness, presents happenings that science, and even religion, should try to understand rather than disregard.

A paradox cannot exist where full understanding is present. If we look at humanity, paradoxes exist. How is it that physical beings in love, who have nothing in life but love, can be happier than those who have great wealth? How is it that a different thought reality can change one person's trash to another person's treasure? How could physical creature evolve to where that which fulfills is not of the material level of its existence? How is it that the acceptance of a Higher Power can lead to personal peace even in times of duress?

Logic says that there must be an explanation to such questions. These ideas do make sense if humans exist for a higher level of reality of love. In accepting a reality of a higher level of love and acceptance, the apparent paradox is not a paradox at all. If we consider that humanity has a nature above the purely physical, it would only make sense that fulfillment of man's higher nature would also be beyond the physical level. This explanation may seem like a simplification. But as has been often said, the simplest explanation is usually the right one.

The reality of physical life is simplistic. Physical reality is that we were born. Physical reality is the circumstances placed upon our lives. Physical reality is the physical laws of the universe. Physical reality is that we die. Physical reality is that the world eventually decays. But human reality is more than just physical reality. Human reality is that love fulfills where nothing of the physical world can. Human reality is that we can reason beyond the mere physical. As such, human reality is tied to the higher level fixed universal reality of virtue and vice. Human reality is that, in being connected to the higher level fixed reality, we are also subject to the consequences of our acceptance, or lack thereof, of virtue or vice into our lives. The reality of physical life is that it exists for a higher-level purpose.

The concept presented in this book—that personal thought reality is relative to personal experience—is not a new concept. It has led to relativism; that everything is relative. But that belief is wrong. I believe, as did Aristotle, that everything has a purpose. There are some constants and they exist for all levels of reality. They exist for any alien beings that may exist, as much as for humans. They are the fixed realities of virtue and vice. Virtue begets order and joy, while vice begets chaos and eventual despair. Humans need to understand that only the highest virtue—love—truly fulfills. But it should be realized that for virtue to be of a fixed higher level, vice and evil would also exist at all levels of reality. And if the Higher Power of love can influence and alter physical existence, it is also likely that a higher level of vice and chaos can influence and alter physical existence.

To move forward in this worldly existence, humans must become more loving and accepting. That will not happen unless there is a purpose for humans to develop a loving morality. If there is an understanding that acceptance of a Higher Power of love will bring love and order, there is such a purpose.

The existence of another level of reality opens the door to the existence of a Higher Power or Supreme Consciousness. One thing that is confusing to me about people rejecting the concept of a Higher Power, of some unknown nature, is that it risks nothing in terms of what is most fulfilling—self-worth and inner happiness.

Yes, it risks the temporary goods and pleasures of the world that do not assure happiness. But then those people who accept the Higher Power can be very happy even without worldly goods and pleasures. In accepting even the possibility of a Higher Power, each of us could be removing the shackles holding us back from possibly a greater understanding of life. We limit our knowledge and our basis for understanding when we do not open our minds to new thoughts and possibilities.

It would be wise to contemplate that if inner consciousness, virtue, and vice are of a higher level, they would not be affected by physical death. For that reason, it would make sense that virtues and vices of inner consciousness will remain with it after death and would likely have a positive or negative on any future conscious existence.

In *Human Understanding*, we realize that our knowledge of true reality is limited. In the physical world, about the only thing certain is death (and perhaps taxes). To understand human reality, we need to think beyond the limits of physical reality. We need to explore the reality of inner consciousness and of the fixed reality of virtue and vice and their consequences. Until our consciousness accepts the reality of a higher level, humanity will remain trapped in a world that cannot provide the fulfillment that inner consciousness seeks.

THE REALITY OF AN INDEPENDENT CONSCIOUSNESS

T he big deviation from predominant scientific thought I make in this book is that humans possess a consciousness independent of the body. This chapter presents various reasons to believe that contention. It should be realized that if humans have an independent consciousness, which is not physical, there must also be a purpose for it to exist in the human body. You can choose to believe that there is no independent consciousness and that man is merely a function of evolution, but first you might open your minds to consider some of the things that indicate that people possess an independent consciousness.

I choose to believe in the existence of an independent consciousness or soul because of the abundance of anecdotal evidence and information that supports the concept of an independent consciousness, not because of religion. While I admit to having religious beliefs, I do not rely on religion for my belief in an independent consciousness. What is contained herein is recorded information, which I accept as reasonable, though not proof of independent consciousness. It is not recognized as evidence because, as Thomas Kuhn explained in *The Structure of Scientific Revolutions*, it does not concur with the presently accepted paradigm of human life being entirely physical.

The engineer in me cannot overlook important information, even if it does not agree with accepted scientific theory. This chapter not only looks at reasons to consider an inner consciousness, it also gives some historical insight into the demise of the concept of reincarnation in Western civilization.

In most of ancient Western civilization, a major religious belief was reincarnation. The Egyptians, Greeks, Gauls, Celts, Norse, Druids, and Romans all believed in various forms of reincarnation. Virgil's description of the Roman view of the afterlife was that some individuals get reincarnated and that reincarnation was not endless. The Roman main belief was that upon death, individuals who had committed crimes, were sent to Tartarus to be tortured by the Furies until the debt to society was deemed paid in full. Virgil also wrote about six levels of heaven. The Greek philosophers Aristotle and Plato both wrote about the existence of a soul. Plato also seems to have believed in the preexistence of souls (21).

In Eastern civilizations, Hinduism and Buddhism accept the concept of reincarnation; that consciousness survives physical death, and can appear again and again in other physical bodies. What is not well known is that the concept of reincarnation, or at least the preexistence of souls, was an accepted belief by many early Christians. Origen (considered a doctor of the Christian Church) wrote about the preexistence of souls in his *First Principles* (22).

So what caused the concept of reincarnation to disappear from Western civilization? The answer is Christianity. The Christian church informally rejected that idea of reincarnation at the Council of Nicaea in 325 convened by the Emperor Constantine, who wanted to establish a Christian orthodox belief throughout the empire. The belief established included the resurrection of the body, which negated the concept of reincarnation. That belief makes sense for those who believed in the exact words of Ezekiel Chapter 37, although it refers to the Jewish people.

The belief could have been amplified by the letters of St. Paul (23), who seemed sure the end of the world was imminent. Then there are stories, whether true or not, that Constantine was afraid of the consequences of his pre-Christian life and was instrumental in getting a more Roman view of the afterlife, which did not necessarily include reincarnation, into Christianity.

Regardless of who or what brought it about, the orthodox Christian belief is now that humans consist of a physical body with an independent soul that comes into existence in the womb at conception. It should be realized that the decision to accept this belief was made by people who considered the earth to be the center of physical reality. I wonder what Christian beliefs about physical resurrection would be today if those people had understood quantum theory, the extent of the universe, that the earth is vulnerable to destruction, and the possibility of more advanced conscious beings in the universe.

Origen's teaching on the preexistence of souls was officially anathematized by the Second Council of Constantinople, convened at the behest of the Eastern Roman Emperor Justinian in 553 A.D. (24) The necessity to anathematize it indicates there was still a belief of many people and a problem for Justinian. There remains much controversy about the Council (25). The endnotes in this book, as well as information available on Justinian and the Council itself, which the pope boycotted, make for interesting reading.

One of the ironic effects of this Council was that the possibility of preexisting souls and/or reincarnation, which would require the belief in an independent inner consciousness or soul, was lost to Western civilization as it converted to Christianity. Though the concept of some form of punishment or restitution for wrongs done remained at that time, belief in reincarnation was now off limits for the faithful. The concept of Purgatory came to Christianity about the 12th century to explain how not so holy people could still get to heaven. However, no decision or belief of humanity has had any actual effect how people can actually get to heaven.

In keeping with the Buddhist belief that physical life is about suffering, perhaps Purgatory does exist as another lifetime. Thinking changes with time. The Catholic belief in Limbo is now in limbo. So what happens to the souls of infants who die just after birth without baptism, or even those who die in the womb if the soul originates with conception? What happens to those with im-paired brains? Perhaps, in modern technical lingo, their souls are "rebooted" into other bodies.

Science actually makes one of the best unintended arguments for independent conscious with quantum mechanics theory. In quantum theory, matter does not actually exist without conscious-ness, so consciousness must have come first. How could a physical being evolve consciousness if consciousness is necessary for human physical existence? There must also be an overall consciousness that caused the matter of the universe. Even if the universe is a quantum hologram, as some theoretical physicists are now suggesting, how was it created? Science indirectly tells us that physical reality is the result of a higher reality of some nature, while seemingly rejecting the possibility of such a higher reality.

In the last chapter, I mentioned ghosts, possession, poltergeists, out-of-body experiences, and exorcism— none of which cannot be adequately explained by physical science. They all seem to be related to a consciousness, or spirit, independent of the body. But there is much more information and many occurrences that conflict with modern conventional thought and point to an independent consciousness in humans.

In the chapter on Spirituality, Near-Death Experiences (NDEs) were mentioned. They indicate a consciousness independent of the body. A commonly referenced NDE source is Dr. Melvin Morse M.D., associate professor of pediatrics at University of Washington. Dr. Morse recounted a girl, dead for 19 minutes who, when she did come back to life, gave details of what the doctors did to resuscitate her. She said she watched while floating above the revival effort (26).

There are many other similar stories. Science has attempted to discredit NDE experiences by saying that near-death experiences are likely due to temporal lobe epilepsy. The ability of the peo-ple, unconscious or clinically dead, to actually know the medical procedures used on them, is ignored.

The concept that an NDE is a function of the brain is contrary to evidence recorded by Jean Jacques Charbonier M. D. in his book, *Seven Reasons to Believe in the Afterlife*, as translated by Jack Cain. He tells the story of Pamela Reynolds, whose body was in an induced hypothermic condition at 59.9° F and whose brain was then completely drained of blood. All brain activity ceases at about 62.6° F. The EEG quickly flat lined and stayed that way for almost an hour. Yet she awoke able to say what had been done, having observed her body from outside it. She also had visions of relatives. What she experienced was related to a consciousness that could not have been initiated by her brain. There are other similar NDE stories recounted in numerous books and also on the Internet. Statistics indicate that about 66 percent of NDEs involve out-of-body experiences.

Many people who have had near-death experiences (NDEs) have also experienced what they describe as heaven and hell. Many say quite bluntly that heaven and hell exist and that the experience changed their physical lives. Their stories are also in books and on the Internet. One online reference I reviewed, which I particularly liked, was *Testimonies of Heaven and Hell*, on the web at http://eternityinourheart.com/. These testimonies, in personal video form, speak of the unbelievable beauty of heaven and the cruelty of hell. These very descriptive encounters do not seem to be due to temporal lobe epilepsy.

Then there is a question of how blind people have been able to provide information of their resuscitation that could only come through vision. Dr. Ken Ring investigated 31 blind people who had NDEs (27). Eighty percent of them said they were able to see when out of their bodies, even those people blind from birth. In the chapter on the Concept of a Higher Power, we will look at the clairvoyant, Edgar Cayce, and the knowledge that came to him not related to time or distance. Most of, if not all, the cures he gave were unknown to science. His consciousness became aware of information scientifically impossible to be obtained by the physical brain.

In the chapter "Concept of a Higher Power," we will also look at such miracles as incorruptible bodies and people going without food or water for years. These are not a direct indication of an independent consciousness. However, they do indicate that physical bodies can deviate from the laws of physical reality.

Although remote viewing is not accepted scientifically and not reliable enough for much practical use, it is interesting to read a review of it by American physicist H.F. Puthoff, PhD, who directed the CIA's studies on remote viewing at Stanford Research Institute. (28) In his written review of the research, *CIA-Initiated Remote Viewing at Stanford Research Institute*, Dr. Puthoff wrote, "Despite the ambiguities inherent in the type of exploration covered in these programs, the integrated results appear to provide unequivocal evidence of human capacity to access events remote in time and space, however falteringly, by some cognitive process not yet understood."

Of much interest related to the subject of consciousness is neuro-imaging research. Dr. Andrew Newberg has conducted significant research in neuroimaging. (29) His tests include religious people and the evaluation of mystical experiences. In his book, *The Spiritual Brain: Science and Religious Experience*, he points out that mystical experiences differ from normal or even abnormal experiences in that people who have such experiences perceive what they experienced actually represented true reality. They described the feeling of oneness with everything "as being more real than every other reality experienced." There is no perception of objects and "there is no experience of self." They "have the perception of going beyond their own ego's thoughts and even beyond their own brain." Such a notion seems highly contrary to the notion that the brain is limited to physical reality.

Rene Descartes, considered the father of modern philosophy, introduced the concept of dualism between mind and body. That theory held sway for a long time. However, it was eventually accepted that the brain and body actually function together for a purpose, rather than acting separately. Because function may exist for any intended mental purpose, the more acceptable term is "metaphysical fundamentalism."

I do not have problems with the concept of functionalism. But again, science has chosen to ignore another possibility. That possibility is the dualism of function: function for purposes of worldly reality and function for purpose of higher level reality. The physical brain's function is for physical reality. The inner consciousness function is for a higher level of reality. With an independent consciousness, functionality can exist at two levels for two different realities. As such, dualism can, and I believe, still exists.

The problem for humanity is that inner consciousness functions through physical consciousness. Inner consciousness comes into play in subconscious decisions that in some way involve virtue and vice and other intangibles such as faith, hope, and love. Unfortunately, inner consciousness can be ignored or even closed off by ego physical consciousness. The more we rely on the physical consciousness, the less we are in touch with our inner consciousness and the more likely we are to lose track of our inner consciousness's purpose in physical existence.

Science suggests the brain could be a quantum computer. I agree that the brain is a complex computer that controls all our physical actions. Computers can follow instructions to analyze what may be very complex. Computers can be programed to analyze and to make rational decisions. They can be programmed to make choices based upon soft logic. But they do not have consciousness. A computer cannot, through prayer and meditation, transcend space and time and even affect change in physical reality. Various studies, some of which are noted in this book, show that such is possible for human consciousness.

I do not know for sure if reincarnation exists, although there are good reasons to believe it does. Actually, it is not important for me or for this book whether it exists or not. But research on the subject should not be ignored. For example, scientific research by Dr. Ian Stevenson into the subject strongly suggests that reincarnation of some nature exists.

Dr. Stevenson's research has been with numerous children remembering past lives and does not involve hypnosis. The very young children involved remembered names and places and even events they had no way of knowing about, which were subsequently verified. As the children aged, the memories tended to fade. His research also found that children who remembered being people who suffered violent deaths, had birthmarks in the location of, and that mimicked, the wound(s) that ended the life of the person whose name they remembered being. In one case, this included a series of birthmarks on the child, which exactly mimicked the shotgun wounds on the homicide photo of the man whose name was the same as the child remembered being. The most noted case of past life memory is that of Shanti Devi. In this case, past memories never faded. It is a most interesting case for those people who are willing to open their minds to other possibilities.

Author of *Many Masters*, Brian L Weiss, MD, found that regressing people hypnotically to previous lives, which seemed to have initiated the phobias, could relieve those phobias. (30)

Dr. Helen Wambach's research began in the 1960s in an effort to debunk the concept of reincarnation. Besides coming to the conclusion that reincarnation exists, her research strongly suggests that people who are reincarnated sometimes change sexes and even races. For religions that accept reincarnation, the concept of carryover from previous lives is the explanation for many inborn talents and personality traits, including homosexuality.

In her book, *Reliving Past Lives: The Evidence under Hypnosis*, Dr. Wambach recounts her experience with a 5-year-old girl. She did not speak nor allow human contact. She could read without being taught and demonstrated amazing math skills. When Dr. Wambach finally got through to her and she first began to speak, she began to lose her ability to read, as well as her math skills, which soon completely disappeared and she became a "normal" child.

You might want to look up James Leininger's Soul Survivor on the Internet for a story of supposed reincarnation that made national news. There are many additional books on the subject for people willing to check out the possibility. If reincarnation exists, independent consciousness also exists.

I have given but a few reasons to believe in an independent consciousness and an afterlife. There are plenty of other sources that give even more reasons. It would be important to look at the all the evidence before choosing to believe or not to believe.

A Dec. 9, 2009 Pew Forum of Religion and Public Life report found that 25 percent of all Americans and even 24 percent of Christians believed in some form of reincarnation. A 2011 study by the Roper Center for Public Opinion found that 20 percent of Americans believed in some form of reincarnation. Protestants' belief was listed as 15 percent, while Catholic belief was listed as 25 percent. In that reincarnation is not a belief of Christianity, yet it is believed by a large percentage of Christians, it is a controversial subject that cannot be ignored. The concept of reincarnation is considered reasonable to many Christians. That is likely because of the seeming unfairness of life and because of the belief that a Higher Power of love would afford all peoples a fair opportunity for salvation.

Obviously, the concept of reincarnation is very controversial to traditional Christians and other religions that do not accept the concept. Because of the mounting evidence of reincarnation, I thought that rather than deny its existence, it would be best to see how reincarnation may actually fit into the context of more traditional non-reincarnation beliefs. It should also be realized that although the majority of Jews and members of the Islamic faith do not believe in reincarnation, there are sects even within these religions that accept reincarnation, although not in the same context as in Hindu and Buddhist belief.

In more traditional reincarnation, Hindu and Buddhist, a certain amount of perfection in physical life is required to reach heaven, or Nirvana. The implication is that a higher state of existence must be earned and it takes many lifetimes to learn and earn. In Christianity, the belief is that a higher-level existence, labeled salvation, cannot be earned. The belief is that salvation is a gift to humanity made possible by the physical death of Christ. Christians believe that salvation is a gift. The concept is that it is the acceptance of the gift of unconditional love into one's being that makes full salvation possible. Actually, the perfection assumed necessary by Buddhists and Hindus may be no different than the full acceptance of unconditional love.

In Christian belief, a person does not have to be perfect to attain salvation after death, at least a level of salvation consistent with the degree of acceptance of unconditional love. Since not everyone is committed to the total acceptance of love at the time of death, the more traditional Christian belief has been that there is a purification process for those not yet worthy of full salvation. However, that belief does not extend to all Christianity. Some of Christianity suggests that any such purification process is voluntary. The question is: If unpurified, where do non-purified souls exist? Perhaps there are different levels of heaven and hell. The belief in different levels of heaven and hell exist in religions that accept reincarnation, as well as in many ancient religions.

Christians should be aware that St. Paul in 2 Corinthians 12:2 uses the term "third heaven." Are there various levels to heaven (and hell) as reincarnation religions believe and as Edward Cayce saw in his healing trances? There are many questions about life after death for which we have no absolute answers.

If hypnosis is believed, there are partial answers. In her book Life before Life, Dr. Wambach notes that 81 percent of the 750 people hypnotically regressed back through their birth said they chose to be reincarnated, and that to some degree they chose the life they were reborn into. Reincarnation is not a subject that should be disregarded. Even if reincarnation does exist, it does not eliminate the possibility of heaven or hell after one lifetime. Perhaps reincarnation occurs until a person makes a knowledgeable choice between selfish control or relinquishing control to love that would be necessary in a true heaven. And even if heaven or hell exists after one physical lifetime, as Christians believe, that does not rule out reincarnation and/or various levels to heaven and hell. It also does not rule out a last judgement. Perhaps reincarnation could be a voluntary way to try to move to a higher level of heaven, or even help those who remain in the physical level.

It is important to realize there is something about death that is consistent in all religions, including ancient ones. There are consequences for how life is lived. I would also think that if there is another physical life, the consequences for a life previously lived would likely also affect the circumstances of any new life. Karma could be a reality. That would be a very good reason not to be bigoted or to take advantage of other people. It would also encourage generosity.

Reincarnation or not, I believe there are consequences for how any life is lived. I also believe that heaven or hell of some nature or level awaits each human entity upon physical death. Even if reincarnation exists, in any additional lifetime, I would still need to be working to achieve final salvation rather than working in the other direction. Also, if reincarnation does exist, it does not rule out permanent salvation or hell after one lifetime. Therefore, I live this life as my only life. I choose to work toward fulfillment in love rather than ultimate chaos.

I have come to believe that life is all about inner consciousness's desire to be fulfilled. One life or many lives, the end game is the same. The fulfillment desired by inner consciousness is probably best described by Aristotelian teleology, in which everything in reality strives toward a perfect, unchanging state. Teleology is the study of the ends of purpose that thing serve. Aristotle believed there is a reason for everything and that the best way to understand why things are the way they are is to understand their purpose they are designed to serve. For consciousness, it would be to unite with the Supreme Loving Consciousness (although some people consider it Paradise.) Perhaps that fulfillment is being united eternally in the state of ecstasy, as mentioned by Dr. Newberg, who is particularly involved in the study of religious and spiritual experiences, and the relationship among the brain, religion, and health, and author of *The Mystical Mind: Probing the Biology of the Religious Experience*. This would also be like the state of Nirvana referred to in Buddhism.

Once consciousness exists, regardless of origin, it looks toward fulfillment. And that fulfillment is to be one with unconditional love. We get to salvation, by accepting unconditional love and forgiveness into the essence of who we are.

I bring up this controversy to point out that we really do not know for sure what exists beyond physical life. We can argue about the existence of reincarnation, as we have for thousands of years, or we can argue about various levels in heaven and hell. But there still will be no fully understood or accepted resolution. We can even debate the reason for a belief in the preexistence of souls. But it will solve nothing. What people need to consider is that whatever they choose to think will not change what actually exists.

Additionally, it will not change the purpose for human existence nor the basics of **human understanding**. When we accept the fixed realities of the universe as presented in this book, whether we choose to believe in reincarnation or not is not important, unless a specific belief itself influences how life is led. In that case, I believe it best to accept that which will lead a person to be the most accepting and loving person possible.

To be even more controversial, I will bring up another thought on the preexistence of souls. Time, as we understand it, is an aspect of physical reality that does not have to exist in other realities such as quantum reality. Once that concept is realized, it should also be realized that things can exist which are not affected by time as we know it. That concept should be accepted by all Christian denominations who believe that the body of Christ is actually present in Communion. It could be that the non-existence of time beyond physical reality, as we know it, makes such presence in Communion possible. Once the concept of there being no actual time at the quantum level is understood (that time only exists in physical reality), it is reasonable to assume that anything that exists outside of physical reality is not affected by physical time.

As souls, assuming they exist, are not of physical reality, they likely existed before the creation of physical matter which is related to physical time. If immortal souls exist, that is a rational evaluation. Again, there is no proof one way or another, and again, it does not matter in this existence. But it should open minds to realize there is much we really do not know beyond physical reality.

Another important issue to ponder, related to inner consciousness, is the potential power of an independent inner consciousness, not considered possible in normal physical reality. Should an inner consciousness exist, it would likely have some type of connection with the Higher Power (or Supreme Consciousness). That connection provides an explanation of happenings impossible in normal physical reality that are attributed to people.

Quantum reality consists of wave energy, which becomes coalesced into what is perceived as physical reality. Any consciousness responsible for initiating wave energy (a higher-level consciousness) should also be able to control and to modify it. Any such modification to normal wave frequency could cause a change in physical reality. Should inner consciousness become coherent (temporarily unified in some way) with such a higher-level consciousness, inner consciousness could have the ability to affect change in quantum-level energy waves and alter normal physical reality.

The experiment with coherent meditation, mentioned in the chapter on Prayer, to reduce crime in Washington D.C. showed a relationship between prayer and meditation and the reduction in crime. It provides a prime example of how conscious coherence with love and peace can change normal physical reality. This would also be a rational explanation for miracles and sudden unexpected cures that result from personal prayer or group prayer, and even from the touch of truly holy people.

The other explanation is that consciousness, which causes wave energy to become matter, can, with intense belief, affect the wave vibrations at the quantum level differently than what would be normal. For instance, intense conscious belief could affect quantum waves that create quantum wave frequency vibrations that neutralize the heat on the feet of people walking on hot coals. However, intense belief that is not directed beyond self in love seems to be limited to one's own body. But in either case, it would be conscious belief that would affect quantum reality. I do not believe that ability is initiated at the physical level of reality. It is initiated by inner consciousness.

Along that line of thinking, perhaps the concept of curses and blessings affecting physical reality is also real and explainable at the quantum level. If something could affect the quantum wave frequency of an object, it might also be able to infuse positive or negative wave energy into it, which could cause it to affect normal physical reality. And at the quantum level, where time is not a factor, once objects are blessed or cursed, they could continuously give off positive or negative wave energy until such is nullified at the quantum level. Therefore, a blessing could actually help protect a person.

Keep in mind that since vice can also exist at a higher level, humans' independent consciousness coherent with evil could also project evil changes at the quantum level, such as curses. Although this explanation of miracles, blessings, and curses may seem far-fetched, it is a rational explanation of how human inner consciousness could affect the quantum level and bring about what are referred to as miracles. Science has not offered any rational explanation. It is interesting to note that this explanation is very much in keeping with religious traditions of blessings and sacraments helping direct and protect those that receive them.

The concept that humans have a higher consciousness that can potentially affect changes in physical reality at the quantum level is one that science, as well as all of humanity needs to check out. Some research has been done in this area and has given rise to the "unified field theory," sometimes referred to as the "collective consciousness." There appears to be a basis for this theory, although it is not an accepted theory.

The concept of universal consciousness is enhanced by the study of ice crystal formations as noted the book *Messages from Water* by Masaru Emoto. After distilled water was placed between speakers that subjected the water to various repeated sounds, such as music, words, prayers, and similar, drops of the water was observed under a microscope forming ice crystals. Pleasant music, kind words and prayer resulted in beautiful ice crystals. Hard rock music, and unkind to harsh words resulted in ice crystals that were ill-formed to grotesque.

As was attested to by evidence mentioned in the chapter on Prayer, the coherence of the consciousness of many people has an effect on what happens in the world itself. The theory is the quantum level is affected by the combined quantum level vibrations produced by human consciousness. Vibrations that result from consciousness centered on love create peace and harmony. Vibrations from consciousness desire to control and take, rather than love, produce vibrations that upset the overall harmony of quantum vibration, which leads to disaster. The theory says that as the world turns away from love and prayer, chaos will follow. The way to world peace is not through wars and fighting or even arguing. The way to world peace is through the love of neighbor, prayer, pilgrimages, novenas, and sacrifice for the betterment of others. Unfortunately, the world seems to be headed a different way.

I am concerned that science has ignored information that is important to humanity because it does not fit the existing scientific paradigm about what constitutes humanity. Questionable unknowns regarding independent consciousness and what consciousness is capable of, need to be investigated rather than being discarded, just because they do not fit into prevailing paradigm. Opening the mind to the concept of independent consciousness can potentially open an all new understanding of what is important to humanity. My research on an independent consciousness has caused me to question some of my religion's beliefs. However, it has actually given me a deeper belief in spirituality and the basic fundamental of all relevant religion—love

In *Human Understanding*, we believe in the existence of independent consciousness. Although not physically provable, the sheer amount of unexplainable happenings, miracles, and other unexplained phenomena says there is a level of consciousness beyond physical reality. It is time for science to consider that humanity functions in dualism of realities. We function in a physical reality for some purpose of a higher reality. We also realize that in the goal of life is fulfillment in love. And that how we live our lives, reincarnation or not, will eventually determine if what happen to us after physical life.

THE REALITY OF CHANGE—
A CHANGE OF THOUGHT REALITY

The more that we investigate how thought reality becomes the reality that people believe exists, the more we should realize that the reality of fears and beliefs, as well as happiness, can change if our basic thought reality changes.

How what we experience forms our thought reality is best visualized in the Indian legend of the six blind men and the elephant. The men all felt different parts of the elephant and so each thought it was something different. The different things were wall (side), a snake (trunk), a spear (tusk), a tree (leg), a fan (ear), and a rope (tail). In at least one version of the tale, they actually begin to fight over who is right. The point is if we do not open our eyes to see the entire picture of life, we will remain ignorant about life and may even be willing to fight rather than to question or change our present beliefs.

Changes in thought reality are not all that easy. Like some scientists, educators, and politicians who ignore whatever does not agree with their beliefs, we typically hold on to the security of our present thought reality as long as we can. Maybe it is because of fear of change or because we have been trained to think within the confines of what we already know. It typically takes some form of pain or embarrassment to instigate real change, because it is then we may be willing to question the values of our beliefs.

Consider the baseball player who believes he is worth $10,000,000 per year and only gets offered half that amount. He is unhappy because his thought reality says he is worth $10,000,000 a year. With a different thought reality, he might realize that 100 years

---

ago, his talent would have been worth almost nothing and consider himself very fortunate and be very happy, although he could still hold out for the ten million. Reality is not always what we think it should be. There are baseball cards considered to be worth a hundred thousand dollars, or paintings worth millions. They may be worth that in someone else's thought reality, but not in mine or that of most other people.

Although there is nothing wrong with a ball player wanting $10,000,000 pay per year or with people having expensive hobbies, the happiness and self-worth and love we seek will not come from income level or material goods or pleasures. That understanding is important to happiness in life. Part of a quote of Ms. Wheelchair America 2014, Samantha Schroth, goes: "Little things used to be a big deal, when now they are really not." The depth of our worries or unhappiness is often just a reflection of the importance our thought reality places on worldly values.

Thought realities on what brings real happiness and inner peace differ for most people, because they have no understanding of basic principles from which to understand life. To have the best opportunity for self-worth and happiness, it is important to have a thought reality based upon actual, fixed, basic principles that promote self-worth and happiness. For many people, that will require opening their thought reality to new purpose and new values. It may be difficult, but it can also make life less complicated and easier to accept.

By being willing to open our minds to new ideas, we can change minor, as well as major, beliefs. An example of a minor change that saved me much aggravation, occurred to me when I allowed myself to think differently. When I was young, I was easily embarrassed. I was even afraid to make long-distance phone calls where I might have to speak to an operator and not know what to say. I believed making any mistake was a sign of stupidity. I made a number of such mistakes and got upset with myself.

When I got a bit older and thought more logically, I realized the embarrassing moments of my youth were now stories I could tell and laugh at. I could also remember those incidents better than many other things in my life. Finally, I realized that the reality of those embarrassing moments were memories I could now share in humorous ways. I also realized how much enjoyment my worries had been costing me. At that point, I decided to look at embarrassing incidents as I would think about them five years in the future and I learned to laugh at them right away. Worry can change to enjoyment just by changing thought reality.

To visualize how new views of reality can cause even major changes in thought reality, we only need to look at how cult exposure can change people. Given enough time for verbal and mental indoctrination, a charismatic cult leader can convert almost anyone insecure in basic beliefs. The cult leader will distort the existing basic realities of belief and then present a replacement reality that covers the distortions. Repeat distortions often enough and they can become real to thought reality. The charismatic Hitler was able to affect the mental reality of millions of Germans with his distorted views. Too often, the distorted views of some controlling political and religious leaders have led people astray. History tells us the consequences.

It's scary to think this has happened and will likely happen again. If you think it cannot happen to you, consider that most of your thought processes have already been shaped by others. The fact that many people of different religions are all sure that their beliefs are the right beliefs proves mathematically that there are millions, or perhaps billions of people, who believe something that statistically cannot be true. The realization that thought realities are shaped and can be reshaped might be scary, but that fact is also one of humanity's greatest blessings. Human purpose, values, and habits can change to something better if humans are willing to search for new thought realities that will lead to self-worth and inner happiness. But it also requires working on accepting the new thought reality.

Because thought reality habits and values are based upon the purpose or purposes for which a person lives, real change most often requires a change in purpose for which one is living. Unless purpose changes, what is important to thought reality most often remains the same. Effective change in thought reality first requires an evaluation of the purpose in life. The greatest change in purpose for thought reality is change from "what is in it for me" to "what is in it for the good of all." A person with an understanding of the fixed realities of the universe would realize that "what is in it for me" is the greatest when what that person is doing is "for the good of all.

It is interesting to look at the steps to recovery in Alcoholics Anonymous. The first step is to admit we are not in control—our wants are controlling us. Because I believe the desire for control is perhaps humanity's greatest flaw, I also see giving up the thought of the need to be in control as the most significant change thought reality can make.

The second step in AA is to accept the existence a benevolent Higher Power. It can restore hope and sanity. It provides a rational reason why there is no need to control. These two steps are the basic steps that have changed the lives of tens of thousands of people for the better, in most cases when nothing else could. The change from a controlling thought reality to accepting thought reality allows us to open our minds to new ideas and beliefs. As it is the reality of what we think that brings us inner happiness or unhappiness, when we are unhappy, it is time to change thought reality to something that will make us happy.

Very important to AA is the need to constantly go to meetings. The repetition helps bring new, positive mental notions deeper into thought reality, until hopefully some day they take over. Any significant change in thought reality requires the repetition of thought over and over again. I purposely keep repeating that for changing the importance of anything, it is imperative to contemplate the changes to be made and the purpose for them many times a day.

The concept of a Higher Power is more important to people who make the habit of praying a number of times each day. The repeated repetition of prayer makes the concept of a Higher Power more important to thought reality. You might want to consider how important the material world would be to you if you contemplated death five times a day. Your happiness in life is greatly dependent upon the thought reality you choose to repeatedly focus on. You get to live with the consequences of your choices.

For effective change, it is most important to understand there are fixed basics in life which are given in the final chapter. Perhaps the most important to understand is the reality the of virtue and vice and their consequences. Virtue, especially the virtue of love, begets order and happiness. Vice, which is a result of selfishness, brings eventual distress and chaos. If you want real self-worth and inner happiness, purpose must be based upon virtue. But any change in thought reality about virtue and vice will happen only when a decision is made to repeatedly focus on virtue and its importance to self and to the world.

A thought to consider when working on changing thought reality is that even in a materialistic world, it is people who are the most unconditionally loving who tend to be the people most happy and content with themselves. They are the people whose happiness is focused beyond the material world. Monks and sisters, for example, can willingly give up worldly possessions for the sake of other people and remain happy. They may seem poor to the material world, but many end up being revered and called saints. And, assuming there is an afterlife, they gain perpetual happiness.

Wisdom requires that rather than accepting the reality of what we have been led to believe, each of us carefully evaluates purpose of life and the potential consequences of how we live our lives. It may not be best to rely on an ego illusion of happiness. In the concept of eternity, a lifetime of material wealth, for the few who will attain it, is nothing.

In *Human Understanding*, we realize that our thought reality forms the basis for all we do and say It also forms the basis for our happiness, as well as our wants and fears. As such, if we are not happy with life or have little self-worth, it is time to change the thought reality that holds us from real happiness and self-worth. That requires opening thought reality to the reality of the fixed basics. It requires repeatedly doing and thinking in ways that make those basics important. It is in working on new purpose and value images many times a day that real changes in life can be made. If we want and are willing to make the effort, we can change an unsure and possibly unhappy thought reality to thought reality in which we attain self-worth and happiness.

PART III

RELATED CONSIDERATIONS

THE CONCEPT OF A HIGHER POWER

I n this book, I often reference a Higher Power. The term "Higher Power' is meant to be non-specific in that there is no defined nature attributed to the Higher Power. Whether the Higher Power is, or is thought of as, a God, as love itself, as universal Supreme Consciousness, or in some other way, is not important to what is being presented in this book. What is important is to realize that there is a Higher Power of some nature

I choose not to look to religion or to religious scripture to bolster my contention of a Higher Power. Although there could be much truth in religious beliefs and doctrine, I believe religion is made up of beliefs and doctrine based upon what man has "interpreted" as being divinely inspired. While I do accept the concept of "inspired writings," this book is meant to be independent of religious beliefs and doctrine.

Some important questions about the concept of a Higher Power are: "Where did the concept of a Higher Power originate" and "is the concept even valid?" The concept of a Higher Power, God, or Great Spirit appears to have existed in all recorded civilizations. For ancient civilizations, it was more "the gods" than a single Higher Power.

There are a number of explanations for the concept of a Higher Power. The most basic explanation is that it is a way to explain the unexplained, including how the world came to be. Another explanation is so humans could believe in something beyond death. There is also the explanation that the concept was promoted by those in power to exploit their subjects. Still another explanation is that the knowledge of a higher reality was instilled in humanity by the Higher Power. And there are still other explanations. But it is not important how the concept came about. What is important is whether or not the concept of a Higher Power is real or at least reasonable enough for the purpose of belief.

When it comes to the concept of a Higher Power, we have choices. We can choose to believe there are only the laws of the physical universe, many of which we do not yet understand. We can also choose to accept the concept of a Higher Power of some unknown nature. Or we can say maybe or maybe not. We are all subjected to a litany of reasons why we should believe in a Higher Power and have probably heard counterarguments.

Without any specific way to physically test a hypothesis, it is necessary to evaluate the issue in a way similar to the ways the basic laws of engineering evolved. Solutions to engineering problems were developed without preexisting knowledge or scientific data to check against. They were developed by trial and error. Walls were built until they fell over. The next time, they were built shorter or thicker and stronger. Eventually the trials and errors developed into an understanding of the science of building walls.

When there is no existing scientific way to evaluate something, science that requires proven facts before hand, is of no help in that evaluation. If proven scientific facts were necessary before evaluation could begin, worldly progress would never have started. Just because something is not scientifically understood does not mean we cannot build some understanding of that issue in the same manner that humanity learned how to build walls and eventually tall buildings. We may not be able to scientifically prove a hypothesis that is beyond physical reality, but we can work on the validity of a concept by evaluating all the bits of information available to us. All evidence, including circumstantial information and potential conflicting facts, must be included in that evaluation. Should a hypothesis fit all the available information and fact, such a hypothesis is likely correct.

One of the arguments for a Higher Power actually comes from science. Modern quantum theory says that physical reality only exists because it is perceived by consciousness. For that to be true, there had to be an initiating consciousness before matter came into existence.

Because of personal experiences, there are many people who will testify to the existence of spirits or ghosts. There have been clairvoyants, such as Edgar Cayce, who expressed knowledge that defied all scientific explanation. (31) Cayce is spoken of as America's greatest psychic and best known for his work as a psychic medical diagnostician. Just knowing the name of a specific sick person and where that person lived, he would accurately describe the illness and the prescription needed for a recovery. Many of his hundreds of prescribed cures were beyond known cures of the time. His life is worth the time to read about.

There have been many recorded anomalies (called miracles) that have been related to those people with a strong belief in a Higher Power. A more convincing miracle that indicates a higher level of reality and humanity's connection to it is that of incorruptible bodies. An "incorruptible body" is one that does not decay after death, even after years with nothing done to preserve the body. These bodies also give off a sweet floral aroma. Although no longer fully fresh, the body of St. Silvan is over 1,700 years old. Even more than a year after death, the body of St. Francis of Xavier bled fresh blood when touched. There are more than 150 such bodies. These are bodies of holy people of prayer and penance normally associated with the Catholic and Eastern Orthodox churches. (32)

Then there is Therese Neumann, who died in 1962 after only ingesting a communion wafer once a day for the last 35 years of her life. After losing 6 to 8 pounds weekly from bleeding of the stigmata, she mysteriously gained back the weight she lost, while under 24-hour surveillance. She said that her existence was to prove that man can live by the invisible light of God. (The life of Therese Neumann is well documented in books and on the Internet.)

As previously noted there are other people recorded as living for years without eating or drinking. Again, these anomalies, or miracles, were manifested through people of different religions with a strong belief in a Higher Power. People who instigate miracles normally consider it is the Higher Power acting through them that actually causes the miracle. There have been thousands of scientifically impossible cures recorded attributed to a Higher Power. These unexplained happenings, which defy known physical laws of the universe, have occurred in various religious realms. That such happenings occur, of which many have been recorded and attributed to a Higher Power, does not provide actual proof of a Higher Power. But it does provide a good reason to consider the existence of a Higher Power.

The chapter "Reality of an Independent Consciousness," in providing significant evidence of humans possessing consciousness extending beyond physical reality, indicates that something exists beyond the physical level. The existence of an independent consciousness within humanity indicates a higher-level purpose for humanity exists. That did not likely happen without some assistance of a Higher Power.

As to the Higher Power being of love, there is also anecdotal evidence to look at. The biggest piece of evidence is that humans have free will. We are free to accept and reject what we want. That ability would not be given by a controlling power. If we review the lives of people of various beliefs and different lifestyles, we find a relationship between holy and loving people that profess the belief in a Higher Power and what are termed miraculous occurrences. Also, if we accept the hypothesis of a Higher Power of love, it is not surprising that people who are loving and accepting are the most loved people and that these people seem to be at most peace with themselves. Such relationships point to any nature of the Higher Power being of love.

Science, as we now know it, is not able to prove or to disprove the existence of a Higher Power. But science can still be of some value in determining that something exists beyond our understanding. Science has raised many doubts about the existence of a Higher Power in that it has explained many previously unexplained mysteries. But it has also opened up such uncertainties as quantum theory, string theory, the concept of parallel universes, and the concept that both matter and time only exist when measured.

With new technology, science has been able to measure unexplained temperature and energy fluctuations where ghosts are said to be present. This does not prove there are ghosts, but it shows that things exist that are beyond what is presently accepted as physical reality. The world is unbelievably more complex than it once appeared to be.

Science has also shown us that the theory of relativity, which applies to the physical world, does not apply to the subatomic level. Science has been used to try to disprove the concept of a Higher Power. But it has actually raised new questions which science itself cannot explain, but which can be explained by the existence of a higher level of reality. That a reality exists beyond physical reality doesn't mean there is a specific Higher Power, but we have not specifically defined what is meant by that term.

With the number of physically unexplained happenings of many different types, even a rudimentary engineering analysis would suggest there is likely another level of reality that can interact with our physical level in a way that is difficult to detect or may not even be physical detectable. Of course, it is possible to close one's mind and deny the existence of anything that does not agree with physical science. But unless you open your mind to the possibility that things are not always as they seem, don't laugh at those who still believe the world is flat.

There are some very smart people who have written about the existence of a God. The writings of Thomas Aquinas would be a good place to start. In his *Summa Theologica*, Aquinas (33) gives five good arguments for the existence of God. The arguments are based upon motion, effective cause, possibility and necessity, graduation of being, and design. The arguments, given in a step-by-step progression of rational thought, are too lengthy to be listed here, but can be reviewed for those interested. (34)

There are also many books written about paranormal encounters and there are many individuals who have had encounters that can only be explained by a reality beyond that which physical laws control. Although these do not provide any proof of a Higher Power, they do augment the concept of a higher level of existence.

I personally had a ghostly encounter almost 60 years ago. While spending the night by ourselves in a century-old farmhouse, my older brother David and I heard some noise on the other side of a closed door. Dave grabbed a rifle and covered the door as I went to open it. Just as I was about to open the door, the handle turned without my touching it. I immediately grabbed the handle and pulled the door open. No one was there!!! That experience had an impact on what I now believe as related to a different level of reality.

But what made a bigger impression on me about a higher level of reality and about life beyond this life were the last moments of my youngest son's life previously detailed in the Introduction. From the last moments of my son's life alone, I choose to believe there is existence beyond death. You can choose to believe what you want. But, as the ancient knight said in the movie *The Last Crusade*, "Choose wisely." There is no scientific evidence that proves a higher level of existence, but based upon my experiences and research, the odds tell me there are just too many things that can only be explained with the acceptance of a Higher Power of some nature.

Another thought on the existence of a Higher Power is creation. There is no doubt in my mind that evolution exists. But is all that exists really the result of evolution? An argument often used to justify total evolution is the "Infinite Monkey" theorem: "Given an infinite amount of time, a monkey could eventually type the Bible." That argument is misleading, as related to the perception of the time required for sophisticated evolution of humanity. Given the scientifically estimated lifetime of the universe (13.7 billion years), a monkey randomly typing on a 42-character typewriter, at a rate of striking one key per second, may have correctly completed one-quarter of the first sentence of the Bible (eleven letters and spaces), although the monkey would not realize it. (35)

Given one trillion years, the odds say the monkey mathematically may have, at some point in time, actually gotten the first 13 letters and spaces correct, but certainly not the entire Bible. The presently assumed scientific age of earth is 4.54 billion years. And science says that microscopic life would not have begun on earth before at least 3.9 billion years ago. When the odds are properly understood, the concept of constructive randomness resulting in such complex things as the eye, the brain, or consciousness (considered a quantum computer), all of which are even individually complex, seems very unlikely. Also unlikely is the evolution of one being from a microscopic seed that takes two individuals to make happen.

Sir Fred Hoyle, noted British astronomer and one of the 20th century's most distinguished scientists once said, "The chance that higher life forms may have evolved is comparable to the chance of a tornado sweeping through a junk yard assembling a Boeing 747 from the materials therein." (36) Although most scientists say this statement is an exaggeration, it speaks of the odds against total human evolved within the life time of earth. Even if the brain could evolve, where did consciousness come from? How could consciousness evolve?

Probabilities on the origin of human life greatly favor either creation or that life on this planet came here from somewhere else in the much older universe. And then there is new scientific research that questions the currently accepted actual age of the earth, which could reduce earthly time in which evolution is supposed to have taken place. Based upon probabilities, creation of humans should still be considered a possibility, rather than being rejected.

Another theory for the origin of humanity is DNA manipulation or actual inbreeding by extraterrestrials. The odds much favor that theory before full evolution on earth. That theory is possible, without changing the universal basics of life as presented in this book, as extraterrestrials would also be subject to the same basics. That theory is growing in acceptance. It is interesting to note that in Genesis Chapter 6 of the Bible mentions the sons of God mating with the daughters of men. The early Gnostics also believed that humans were created by lesser beings than the one unknowable God, who put material bodies on already existing spirit entities to make them forget about their relationship to the divine.

As an engineer concerned with the basics, I do not find it important whether or not the physical nature of humanity evolved or was created. What is of concern to me is the inner consciousness of humanity and the purpose for its existence. Because I believe in a higher level of reality, the question of why human consciousness exists comes long before being concerned about how humanity came to exist.

When my son Andrew was at Children's Hospital in Milwaukee, I had the privilege of spending some time with a man named Lee Horsman. Lee's job was to comfort the dying children and their families. On a few occasions, he spoke of a large number of out-of-body experiences the very young children would relate to him. He said that these children normally met a peaceful being of light that they seemed to recognize as loving and "special" in some way. This held true even for children who had only recently learned to speak, and for young children whose parents did not believe in a God. Some of these children had not been predisposed to the idea of a Higher Power or, for some children, to the idea of an afterlife. These children were not influenced by previous images. Mr. Horsman said the young children related that they sensed the presence of a loving entity. This is another example that supports the presence of a Higher Power of love.

The following is one possible way to visualize a Higher Power of love. The Higher Power of love can be thought of as a father. Since the father of love would endow his children with the gift of love, surely his children would be expected to nurture that virtue and cause it to grow. But he would not force them to be like him because he loves them and gives them free rein to be and to do what they would like. What would be the consequence if his children did not use the gift of love and decided to be selfish instead? The father of love would continue to love even those children who turned from his love to selfishness. But he would not be able to give them the inheritance he planned for them. Not because he would not what to, but because the precious inheritance he has for them is his love and all the wonderful things that result from love. Those who are not of love or who do not return to love forfeit their inheritance of love. It is likely so with any Higher Power of love. To receive the total gift of love offered, the heart must be open to that gift.

The question is often posed: How can any Higher Power be of love if souls are being cast into hell for a single mistake, when others have led terrible lives and repented at the last moment? That is a hypothetical question which itself is based upon an assumed outcome, which is not possible to know. In the chapter on the Reality of an Independent Consciousness, I specifically point out that we do not know what happens after physical death. Even the existence of hell is based upon human interpretation of scripture. So is the existence or non-existence of reincarnation.

In Origen's *First Principles*, all souls will eventually be restored to a state of dynamic perfection with the Godhead. As to why the Higher Power of love allows the terrible events to occur, possibly it is because humanity was given free will, as well as the gift of pain from which to learn. Interference would negate the effects of free will. Questions about the love of the Higher Power are based upon human assumptions about a level of reality of which there is little to nothing really known.

There are reasons, other than just religious teachings, to believe in the existence of a Higher Power. But are there any reasons, other the lack of positive scientific proof, cynicism, and skepticism to believe there is no Higher Power? There are people who will deny the existence of a Higher Power as a revolt against the way religious leaders have, all too often, used the concept of God to manipulate other people. And there are those who will use the seeming unfairness and the injustice in the world as a reason to say that no loving Higher Power exists. But the main argument for those who do not believe in a Higher Power is that science has not proved the existence of a Higher Power. Unfortunately, when it comes to the existence of a Higher Power, many people ignore recorder facts and anecdotal evidence that do not agree with their thought reality.

The question every person needs to think about is: Is it sensible to choose to accept that for which there is no proof and conflicts with recoded facts and arguments over the likelihood of a Higher Power, the existence of which provides an explanation of unusual recorded facts and information? Murphy's Law would recommend against it.

Although there are people who reject the possibility of a Higher Power, it should also be realized that many people labeled as non-believers or atheists just do not want to feel forced into believing something they have doubts about or do not believe. But they can still be loving, spiritual people. I believe that salvation is about accepting unconditional love into one's heart, which does not necessarily mean pursuing an active religious life. However, it is difficult to be spiritual without a sustained purpose for being spiritual and repeated spiritual activity.

As to the actual existence of a Higher Power, all we can do is analyze the information we have to the best of our ability, and based upon that, accept what makes the most sense. We can choose to utilize, to question, or to ignore various, so called, proofs, facts, and information available to us. The engineer in me says that, with no specific proof, anecdotal evidence and facts available are the best indicator of what actually exists.

We can search for unworldly evidence in the physical world. But maybe the best evidence is simply that we possess the ability to love. Love is not of the material world, nor of normal evolution, although some brain researchers will claim love is just a brain reaction to factors that influence the brain. I reject that opinion as will be explained in the chapter on Love. Love is a virtue, not a feeling, although feelings result from love. Love is the highest virtue and all other virtues spring from and culminate in love. It is from the source of unconditional love, referred to as the Higher Power, that we are given the ability to love. And it is in love that humanity is connected to the Higher Power. As a result of the importance of love alone, I embrace the concept of a loving Higher Power.

In *Human Understanding*, although there is no scientific proof of a Higher Power, there are many reasons to accept the concept of a Higher Power; even though what that Higher Power is we do not know. It may be that the Higher Power is pure love. My common sense tells me that when I have to make the decision that is not a sure thing, I should go with the odds. In this case, the odds are in favor of a Higher Power.

IMAGES AND LIFE

Most important to thought reality is our mental images. We relate to each other through words. But it is the mental images of our thought reality that have the greatest influence on what we value and how we function. Words are just used to transmit images and thoughts. As infants, it is the images we observe, not the words we hear, that have the greatest influence on thought reality. These initial images form the basis of our thought reality notions and the basis for all additional thought.

Later in life, when faced with different situations, if we do not act out of habit, we rely greatly upon on our thought images on how to handle each situation. Perhaps we become overwhelmed by what we imagine, which will likely result in worry or fear. It is mental images and resulting mental notions, not words, that most influence our major decisions and actions in life.

When I was young, I was told that I was made in the image of the Creator. At that time, I gave that concept a good bit of thought. For some reason, I couldn't picture my Creator as another human form. But as I analyzed the concept, I realized that, even if people are not physical duplicates of their Creator, people's lives are still influenced by the image they have of a Higher Power or some surrogate higher power. I also realized that in the ability to love humanity has been given something beyond normal physical reality. Perhaps it is in the ability to love that we are made in the image of the Higher Power.

Historically, when humans could not find the answers to questions about life and the universe, they looked to some form of Higher Power for an explanation. Humans have typically visualized the concept of a Higher Power in forms they can comprehend. Most often the Higher Power is imagined or believed to be some form of god, super-human, a powerful spirit, a super-being, or even a king. But the Higher Power can also be thought of in terms of love, order, consciousness, or nature itself. Humans have no way of truly knowing.

It is my contention that the temperament of whatever Higher Power or surrogate higher power we imagine has an effect on our morality and our value of life. Even the morality of the societies, or lack of morality, is affected by the image (belief) each society has of a Higher Power. People brought up with the image of a Higher Power as powerful and controlling tend to be controlling. Most people brought up around the image of a Higher Power of judgment and vengeance will tend to judgmental and vengeful. Those blessed to be brought up with the image of a loving Higher Power will tend to be more loving and forgiving. And even if people do not have any image of a Higher Power, their lives will still be influenced by the morality of the society in which they live. It is important to realize that the images we project are a reflection of the wants, fears, and beliefs of our thought reality. These images affect the way we think. But the opposite is also true. We can influence our thought reality by the images we allow ourselves to project and focus on. Project and concentrate on an image often enough in your mind and it becomes part of your thought reality.

When I was young, while hiking in a marshy area near the Wolf River in Wisconsin, I made up a story of seeing a dozen deer running and leaping through the tall grass, and I pictured the scene in my mind. In imaging the story and repeating it many times, the image became real to my memory. To this day, I can still visualize that scene and almost forget I made it up.

That being the case, I realized that it should be possible to help develop happy thoughts and memories by spending time thinking about happy times and good things. If we spend more time imaging the good things we have done in life, we will think more of ourselves. With effort and repetition, thinking happy can become a thought habit. Conversely, it is possible to develop or reinforce sad thoughts and memories simply by spending time imaging them, or even imaging bad things that might happen.

People become influenced by the images they repeatedly focus on. This goes back to learning though repetition. Repeat something often enough and it becomes part of thought reality. That includes mental images. The expression that "a picture is worth a thousand words" does point out that images are more impactful than words.

As repetition of positive images can be the back door into thought reality, they can also be the back door for negative images. Provide the mind repeatedly with images of power, wealth, sex, revenge, and other adverse images, and they can take over thought reality. We can see the result of repeated images in the desensitizing of society on what was taboo only a generation ago. This is something important to consider, especially where glorified violence and pornography are easily accessible. Negative images and worldly images can block out offsetting images of love and acceptance and their importance. Such things will decrease the feelings of self-worth and love which inner consciousness desires. We need to expose ourselves to images of love.

It is interesting that in Alcoholics Anonymous' acceptance of personal lack of control and turning control over to the Higher Power are the first two steps to overcoming addiction. This process may not involve specific imagery, but it does involve some personal imagery. AA has proven to be about the most effective method of actually overcoming addiction. By repeatedly going to meetings, people are able to develop the thought image that there is a Higher Power and that it would be better to turn their lives over to the Higher Power.

Any image of a loving Higher Power, caring about each of us, is also helpful in developing more self-worth. Also, with the acceptance of the image of ultimate loving justice, people can more easily accept life as it is handed out to them. How we image a Higher Power, or just the image of how another person or persons have sacrificed for us, can affect how we think about life, love, and fulfillment. Conversely, sustaining an image of a judgmental Higher Power, or the image that worldly control is important to personal success, will most often promote anger, revenge, or even war.

The brain has been the subject of many neurological studies in the last decade. That is important to this chapter because the images we have come from our brains. But what the brain images comes from though reality, from what we allow ourselves to focus on. Much research on how the brain functions has been conducted by Andrew Newberg, MD of the Myrna Brind Center of Integrative Medicine at Thomas Jefferson University Hospital in Philadelphia. Many of Dr. Newberg's tests have been related to meditation. The best explanation of his findings is provided by Mark Robert Waldman, who has written some books with Dr. Newberg and produced some short videos that can be viewed online. (37)

In the first chapter of *How God Changes the Brain*, Dr. Newberg points out that long-term contemplation of God and other spiritual values appears to permanently change the structure of those parts of the brain that control moods and give rise to our conscious notions of self and shapes our sensory perception of the world. The book points out that this can be done in eight weeks on as little as 12 minutes a day. Waldman states, "If you create a negative image of God, it's very neurologically disruptive. If you create and maintain a totally optimistic vision of God, all our research shows that it's very neurologically and psychologically enhancing."

Positive imaging and contemplation can change the aspects of negative thought and help promote positive thoughts such as empathy and compassion. One of the statements given by Mr. Waldman is that based upon their neurological study, such meditation "is the most effective way to treat severe anxiety and depression."

If focusing 12 minutes a day on something can make major changes in the brain, we should realize how important it is to focus on the good images and ways of thinking. Focusing on the right images can make life more rewarding and can lead to inner peace and happiness.

In *Human Understanding*, we realize that the images we repeatedly think about form the notions of thought reality and are important in all our mental evaluations. Projecting positive or negative images will lead to positive or negative mental notions in thought reality. To a great degree, how we live our lives will follow the images that are important to thought reality. We may or may not be made in the image of the Higher Power. But most of us live somewhat in relation to our image of the Higher Power, or that of the morality of the society in which we live. Hopefully any image you have of a Higher Power or higher purpose will be one of love. If not, you can develop positive images about life by focusing on positive images and upon love.

LOVE

There are many definitions for the meaning of the word "love." Love is an intangible virtue and difficult to specifically define. The problem with being human is that we do not easily grasp the reality of love. Love is a virtue that can transcend through all levels of reality in which consciousness exists. Love gives a real, purposeful meaning to life; yet many of us do not know it. Love brings inner peace; but most of us do not realize it. Love sustains us as humans; but most of us are blind to that fact. Love fulfills us; but most of us are not willing to extend love to be filled with love.

Real love is not of the material world, so it is something not well understood in a material world. There is probably no way for a human to truly understand or to adequately describe love, although there have been some good attempts. I have heard it said that unconditional love must create in order to share the joy of love. It is also said that love is the sacrifice of one's self for another. There is also the belief that salvation is the acceptance of unconditional love. As there is no real adequate definition for love, what I attempt to do here is to just give a wider insight into a reality beyond physical existence. Some of what I present is common sense; some of it goes beyond.

Love is thought about in many ways, mostly based upon the perception(s) of love we have been exposed to, or by love that has been extended to us. We may view love as portrayed on television or as books state it should be viewed. Some people view love in the form of physical relationships. Some people will act irresponsibly to express some form of attraction or infatuation they consider to be love. There are also people who control their emotions and are more likely to express love in the form of responsibility and loyalty. Not everyone is comfortable with hugging, especially when hugging was not part of how they grew up. We are human. We are all different and we are not perfect. Love, or what may be perceived as love, will therefore be viewed in myriad ways and attempted to be gained and shared in just as many.

Love is not sex. Love is not infatuation. Love is not a good feeling about someone else. Love has nothing to do with the feeling of needing someone or of being needed. Love cannot choose. Love does not exist for a worldly reason. Where real love exists, it just is. Love is a virtue of a higher level extended to humanity. It is ours to accept. And we accept it to various degrees by how we share of ourselves and how we open ourselves to others.

On the human level, love is more an unconscious commitment to sharing of one's self with others without judgment. Where real love exists, commitment and acceptance are so natural, love happens without conscious consideration. Real love is experienced like an essence of inner warmth generated by mutual acceptance and commitment. In the willingness to give of self, love comes to exist. Love sees the goodness of all in creation and in all people. In love, total acceptance and sharing, we find the greatest fulfillment as humans. Conversely, where there is judgment and lack of forgiveness, real love cannot exist.

This description of unconditional giving of self is difficult for many of us to comprehend because we are almost always conditional in what we do. We look to gain value. But love does not exist where the desire is to gain. It exists where the desire is to give. It is particularly hard for rationalists like me to grasp. I used to think love was something that could be rationalized. It took most of my life to finally realize it could not be.

Unconditional love is almost impossible to understand in the physical world because unconditional love seeks no value. Unconditional love has no reason to seek value because unconditional love is the greatest value there is. And for the same reason, love has no reason to judge or get angry. Some scientists try to define love as a reaction of the brain to specific circumstances. I reject that notion because love is not a rationalization. It is a virtue that either exists, or doesn't exist, to different degrees in different people, regardless of the brain's reaction. It is a reality above physical evaluation. As difficult as this is to understand, we all need to realize it.

Love, on a level that most of us can comprehend and experience, is best described as the opposite of selfishness. For people who think of themselves first, real love cannot exist, for their hearts are too full of themselves. It is the story of Adam and Eve all over again. When we want for ourselves, love is lost to selfishness, along with our personal peace and the ability to experience joy. Selfish wants and the selfish desire for control eventually result in disharmony for us and for those close to us. It is worldly concerns that keep us from experiencing joy. It is the acceptance of love that connects us to the Higher Power of love. And it is judgment and selfishness that keep us apart.

Real love does not cause a person to give so as to feel good. Love just gives. Love gives the extra smile, the words of encouragement, the extra effort, the thank you, and all the little things that are important without having a reason to do so and with no expectation of getting anything back. Real love wants each and every person to develop to the best of his or her abilities. Therefore, love understands and accepts the pain (for self and of others) that comes with helping to nurture talent and accepts responsibility even when it means the loss of a relationship. Sometimes it is in feeling the pain of others that we better come to understand what love is.

People who say, "I don't love you anymore," have no idea of what real love is. Love does not suddenly appear and fade like infatuation. People who do not feel love are people who do not know how to extend love. In giving of oneself, especially in difficult situations, real love is understood and felt. Be aware that people can also be kind, courteous, and even generous without love. For them, generosity can be an environmental response or even for a value to be gained.

Conversely, love requires putting others before self. Do you decide what to watch on TV or do you first ask what others would like? Do you schedule your free time about what you want or do or first ask what others would like to do? Do your wants control what you do or do you consider the needs of others? Where personal wants control, real love is lacking. Realize that people can use self-righteousness in place of love to justify personal decisions and the lack of forgiveness. The desire for control is almost the opposite of love and in the end, can destroy relationships. I speak from experience.

Love itself is more than a feeling. The wonderful feeling we experience when we think we feel love, is not itself love. Rather what we feel is the joy of inner consciousness, which is a product of love. We need to distinguish between feelings and real love or we will not see where commitment, acceptance, and responsibility are necessary for love to exist.

When a real, committed love exists, it produces a wonderful feeling that everything is okay. That is brought about by freedom from fear, which accompanies the acceptance of love. It is similar to how, as will be addressed, the appreciation of *"what is"* brings happiness. The greater the depth of acceptance, of purpose beyond self, and of the responsibilities of that acceptance, the greater the resulting feeling of love will be. When love is great, it can overwhelm us and cause us to spread love beyond ourselves. Think of love as the virtue from which all other virtues spring forth. When we think of how powerful love can be on a flawed human level, we should consider what love could feel like in the unconditional realm of the Higher Power of love.

A good understanding of love opens a person's mind to what he or she is missing and what he or she can have if willing to give rather than take. However, that understanding alone changes nothing. I have found that just because a person discovers a reasonable understanding of love and its importance to inner peace and happiness, it doesn't make giving of self any easier or reduce temptation to selfishness. It takes a commitment to extending one's self in love to really grasp the difference it can make in self-worth and finding purpose in life.

In *Human Understanding*, we realize that although love may be manifested in a feeling of serenity and joy, love is more the reality of serenity and joy that comes with giving. As humans, our expectations limit our understanding of love and even the love we experience. Our understanding and experience of love will only grow when we expect less and give more so as to touch upon the unconditional love of the higher level. With love, the greater the selflessness, the greater the inner serenity and joy experienced. Love is the culmination of all virtue and it is love that our inner consciousness seeks.

RELIGION

EARLY RELIGION AND MORALITY

When looking at religion as a subject, it is important to understand more than the beliefs of religion. The engineering approach to understanding of any subject does not come about by looking at just one segment of the subject. Rather, it starts by looking at the known subject history and objectively proceeds to such things as the purpose of the subject, the success of the subject, the failures of the subject, and other things that affect the subject or which the subject affects.

A good place to start in looking at religion is at what we know about the general history of spirituality and religion. The first evidence of belief in something beyond the physical world is a 26,000-year-old burial site in Dolni Vestonice in the Czech Republic. There are other ancient burial sites with preserved bodies and valuable artifacts that indicate a belief in something beyond physical life. With poor transportation, the specific beliefs of ancient societies were likely limited to local tribes. We might guess, but do not know for sure, that there were local shamans in ancient times, similar to those who have existed in smaller wilderness societies, even recently. Shamans keep people in touch with the spiritual world.

What is known of religious history, of actual beliefs and practices, begins with major ancient civilizations about 5,000 years ago. What is most interesting about all the major ancient civilizations is that all had belief in gods, most of which appear to have been related to forces of nature. Regional civilizations appear to have been united by a common belief in gods. All the known ancient civilizations had gods they worshiped. The Assyrians had Ashur and others. The Canaanites had Baal and others. The Greeks had numerous gods, as did the Norse.

Not much is known about religion in ancient China but, according to Dr. Mark W. Muesse, PhD, director of the Asian Studies program and chair of the Department of Religious Studies at Rhodes College, bone inscriptions reveal that ancient Chinese believed there was a close relationship between the spirit realm and the human realm. Ancient India had the Vedic deities. Ancient Egypt had dozens of gods to worship. Even the Aztecs, Mayans, and Incas of the Americas had gods they worshiped. Additionally, the powerful leaders of these nations were often thought of as gods or descendants of gods.

Although different civilizations had various gods, ancient wars appear to have been mostly about empire building and control of conquered territories, as well as ethnic expansion and cleansing. Ancient wars do not appear to have been about religious beliefs, although they called upon their gods for help. Some of the same gods were worshiped in civilizations that fought each other.

An accepted belief in one supreme Higher Power, seems to have originated with Zoroaster (38), who is believed to have lived somewhere around what is now Southeastern Iran. There is disagreement on exactly when he lived. The likely time would have been between 1600 and 1000 BCE, although some historians believe it was toward the latter. Zoroaster introduced such concepts as a universal conflict between good and evil; other levels of beings above humanity, which we would call angels; devils called deavas; free will; personal and final judgment based upon the moral quality of one's life; resurrection of the body; heaven and hell; a savior born into the world; and even an apocalypse culminating in the triumph of good over evil. Zoroastrianism spread throughout the Middle East under the Persian Empire, which allowed religious freedom. That Zoroaster's concepts now exist in other religions tells us it had significant influence on religions that followed.

Monotheism, belief in on god, is often attributed to Judaism from the time of Moses and to some extent it may have been accepted at the time of Moses. But monotheism does not seem to have fully taken hold with all the Jewish people until after the Babylonian exile, a time of Persian and Zoroastrianism influence. Even the Book of Genesis says: "Let **Us** make man...." After Judaism, the belief in one God spread with Christianity and then Islam, although Zoroastrianism had an effect on these religions as well.

Ancient temples, statues, and evidence of sacrifice, sometimes human, tell us that beliefs in the ancient gods were important. It appears that ancient religions were based upon cooperation with, or fear of, the divine forces normally associated with different forces of nature or other powerful forces.

According to Christopher Dawson, author of *Dynamics of World History*, civilization began with agricultural groups getting together for the better prosperity for all. While that is likely true for small communities, it is not likely for large civilizations. Disagreeing with Dawson's assumption, a June 2011 *National Geographic* article about 11,000-year-old Gobekli Tepe in Turkey, suggested that religion is the cause of civilization. That suggestion, based upon archaeological evidence, was made by archaeologist Klaus Schmidt of the German Archaeological Institute and others involved in the discovery. This concept cannot be easily dismissed.

Theoretically, there could be a number of reasons for civilizations to begin, the most likely being fear, security, and force, as well as betterment. If we look at civilizations before the United States, we find that all large civilizations arose through force, or religion and force. In more primitive cultures, those we actually know something about, we find tribal societies that tended to fight with each other. Even in more advanced countries, history has shown us that, other than civilizations advanced by force and religion, societies remained tribal, clannish, or in smaller, independent city states.

For any large civilization to have formed and continued to exist for a long period of time, there had to have been a common code for how people could live together without constant fighting. The common unwritten code of how people in large civilizations get along is called morality. Morality is the code of conduct within a society or civilization that promotes trust that other people will act in acceptable ways. Morality within a civilization exists because of common purpose and values. Without common purpose and values, there is distrust, factions, and eventual fighting. So, what is it that initiated the morality of common purpose and common values that resulted in large ancient civilizations?

Ancient societies appear to have been very superstitious. Either that or there were actual beings of unnatural power at the time. The belief that the gods controlled the earth made it reasonable for larger groups of people to get together to pay homage to the gods. The things most likely to have brought various tribes together were a common belief or common fear. Worship and/or sacrifices to the gods to appease the various forces of nature were perceived as important to ancient peoples. Even the weather responsible for good crops was seen as influenced by the gods in many ancient societies. Ancient writings and pictographs tells us that there was also belief in an afterlife of some nature, although specifically what that was varied between civilizations.

Rather than smaller clans getting together for social betterment, I believe it was fear of the unknown, especially fear of the gods, and communal worship, which created common purpose and values that allowed civilizations to grow. Would large, what appear to be temples of massive stones, structures have been constructed just for social betterment, as at Gobekli Tepe? As will be pointed out in the chapter "Addiction," the percent of people committing crime is much smaller for those who fear hell than those who believe in heaven.

I suggest the initiating cause of morality was more fear of the gods and fear of a bad afterlife than a common social purpose. While it is true that common social purpose and values are factors in the growth of civilizations, because of limited communication at the time, the odds of establishing common social purposes, as the reason for large ancient civilizations, is poor. Only a few hundred years ago, local tribes had different languages and dialects. In India, where there are hundreds of languages, the people are still united by their belief in their religion.

It is also important to realize that without fear of something substantial or a common belief in something substantial, there is little reason for individuals within large civilizations to follow a moral code. The individual desire to control can only be overcome by love or fear. And, as I have pointed out, love is not the controlling factor in how most people function. My analytical belief is that the substantial something, that initiated morality into large groups of people, was fear—especially fear of the unknown that was attributed to the "gods."

Theoretically, tyrants, ruling over large areas, could have imposed common laws of behavior that people got used to over time and created some form of common behavior. However, unless such rulers were respected as gods of some type, they would not have been respected by the people and no accepted morality would have likely developed. In Egypt, China, the Americas, and even to a degree in Rome, the rulers appear to have been considered divine. It was belief in and fear of the "gods," along with behaviors to please the "gods" which brought about regional morality and resulted in what is referred to as religion. For that reason, religion should be considered the basis for civilization

Another possibility for a belief in and fear of "gods" is perhaps that they actually existed. A recent survey of Americans by Chapman University found that 27 percent of Americans believed that aliens visited the earth in our past and 20 percent of those polled believed aliens impacted human civilization in ancient times. A 2008 *Huffington Post* online poll found that between 33 percent and 48 percent of 18- to 24-year-olds believed aliens impacted ancient civilizations. The belief grows as more ancient discoveries are made. Perhaps what science has considered mythology may be more actual history than present science has told us it is.

New discoveries, such as at Gobekli Tepe in Turkey, are rewriting what science has said was the chronology of human development. The discovery of the 10-square-mile city about 170 ft. below sea level 20 miles off the shore of the city of Dwaraka in India is another good example. Items retrieved have been dated as old as 9,500 years ago. The discovery actually gives credence to the Sanskrit epic *Mahabharata*, which says the ancient city of Dwaraka was destroyed and submerged below the sea.

Ancient flying machines are also mentioned in the *Mahabharata*. The possibility of alien DNA manipulation, and fear of such aliens as gods, would also go along with my explanation that fear of "the gods" is most likely responsible for the development of both religion and morality and the growth of civilizations. This in no way is meant to say that any such aliens existed. Even if they did, they would not have been actual gods and would be still subject to the same fixed realities of the universe as humans as listed in this book.

Just by looking at present civilizations, we can see that religious beliefs play a big part in the moral nature of those civilizations and in the laws of those civilizations. The morality resulting from religion is the key ingredient for how people within each civilization can live and work together. The more peaceful the overall morality resulting from religion, the more peaceful that civilization will be.

The nature of religion seems to have changed beginning with Zoroaster. Religion changed from worship of the "gods" to something more internalized. He was followed by the Hebrew prophets, the Greek philosophers, Confucius, Lao-tse, the Upanishads of the Hindus, Buddha, Christ, and Mahammad. An example of the degree of change in thought is that Plato not only suggested the preexistence of an independent soul, but also wrote that, before an incarnation into a body, each pre-existing entity got to choose an unseen guide for life. (Today, this would be referred as a guardian angel.)

With the prophets and philosophers came the realization of personal responsibility and consequences for how life was lived. Slowly this realization became more pronounced and associated with new beliefs we now call "religion," and different moralities developed with different religious beliefs.

With the introduction of more specific religious beliefs and personal internalization, people became more concerned about how they lived and the rules they lived by. But as a result of trying to do the right thing and relying on leaders to instruct them in right and wrong, many people have been misled by the greed and ignorance of religious leaders. That greed has resulted in a bad image for religion.

For example, Friedrich Nietzsche, in *On the Genealogy of Morality*, basically says religion and the resulting morality are a scam of the higher class, including priests, to control the people. I can understand why he thought that way. Religion has been used like a scam in many instances. However, I see religious morality as the basic ingredient of civilization and key to its survival. Not all higher-class people and religious try to scam the populace. Many religious people forfeit their lives for the religion they believe in. I further reject Nietzsche's beliefs because I believe there is a purpose for life, while Nietzsche did not so believe.

It is important to realize that just as religious morality brought about civilization, the loss of that morality will bring about its eventual collapse. Problems begin for civilizations when the basic fears and beliefs that established morality are lost. As morality is lost, along with its purpose and values, cooperation and trust within civilizations get lost.

I do not believe that humanity has evolved to the point that people will cooperate just out of acceptance and love. There is too much reliance on personal control for most people to accept the concept that love is the answer to the world's problems, even though it is. Without a basic morality that promotes responsibility to others, there are only governmental laws and consequential fear that hold civilizations together.

Without morality, initiated by religion, the unwritten laws of morality that create trust between people will disappear and society will become one of "anything is okay if you don't get caught." Religion is important for civilization. And it is most important for religions to focus on love. But until people realize the importance of love, religions need to remind the faithful that there will be consequences for bad living.

In *Human Understanding*, we see that the key ingredient to civilization is morality. Morality likely originated along with common behaviors to appease unknown forces and developed into religion. Society today is still dependent on morality. And as it is only religion that effectively promotes morality, religion is critical to civilization.

RELIGION AND SCRIPTURE

The purpose of a religion is to direct humanity to fulfillment with the Higher Power, or to enlightenment, in the case of Buddhism. Because most of us are busy with many other things besides religious concerns, most religious people rely on the research and wisdom of religious leaders, who spend most of their time with religious study and giving direction to people of the same religion. Where there is a belief in a higher level of life, religion is natural. What follows is not intended to study, promote, or degrade individual religions. Rather, it is written to give a better understanding of the subject of religion and the fallibility of all religions, as well as their importance. Engineers must look at all the evidence, even when the evidence is not what they would like.

I believe the best way to look at religion is to consider each religion a family. Children rely on the parents for direction. However, parents are human. Even when they try their best, parents make mistakes, and hopefully they learn from their mistakes. Just as children rely on parents for direction, the populace relies on religious leaders for spiritual direction. And because religious leaders are human, they also make mistakes, even in trying to do the right thing. Religion reminds us the purpose for our existence is related to a purpose higher than this physical existence. But the fact that there are different religions that vary in what they preach tells us, that like parents, religious leaders make mistakes. That is not surprising since no one knows for sure what actually exists beyond physical reality.

The populace is seeking answers to so many questions. People want some fixed belief so as to know what life is about and what is important to how they can be the most fulfilled. Without a personal belief in some fixed reality, many people feel lost. They are like children who want answers. Where are we going? Are we there yet? Even for people who believe in some type of existence after physical death, the questions are numerous and diverse. What occurs after physical death? Will we ascend to a higher level after death? Does hell exist? Will we be reincarnated? Will we be resurrected at the physical level? Is there an actual paradise? What will paradise consist of? Are there different levels of heaven and hell? What is it to be united with the Higher Power?

Trying to understand the unknown is natural. But when it comes to answering questions beyond what can actually be measured, religions are restricted to opinion based upon what is considered inspired scripture and the words of those people considered prophets, rather than upon proven knowledge. Therefore, based upon what is considered the best information available, educated opinions are voted on and proclamations given to the religious faithful. This is no different than parents answering their children's questions the best they can without actually knowing everything about what they are saying.

It is critical to understand that religions are based upon human interpretation of the information available to them. Although religions can be helpful in directing people to lives of virtue, they may not be correct in defining that which is beyond humanity's ability to actually know. Because of the questionable nature of religion, people, like confused children, often reject what religious leaders say because it doesn't make sense to them.

To maintain the respect of those they direct, it is most important for parents and religious leaders to be willing to learn and become relevant to all their children. That includes admitting mistakes and, in those instances, making changes needed to regain the confidence of their children. As knowledge grows, which includes new historical knowledge, religions must also be open to change when and where required.

However, as will be pointed out in the chapter Idealism and Practicality, it is still important that religions remain idealistic.

Religious leaders, and people posing as religious leaders, have fostered love and started wars. They have promoted peace and preached violence. Some religious leaders have brought personal peace to multitudes of people, while others have molested the innocent and fleeced the faithful. It has been said that more people have been killed in the name of God than for any other individual cause. However, I contend that the atrocities, though related to religion, are the fault of power-hungry and controlling religious and political people who misled the faithful in various ways to get what they wanted. They are not the fault of real religion, which is of love.

When religion and politics mix and leaders try to control what people think, people end up dying. For peace to exist, religion should never be mixed with any position of power in politics. Politics is about control. Religion is about love. Love is about learning to give up control. When religions get involved with control, they are no longer centered on love, which should be the essence of religion.

Humanity has abused religion to foster personal or nationalistic goals throughout history. And the spiritually blind have followed aimlessly along. Blind faith, without an understanding of love, has led to idolatry, Satanism, human sacrifice, suicide and mass suicide, war, terrorism, and hatred. Poor religious leadership and unloving purpose can lead followers to distress, unhappiness, disillusionment and even war. Depending upon what is preached within a religion, much acceptance or much animosity and bias can result. It is said the lowest places in hell are reserved for false religious leaders who lead other people astray, which would be appropriate.

On the other hand, the existence of religion has kept alive the concept of spirituality and love and provided morality critical to civilization. Religion has fostered the humanitarian efforts of giving and sharing. The existence of such a large number of religious schools, universities, and hospitals bears witness to that fact.

Religion, based upon love, initiated the concept that all human life is to be respected. While the unborn are not yet respected by many people, at least religious morality did help reduce slavery in much of the world. Without morality of some kind, brought about by religious beliefs, there has been little reason to think of anyone but one's self, especially for those in power.

Spirituality is of love. Religions are human creations. This is important to realize. The concepts of spirituality have been given to humanity through the words of the prophets and great teachers. In almost all cases, the written words, which are attributed to these great teachers and prophets, were words that were remembered by followers and written down, as well as could be remembered, at various time intervals after originally being spoken. Conflicts with the written word exist in all religions. There are plenty listed on the Internet if you are interested. But be aware, they are typically given to discredit specific religions.

Let me preface my concerns about scripture by saying I believe much of scripture was inspired by a Higher Power. But when it comes to believing what actually is inspired scripture and in the specific wording of scripture, my belief decreases substantially due to a number of reasons. The first reason is the accuracy of most scripture is questionable. Secondly, there are often conflicts within scripture and between the scripture of different religions, all claiming to have the correct inspired scripture. The third is that what is contained in scripture can be interpreted in a number of ways, which has resulted in various sects within each major religion. I personally believe that scripture that leads people to love has been inspired. I also believe that without inspiration to love one another, humans would not be much more than animals.

I have listed some concerns about the written word of the major religions to point out there are questions regarding the accuracy of the scripture of all religions. I also point out there are disagreements of interpretation of scripture within each religion, as the various sects and denominations indicate. The intent is not to try to discredit the religions themselves, because I believe they are all important. I do so to open the minds of those people who blindly accept scripture that is not centered on the fixed basic of love, and also so no one can say: "Not so with my religion."

Hinduism is based on "the accumulated treasury of spiritual laws discovered by different persons in different times." There is no agreement as to the origin of the Vedas, (a collection of knowledge, hymns, and other religious texts) which was likely about 1,500 BCE although it could have been earlier. But the origin of Hinduism is thought to be as old as 6,000 BCE. Somewhere between 800 and 400 BCE, a philosophic commentary, compiled orally by priests and referred to as the Upanishads, came about to unify the fragmented beliefs of the Vedas. The Vedas and the Upanishads were transmitted orally in verse form for many centuries before they were written down with the arrival of Islam about the mid-6th century. Over many centuries, sages refined the teachings and expanded the canon. There are numerous denominations in Hinduism indicating different beliefs within Hinduism. A good book on Hinduism, from which some of the information listed is taken, is *Great World Religions: Hinduism*. (39)

Judaism developed over time from the days of Moses to the time of Zoroastrian influence and even more after the destruction of the Temple by the Romans and the arrival of Christianity. With the destruction of the Temple came rabbinic literature and the decentralization of religious expression. These events precipitated the Mishnah and the Talmud. In Jewish tradition, the first five books of the Hebrew Bible, the Pentateuch or Torah, are attributed directly to Moses. But most scholars disagree and will argue that even the first book, Genesis, is a compilation of a number of writers.

Writing, as we think of it today, was not common at the time of Moses. Although early Phoenician writing existed at the time, Hebrew writing appears to have evolved from the Phoenician 400 or more years after Moses lived. Moses' writings would likely have been hieroglyphics. Some things written in the Hebrew Bible do not make logical sense. They begin with the first book of the Hebrew Bible. In Genesis 1: 6-19, water and plants were created before the two great luminaries of the sky to shed light to the earth (and warmth necessary for actual water and for plants to grow). There are many other inconsistencies in the Hebrew Bible. Although I believe most, or possibly all, of the Jewish Bible is based on actual historical events, there are many reasons to question the exact words. The various religious sects in Judaism also indicate different beliefs in Jewish scripture.

Buddhism is more of a spiritual way of life directed toward the realization of enlightenment rather than a belief in a god. It is based upon the multitude of teachings and rules of Gautama Buddha. (40) After Gautama Buddha died, a monk named Ananda, one of Buddha's disciples, supposedly remembered all his discourses and a monk named Upadhi remembered all the community rules. These were initially transmitted through oral teachings for more than 400 years before eventually being written down. The Pali Canon is considered by scholars to be the closest to the teaching of Gautama Buddha. It is very large. It should be realized that the sutras, one of three divisions of the Canon, which were all supposedly remembered by Ananda and handed down orally, alone contain over 5000 discourses.

In Buddhism, enlightenment is considered to be the Wisdom of Emptiness, obtained through a holy life and meditation. The object is to reach Nirvana, which is not fully understood, even by Buddhists. Buddha himself did not answer all the questions directed at him. Even though Buddhism is mostly about self-control and a worthy life, there have been schisms due to different interpretations of Gautama teachings. These schisms point out that Buddha's teachings, even if they were transmitted perfectly, can be interpreted differently.

Christianity is based upon the teachings of Jesus Christ as were spread by His disciples and the interpretation of what the life and death of Jesus means to humanity. The diversity of modern Christianity is mild in comparison with Christian thought during the first three centuries (41). That is because there was nothing in the early writings that defined religious practices or religious requirements. What actually came to be Orthodox Christianity was what the majority of religious leaders decided upon at the Council of Nicaea in the year 325.

The gospels themselves did not appear until the years 40 to 50, and as late as 70 years after the death of Jesus, so they had to have been based upon memory and oral tradition. There is no substantial evidence that the gospels actually were written by the apostles whose names are attached to each. All the gospels are now believed to have been written originally in Greek. Could the apostles even read or read and write in Greek? Their language was Hebrew or Aramaic. The majority of scholars do not believe the gospels were written by the apostles (42).

It should be realized there were books, other than those now attributed to the apostles, written in the names of the apostles and other disciples to give credence to what was written. (43) There is some evidence (the *Muratorian Fragment*, a copy of perhaps the oldest known list of most of the books of the New Testament) that there might have been something like a canon consisting of 27 New Testament books as early as the year 200 or slightly earlier. But it took until the mid-300s before there was general overall acceptance. So, does the New Testament have it all right?

Although the writings actually accepted as correct are very likely correct or close to correct, questions remain. Scholars today are not all together confident that 2nd Thessalonians was written by St. Paul. 3 Corinthians has been eliminated from most of Christianity. Some of what is contained in The Acts of the Apostles is considered to be fictitious, in that it denotes continuous harmony between Peter and Paul (Acts 15: 1-24) which is not consistent arguments over adherence to Jewish law, especially seen in Gal 2:11-14). If the words of Christian scripture were written to be interpreted exactly, how come there are so many different Christian interpretations and Christian sects?

If you want more controversy on traditional Christian belief, you might want to review a different version of the hidden years in the life of Christ than the one Christians typically accept. It says that Christ was off about His heavenly Father's business rather than a carpenter's business. If Jesus was a good Jewish boy he would have gotten married soon after his 12th birthday. (44) It is interesting that the same text was possibly the first written record of the crucifixion. But it was written in India, not Israel. In 1922, the head lama at the Hemis Buddhist monastery in Tibet said the Sanskrit writing held in the monastery, which contained an account of the crucifixion, as well as the hidden years of Jesus, was a copy of what had been written in the Pali language four years after the crucifixion with information provided by traders from Israel.

Islam is based upon the Quran (also Koran). The Quran, as it exists today, supposedly portrays the exact words the angel spoke to Muhammad. But questions about how the Quran of today was actually compiled raises questions as to its accuracy, as do its conflicts with archaeological history. It was two years after Muhammad had an initial vision before he even began to tell others what the angel had spoken to him. After Muhammad began to tell others of his visions, these were transmitted orally for many years.

The original Quran was supposedly assembled by Hadhrat Zaid. Zaid supposedly knew the oral text in its entirety, yet early Hadith literature says that Zaid had to conduct a thorough search of different oral recitations and what writings existed in its assembly. Such literature also states that portions of the Quran were irretrievably lost at the Battle of Yamama.

The Quran written two years after the death of Muhammad in 632 was known as the Habsah Quran. There is evidence that portions of the original Quran have been changed. The *Sana'a*

Manuscript (45), the most ancient segment of the Quran to be found in the Great Mosque in Yemen in 1972, has two layers of text.

The top layer basically conforms to today's accepted 'Uthman text. However, the lower layer has differences. It should be known that Caliph 'Uthman ibn Affan in the year 651 supposedly had the Habsah Quran exactly copied. But then he also had all previous copies of the Habsah Quran burned. Why? There is also political intrigue involving Caliph 'Uthman ibn Affan, who was assassinated in a revolt and the intentional destruction of the original Habsah Quran by the Uncle of 'Uthman. (46) The present Quran also conflicts with archaeological evidence. (47) In addition, the different sects within Islam also point to different interpretations of the Quran.

There are fundamental scriptural questions even with more recently evolved religions. I have chosen Mormonism and Jehovah Witnesses as examples. After "interesting" historically beginnings, which are available in books or online for those interested, these religions have morphed into more classical religions. The origins of all religions, as well as their histories and their founders' histories, should be important for members of any religion to be aware of. But I doubt that most members are aware of such history.

The fundamental basis for Mormonism is the *Book of Mormon*, found and translated by Joseph Smith, which provided additional, previously unknown scripture, if accurate. The *Book of Mormon* claims that the Indians of North America were the lost tribes of Israel. Thomas Murphy (who traces his linage back to the first Mormons in the West), chairperson of the anthropology department at Edmond Community College, was threatened with excommunication when, based upon genetics, he wrote: "DNA research lends no support to traditional Mormon belief about the origin of the Native American.

Richard Bushman, a prominent LDS historian, said, (48) "I think that for the church to remain strong, it has to reconstruct its narrative. The dominant narrative is not true; it can't be sustained." The statement was made by Bushman during a fireside chat regarding whether the traditional understanding of church history is accurate.

The Jehovah's Witnesses base their religion on their interpretation of Jewish and Christian scripture, which itself is questionable as to accuracy as noted above. The fact that the end of the world has been incorrectly predicted numerous times by this religion leads to additional questioning of the ability to correctly interpret any scripture that may actually be inspired. In predicting the date of the end of the world, the words of Mathew 24:36 and Mark 13:32, as well as Acts 1:7, are not taken into account. These words say that not even the angels or Jesus Himself knows the end time. If Jesus and the angels cannot figure it out, it is rather useless for mankind to try.

That conflicts and questions, regarding scripture and scripture interpretation of the various religions, exist does not mean that what is written or interpreted should be disregarded. What it does mean is that we need to be careful about what we accept as true, inspired scripture, including specific wording, as well as scripture interpretation. Besides the question as to the correctness of the older scripture and who wrote it, in general, we do not know the people who later compiled, translated, and edited the works of original writer(s).

The people involved may have had opinions or agendas that could have been added to make a point. Also, for those texts based many years of oral transmission, the extent to which exact words and sentences can vary when passed through just a few people should be considered. Another consideration should be given to how storytellers often expand certain story parts to make those parts more or less important, which could include the original authors. Other changes could have happened when being copied through omission and transposing.

Additionally, it should be realized that in the transposing and translation of documents from one language to another, the original meaning is sometimes lost. The same is true of books with specific written languages that have evolved between the time initially written and the time of latest accepted text. For example, it did not take long for the word "gay" to take on a very different meaning than it had for centuries. The original Hebrew and Islamic writings did not contain any punctuation marks, resulting in different ways they could be interpreted when later rewritten.

In spite of conflicts, contradictions, intrigue, and differences between religions and history, the major religions, other than Hinduism and Buddhism, still claim their sacred texts were inspired by God, or are the direct word of God. Hinduism is considered loosely inspired although more traditional Hinduism arrived though philosophy and also somewhat based upon supposed ancient historical events. Conflicts, in what is said to be inspired, point out that not all can be inspired.

Another thing to consider is that if the exact written word was to be so absolutely important; would not the initiating prophets or great teachers have written it or at least edited themselves? Except for the very questionable possibility of Moses, that did not happen. Because the initiating prophet or teacher did not consider it necessary to write down exactly what they said or to at least edit what was written, it would seem that the exact written word was not as important as the message they were trying to deliver, especially if we consider the different versions of the "exact word." Because of conflicts within the "Word of God" and questions as to wording, blind obedience to the specific words of scripture could lead to some improper beliefs where the scripture is not accurate.

If the scripture of all religions is somewhat questionable, what should be believed? So as not to be misled by the written word, the best way to evaluate inspired writings is to consider that which directs us to virtue and to love one another is inspired even if specific wording is not correct. If the Higher Power is of love, then that which is from the Higher Power would be of love. This may not be a traditional way to look at "Holy Scripture," but it is one that will not mislead. Writings that direct away from virtue and from loving one another or even disliking one another should not be considered inspired by a loving Higher Power.

Because of scriptural conflicts, it is also reasonable to conclude that it is the messages of the holy books that are important, rather than the specific words. We need to understand the big picture of what scriptures tell us. The basic message of the prophets, mystics, and holy people of all major religions is fundamentally the same. The message tells us to pray and/or to meditate and to perform good deeds so as to attain enlightenment or salvation.

It is time to recognize that all religions, which believe one Higher Power, are all praying or meditating to the same Higher Power. The best way to show such recognition is by accepting all people as brothers and sisters. Why is there a need for any fighting in the name of the same Higher Power? It is just another example of the human desire to control. If we live by the great commandments, or even by the essence of spirituality, which is love, we will not be misled in our quest for fulfillment in love.

Most people of specific religions generally accept what they are told by their religious leaders. To question could be considered lack of faith. This applies to doctrine as well as Holy Scripture. It should be realized that if there is anything inaccurate in Holy Scripture, from which religious doctrines have originated, religious doctrine would not likely be totally accurate either.

Another thing to consider about religious doctrine is that most basic doctrines of the major religions were developed long ago when there was limited scientific knowledge and much superstition. Times change and with time, and with new knowledge, so do beliefs. A 2006 poll taken by Scripps Howard News Service and the University of Ohio found that only 36 percent of Christians now believe in the resurrection of the body. (http://newspolls.org/articles/19603).

The earth's being subject to destruction in the future is just one reason to question bodily resurrection. With new knowledge and understanding, beliefs change, whether or not religious leaders like it. But, like science, many religious leaders try to hold onto past doctrine, often for fear of losing creditability. But like stubborn parents who take offence when their children question their decision, they can lose even more credibility for not learning and changing the things which need to change.

As doctrines of a religion become questionable, with new knowledge, it would be best for religions to revisit them or maybe acknowledge the possibility that specific doctrine may not be exactly correct, before all creditability is lost. Religions have proven fallible in what they preach as truth. We have only to look to history to prove that point. As late as 1600, the Dominican friar Giordino Bruno was burned at the stake for professing, among other things, that stars were just distant suns about which there were other planets that could foster life on their own. An open mind can get you ridiculed and in trouble with people who do not open their minds.

It might be wise for Christians to look at the words of Jesus Christ, referring to the religious doctrines of his time. "For the doctrines they teach are the commandments of man." (Mark 7:7) Even Jesus didn't see it necessary to hold to some of the laws of the religion He practiced. So how do we actually know what doctrines to believe? I would suggest that we best look at doctrine as suggested in how we look at scripture. We can believe in doctrines that promote love, prayer, and acceptance in a Higher Power of love. Even doctrines that seem questionable may be best to accept if they promote love among people. Not everything can be explained in physical reality. But that which promotes love needs to be accepted as part of fixed reality.

In paying attention to the essence of love, rather than just words, the followers cannot be misled by those who would abuse religious leadership intentionally—by ignorance or by complacency. The Christian St. Paul tells us that the written law brings death, whereas the spiritual law brings life. The spiritual law is the law of love. There is also the expression: "Love is above the law." This expression reminds us that love is more important than any human law. As St. Paul also says, "Love therefore is the fulfillment of the law." But in paying attention to the essence of love, it is important to understand the concept of love. For that reason, Love is a chapter in this book.

What I suggest could be taken as a gnostic approach to religion. However, what I suggest is not meant that people come up with their own ideas of what religions should be preaching and doing or should choose the religious rules they want to follow. I still look at religion as a family whose members need to stay together and learn from each other. As parents of families can make mistakes, religious leaders may make mistakes. But, like parents who have been through much in their lifetime, overall, they still know much more about life than the children in their family.

When children are asked by parents to do or to believe something the children understand is wrong, they should convey those feelings to their parents. It is smarter to try to change the views of responsible parents than to believe they can find all the right answers themselves. But parents need to respond by making sure that they continue to grow in knowledge, listen, and act in a way that holds the family together through love and understanding. The same is true of religions.

In *Human Understanding*, we realize that religion is based upon human knowledge and human interpretation of what is considered scared scripture. But because of the questionable correctness of sacred scripture, we also realize that we need to look at scripture in a way that is not confusing and not misleading. We understand that we need to focus on that which is important about religion. And what is important about scripture and religious doctrine is how they lead us to love, the type of love that is concerned about others as much as about self. So that we are not confused nor misled by scripture or religious doctrine, each of us has a personal responsibility to be sure that our lives are focused on love, and not necessarily on what we are told.

Other Thoughts about Religion

When they have a choice, people choose specific religions for many different reasons: because they feel comfortable with the religion they grew up with; because of years of searching; because they want to live happily after physical death; possibility to control others; because it seems like the right religion; because of the example of members or leaders; because they feel accepted; or for social or other reasons. Some people join or stay with specific religions to avoid ridicule or persecution. Some people subconsciously join churches that have specific conditions that assure paradise to have some control over their destiny.

For those people concerned with being a member of the so called "right religion," the odds are against them. The greatest percentage of the world's population is Christian at about 32 percent, but that includes all the Christian denominations. There were over 33,000 different Christian denominations and sub-denominations in Christianity in the year 2000 alone. They include 9,000 Protestant and 22,000 independent denominations. The others are Orthodox, Catholic, Anglican and marginals. Those statistics are from Center for the Study of Global Christianity at Gordon Conwell Theological Seminary. (Be aware that the count is somewhat misleading.) The denomination in one country is counted as separate from the same denomination in another country. That is because there is often different leadership and sometimes doctrinal differences in different countries within religions that go by the same name. At the time of counting, there were 238 different countries. But that still leaves many actual different denominations.

When you consider all the different sects in all the various religions, the odds of belonging to the "right religion," should one exist, are not good. Something else to think about is, that because major religions concentrations tend to be geographically located, the religion you belong to has more to do with where you were born in the world than on any other factor. In some geographic locations, there is no choice of religion.

So, if there is a just and loving Higher Power, how can we believe that salvation is only through one religion? Salvation is not through religion. Religion can help lead people to salvation. But salvation only comes through the gift of love of the Higher Power. The "right religion" is the one that best leads us to accept the gift of love into our hearts.

What should be remembered is that spirituality, which religion is supposed to lead us to, cannot be achieved by merely paying lip service to what the religion preaches. Belonging to a religion means almost nothing without some commitment to what religion is there to lead its member to. The love of spirituality needs to be put into people's lives.

An athlete is not successful unless he or she commits to the effort it takes to be successful. It is no different with spirituality. A person's spirituality will only increase with an effort to increase it. The greater the effort, the greater the success will be. Without some form of periodic spiritual practice, our thought reality will most often become caught up in the pleasures of the materialistic world. It is what repeatedly enters the mind that becomes a part of thought reality.

To believe that change can be made by just occasionally thinking about something is like believing that by just occasionally thinking about healthy eating, we will stay in good physical shape. We actually need to do more than think about the things we want and need. We need to work to attain them and keep them. At least the materialistic world, by promoting good physical appearance, gives us some encouragement.

In our everyday lives, we are enticed by material goods and ideas that promote pleasure and selfishness. But there is almost nothing in our everyday material world to encourage us in our spiritual health. Perhaps that is why many people find it an effort to attend religious services, and the opportunity to give thanks and praise to the creator of life and of the ability to love.

If we do not practice something that stresses the importance of love, we will most often overlook the concept of spirituality and the need to respect and to share with others. Other than religion, what source is actively teaching humanity the concepts of love and acceptance needed to maintain civil morality?

The desire to know and understand is most pronounced in children. Childhood is the time of their lives that is most important for their learning, especially as related to morality. They are developing their basic thought reality, as well as the means and methods of interaction they will utilize most of their lives. Without being exposed to a higher purpose and a healthy morality, children's thought reality values will include whatever brings the most perceived happiness and pleasure to the adults they observe.

In society, where the pleasures of escaping life's realities are pushed on the public through advertisements and are readily available for a price, it's no surprise that the youth of modern society are looking more to material rewards than to the inner happiness and satisfaction that comes from being virtuous. Without fear of after-death consequences; why worry? If things get bad, there is always suicide. According to the Centers for Disease Control, National Center for Health Statistics, the rate of suicide increased 24 percent between 1999 and 2014 for people under the age of 65 and is the biggest cause of death in young people.

Children require tangible facts and concrete ideas to arrive at a solid sense of morality. Children unconsciously look for basic fixed principles for developing basic thought reality. They need a point of reference by which to understand what is right and a reason to believe it is right. They need to understand the basic fixed reality of the universe; virtue creates order and joy, while vice creates chaos and despair. That reality would make a bigger impression on children if parents recognized that fact. The concept that there are consequences beyond human life, as well as in life, for how life is led, will impact a child's morality. The lack of a reason for loving and accepting morality will also have an impact on how children will grow up.

A loving religion will teach children that they are all equally loved. It is important that a child's self-worth does not rely on being the best, being beautiful, being handsome, or upon some other physical rating to be of personal worth. An understanding that they are always loved by the Higher Power, and that there will be an ultimate justice, would be of great benefit to those children who do not fit into the world of material values, whose parents do not appear to love them, or who are picked on. It would also help other children realize there are consequences for bullying.

Without positive lessons in morality and without examples of love and spirituality, children will more likely develop thought realities based on the material world purposes and values they are exposed to. Parents may think that since they are good, moral people, their children will be the same. While that may happen, it is by no means an absolute. The reality of humankind's physical nature is to get the greatest return for the least amount of effort. It is important that children learn to think beyond physical wants.

In a society where materialistic achievements are important for acceptance into most peer groups, children's morality may follow that of a peer group rather than that of the parents, especially if the parents pay little attention to moral concepts or even to their children. The greatest effect parents will have on their children's morality and overall happiness is the example they give. For that reason, it is also important that children see their parents acting morally. It would also help to see their parents actively participating in some type of spiritual program. It is also essential for children's friends to be of good moral character. Loving religious programs can provide such friendships.

Even as adults, our likes and dislikes will tend to blend with those with whom we associate. It is important to associate with those people we believe have good values. All of us need examples and encouragement in spirituality. There are some people who claim to be spiritual who do not practice any religion. Yet, maybe they are.

Spirituality lies in selfless actions, not in religion itself. We are spiritual when the purpose for which we actually live is focused beyond ourselves. That is what religion is supposed to lead us to. Our spiritual consciousness needs prayer and/or meditation and acts of love, as much as our bodies need exercise. If we are truly spiritual, we will want to learn more about spirituality and reflect on how it can positively impact our lives and the lives of others. Most often people find and accept spiritual responsibility through religious activity and volunteering. But without acting for causes beyond self or having constant reminders of the need to be spiritual, it is easy to lose one's self to worldly wants and pleasures.

Maintaining religious morality that promotes love is also important for society. Without a belief in a morality based upon love and justice, the only reason to behave is fear of being arrested. In America, as it relies less on morality, as the images of religion are removed from public view, as the concept of free will diminishes, and as Americans rely more on perceived worldly happiness, crime numbers have soared.

As will be cited in more depth in the next chapter, the number of people incarcerated or on probation in the United States increased 476 percent just between 1972 and 2007. We see the lack of morality in those people who promote violent games and even violent songs, at the expense of society, just to make a buck. History is full of stories about civilizations that lost their morality to worldly wants and power. They all ended.

Religions and religious morality can also affect countries and societies in subtle ways. Religions that restrict differences of opinion and independent thought can stifle the very people and the societies they are supposedly helping. Religions that require blind faith discourage people from opening their minds to better understanding and new ideas.

Over the years, I have conducted many interviews and met many people. What I have ascertained is that, in general, people from countries that have strict religious beliefs and practices, do not, as the expression goes "think outside the box." Although not always true, typically they have not been mentally creative. I believe their ability to think, beyond accepted thought reality, was indirectly stifled by having to conform to strict religious beliefs.

Thinking outside the box is critical to creative engineering. It is interesting to review the parallel between religious freedom in the USA and its corresponding rise of creativity. I do not mean to imply that freedom from religion was the cause. Rather, I believe, the cause was freedom to think for self—about religion and about other issues.

Although religions have had, and still have, questionable issues associated with them, what is overlooked is the importance of religion and what religion has accomplished. To get a true understanding of religion and its importance, it is necessary to look beyond the human frailty of religion and look at the positives it has accomplished for humanity, the most important being that has provided a good reason for humanity to think beyond selfishness and about others. As humanity has gone beyond the fear of nature, and even fear of laws, it is only the morality of religion that holds civilizations together.

If you are thinking about joining a religion or changing religions, you need to understand that religion is not what you seek. What you seek is fulfillment in love with the Higher Power of love. The religion you choose should be the one that will best lead you to a life of virtue, especially to prayer and love. Look for religion that is focused on love and forgiveness and allows personal thinking.

Religious sects that speak adversely of other religions or condone violence in any way do not have their focus on love. You might look for visible signs. Religions with miraculous happenings, saints, and very holy people might be something to consider. You might look at what the religions provide in humanitarian help, which is a sign of love. You might also consider sacred scripture that best focuses on love and that best encourages people to understand the message of love.

It is the loving and accepting words and acts and examples of the founders, as well as the loving words and acts and examples of the present leaders that you can believe in. Words mean nothing without actions to show they have meaning. Religions should lead you to understand and believe for yourself rather than tell you what you should believe. The right religion could be different for different people for many reasons.

The fanatical sects of any religion that abuse the message of love and acceptance are not true religion and can give specific religions a bad image. But this does not mean, because a specific religion has fanatical sects, it is not a religion that can lead to salvation. It is interesting that when Catholic visionaries of a supposed apparition of the Virgin Mary at Medjugorje, Yugoslavia, asked Mary who was the holiest person in the village. Mary replied it was devout Muslim women. (49) That response is certainly one that would not be expected of the Catholic children if the vision was made up. It also is a good reminder that holiness is based upon love and prayer, not what religion you belong to, although what religion you belong to can help.

As for fanatical sects that think they have to kill others in the name of God, I wonder why they do not realize that if God really wanted people of other religions to be dead, they would be dead.

In *Human Understanding*, we realize the religion we belong to has more to do with the family and country we were born into than any other physical factor. That tells us that if there is a loving Higher Power, it is not one specific religion that will lead to salvation. That realization also tells us that what is important about the religion is that it leads us to the acceptance of love. Without loving religious morality, there is eventual chaos. Religion, to be effective for us and for our children, has to be practiced to the point that we come to understand the importance of love. That will not likely happen if religion is only an occasional thing.

A final overall realization that ***Human Understanding*** provides, is that religion is about establishing the morality of love. Love is about acceptance and forgiveness. It is only a loving morality, resulting from a belief in a higher level of reality of love that will save humanity from itself. Humanity can destroy itself even with religion if religion is centered on control. Religion, which is important to morality, leads humanity to virtuous living through examples of love and with inspired writing and teaching. The most important thing to realize about life, regardless of religion, is that we must incorporate the virtue of love into our everyday lives. For that, we need to focus on spirituality as often as we can.

IDEALISM AND PRACTICALITY

The concept of idealism is often regarded as old-fashioned in the world today. However, in life, as in all other things, if we do not strive for an ideal, we remain in mediocrity. Therefore, it is important to understand the difference between the two and why idealism is important to us.

Idealism deals with the concept of perfection. The ideal way is, by definition, the best way to think about something or to accomplish something. As an engineer in the building business, I would like to be able to have ideal designs for every project I am involved with. Unfortunately, building projects are limited by such things as funding available, soil capability, construction equipment available, the time allotted to get the project built, worker knowledge, weather, quality of materials, strikes, and other unanticipated things. So, engineering today typically puts together the most practical design or product for what is intended, based upon many limiting factors.

Idealism does not normally present easily workable solutions to many problems. What is needed to make the ideal is not normally available. However, without idealistic goals, there would be no reason to keep finding better solutions. Practical solutions are most often needed to finally achieve the most ideal possible.

The attempt to design the ideal mousetrap has spawned hundreds of different models over hundreds of years. The traps in each era were likely the best that could be made at that time. Materials and creative ideas have changed with time and materials and will continue to do so. Thus, the ideal mousetrap may actually never come to exist. Nevertheless, humans continue working on building a better mousetrap in an attempt to create the ideal trap.

That said, if people are merely satisfied with just the practical, the ideal will never be attained. The same is true with life. Life is not meant to just maintain the status quo; it is meant for us to strive for the ideal. According to Aristotle, life is meant to attain the perfect, unchanging state.

In working toward the ideal purpose in life, we continue to improve ourselves and find self-worth and inner happiness.

Being idealistic is wonderful in theory, but there are problems with it. The first problem is that our day-to-day decisions are almost always governed by the practical habits of our limited thought processing. Another problem is arriving at an accurate understanding of what the ideal is that humans are actually trying to attain. There are certainly enough people telling us what is the idealistic truth and how to live our lives; yet what we hear often conflicts. So as not to be confused about what is important to be attained in life, I point out that there is but one ideal—love. That is a basic reality upon which thoughts and actions can be accurately evaluated.

If we have any desire to be idealistic, it should be to live lives of total virtue and love. However, we are human. Therefore, we will continue to be practical in what we do. We will all continue to make some very smart and some poor decisions in the practical implementation of our beliefs. But the most important issue in making practical decisions is to make those decisions based upon what we believe to be most ideal—what is most loving—for the circumstances involved. If we do make errors in our decisions, may they always be made in the effort to be loving in all we do.

Religions tend to be idealistic, and they are often ridiculed for that idealism. Yet, there is a need for religions to be idealistic. It is to create a goal or purpose for humanity at a higher idealistic level so that we may pursue a higher-level reality of love. Should the idealism of religion be replaced by short-term, more practical concepts, humans would lose much of the desire or requirement to strive for improvement in love and morality. As a result, religion, as well as societies, initially based upon religious moral values, would falter.

Although people will normally be practical with how they live their religion, it is necessary for religion and other important institutions that overall goals remain idealistic. If religions do not maintain idealism, morality will become whatever is practical at the time. Idealism is very important. However, religion should also have tolerance for those people for whom living the ideal is not achievable. For most people, the ideal is only achievable through some amount of practicality. For others, practicality may be the only way to survive.

Although the idealism of religion may be mocked, it is interesting to note that as countries try to replace religious morality with laws, the morality of those countries also declines. The United States of America is a good example. In the last 50 years, the USA has become more secular in its concerns and laws and less concerned with basic religious morality. As stated previously, the result has been less then fulfilling. From 1972 to 2007, the number of people incarcerated or on probation rose 476 percent, from 161 per 100,000 to 767 per 100,000 in the United States, according to *The Growth of Incarceration in the United States: Exploring Causes and Consequences 2014* (National Academies Press).

Without moral idealism, personal wants become most important and immoral acts seem to find a way to be justified. It should be noted that there are religious beliefs that do not promote the ideal of love and these need to be changed. But it is very important for society that religion holds on to the ideals of sanctity of life and a loving higher purpose for life.

In *Human Understanding*, we realize that although a practical outlook can help us toward specific worldly goals, true fulfillment must come from a higher ideal than worldly achievements. We also realize that if we do not accept the concept of the ideal—love—as purpose for life, we will get overpowered by the practical values of the material world. In life, we should be striving for the ideal—for love.

INTELLIGENCE AND WISDOM

A word that seems to be missing in modern society is wisdom. Wisdom and intelligence are different and, if you are concerned about more than this worldly existence, it is important to understand the difference. In the Old Testament of the Bible, the *Book of Wisdom* 7:8 and 7:10 speaks of wisdom as "the most noble and treasured of all possessions." (50)

Wisdom enables the wise to choose the best overall course of action for whatever situation requires a decision. It is interesting that the Holy Books do not speak more than in passing about what can be taken to mean intelligence—yet wisdom was valued enough that one of the books of the Hebrew Bible is called "Wisdom." Why is it that in today's vocabulary intelligence is a commonly used word, while wisdom is seldom-used? And is there a significant difference?

Intelligence is defined in a number of ways: "the ability to acquire and retain knowledge, keenness of mind, cleverness, and the ability to find successful solutions to new situations." Wisdom is defined by the *Merriam Webster Dictionary* as: "knowledge that is gained by having many life experiences; natural ability to understand what most other people cannot understand; knowledge of what is proper and reasonable—a good sense of judgment."

What appears to be lacking in understanding the definition of wisdom is how important the knowledge of history is to wisdom. Wisdom also is concerned about history yet to come. It is knowledge of the past history and past consequences of human activities that best predict the future for humanity.

The sacred writings are concerned with wisdom. They were written over a long period of time and were concerned with lessons in life. The wise are concerned with lasting solutions that bring peace and fulfillment. Intelligence is measured in terms of quick solutions to material or worldly problems. Wisdom is measured in terms of overall understanding of life and justice and it weeps at the futility of many short-term intelligent solutions.

That doesn't mean that intelligence should be discarded. The wise man can also use intelligent solutions for both short-term and long-term benefits. Wisdom does not conflict with intelligence, but sees intelligence as only a part of a bigger picture.

The fact that intelligence is valued over wisdom in today's society is a sign of the shortsightedness of the world we presently live in. Come up with a product or solution to a problem that will make money and long-term adverse consequences that are not immediately apparent will often be ignored. The various recalls of products show this to be true. In the "I want it now" world, intelligence is highly valued and long-term consequences and unintended consequences are often not considered. That seems to be especially true in the world of politics.

One of the best distinctions between intelligence and wisdom is I have heard is: *Intelligence gives us the ability to clone a dinosaur, while wisdom has us stop and ask, "Hey, is that really a good idea?"*

Wisdom asks about consequences, long-term as well as immediate. The wise man does not jump on the band wagon just because it is the "in" thing to do. The wise man will deny immediate desires when he believes there is a greater reward by waiting for something better. Wisdom looks to understand the meaning for what is to be done, as well as any long-term consequences. What long-term lessons of love and life are truly solved without wisdom?

Intelligence may be envied, but it should also be noted that for each difficult question an intelligent person can answer, that same person can probably think of at least one more question not previously posed. It is like breaking down the atom only to find smaller particles. Intelligence can solve specific problems. But by itself, intelligence cannot solve life's problems. It can actually make life more complicated. Also, intelligence is not always right, which can be amusing, as was recorded in a recent *Reader's Digest*. A professor was explaining to his class that a double negative can make a positive and in some languages, a double negative remains a negative. But there is no language in which a double positive means a negative. To which a student responded: "Yeah, right!"

Intelligence, in itself, does not lead to fulfillment. If properly utilized, it can lead to wisdom and to fulfillment. When not properly used, it can lead to internal disharmony and even pride. Because the intelligent person normally works within the limitations of science and the material world, that person tends to accept that intelligence and science can develop the ultimate solutions to human problems. Yet it is people, supposedly intelligent enough to govern nations, who start wars and bring misery to millions. Intelligence has not produced peace because it is focused upon immediate worldly problems and how to control them, rather than on the concepts of acceptance and love.

Intelligence operates within worldly consciousness. Wisdom is in touch with inner consciousness and the values that bring an inner feeling of happiness and peace. The fact that the non-physical virtue of love can be more fulfilling than anything physical is enough to convince the wise that there is more to life than being intelligent and worldly successful.

It is wisdom that accepts and forgives. It is wisdom that brings joy and personal peace. Wisdom is of the world of acceptance and love. There is nothing wrong with intelligence. It may get us someplace in today's society. But it is far better to be wise about that which brings joy, and love, and satisfies the heart. If you are intelligent, you may do well and you may find personal peace. But that is not a given. If you have wisdom, rejoice. Regardless of the level of intelligence, you will know how to arrive at personal peace.

In *Human Understanding*, intelligence is for the here and now, while wisdom is for those who believe in forever after.

CONTROL

In my opinion, if there is any one vice that is the most responsible for the greatest amount of violence and personal unhappiness in the world, it would be the desire for control. I see the desire to control as the opposite of love and therefore as the root of all other vices. While others may consider the desire for control as a sin of pride, I believe that people even without personal pride can partake in the desire to control. I believe the need to feel in control is the biggest factor in such things as addiction, judgment, anger, and even stress, as the following chapters will show. Control is a natural desire of our worldly egos, but it leads to inner turmoil as well as to war, rather than to inner peace and peace in the world. Although we desire control, we need to realize that the feeling of being controlled is perhaps the most despised feeling there is.

Would that I be king. The desire for ultimate control is something that many people dream about. Yet, being king does not of itself bring happiness. A king may be able to attain more physical pleasure and political stature, but inner peace and happiness is based upon the feeling of being loved and accepted. Kings are loved for their benevolence and hated for their control. This is true at all levels of authority. This is even true for how children view parents. Control is a form of exercising one's power over others. Most of us are familiar with the expression, "Power corrupts, and absolute power corrupts absolutely," originally stated by philosopher John E.E.D. Acton. The desire for power and control has wreaked havoc upon humanity for all of recorded history, and probably before that. And it will likely do so again in the future.

The desire for control begins at an early age. As young children, we were exposed to the control of others. Of all values that children are exposed to, the value that likely makes the biggest impression is that people in control seem to get what they want. As children, we observed our parents and other adults doing what they wanted, often while telling us that we couldn't do likewise. We may not have thought about it, but, as children, control was a major value we subconsciously wanted.

The desire to be in control is the subtlest of all vices. The more we detest the control of others, the more likely we are to desire our own control. Like other thought habits (good and bad), the value of having control entered our thought reality in our childhood. Even as children, most of us tested our parents to see ways we could get some control over them.

I'm told that my first sentence was, "Spank me, I'm gonna," in response to my mother when she threatened to spank me if I didn't stop pulling books out of the bookcase. I'm sure each of us has a similar story of youthful defiance. The desire for control is there even if we are not consciously aware of it. Many of us who had a domineering parent or parents vowed we would never be like them. Yet, the very need to escape the control of a parent(s) has typically made our desire for control even greater. Children may lead their lives differently than their parents, but most often the judgment and control of a domineering parent(s) gets passed down between generations in some form. Even children who break off communication with a parent, who they felt dominated or mistreated them, are merely trying to show they are now in control.

The desire for control impacts our lives from infancy on. Based upon my limited observations, I would say that, in general, the more controlling a parent(s) in a family, the more desire for control the children will likely have. Please realize that control can be implemented in subtle ways. It can be implemented through weakness, as well as by power.

Despite all the unhappiness brought about by the need to feel in control, the desire to have control over the situations in our lives remains perhaps the greatest struggle each of us faces in our search for happiness. We would like to have the value of material and mental security we perceive will come with control. But it is the need to feel in control that sustains wants, judgment, anger, and revenge—sometimes to the point of personal vendettas and wars. In so doing, control limits the ability to love.

People do not normally realize how they are controlled by their desire for control. Even many of us, who desire peace and freedom from control of others, would like to control the world long enough to have everyone understand the need for peace the same way as we do. The degree of such a desire establishes the depth of our mental hypocrisy. The need to feel in control robs us of finding acceptance and resulting happiness. It is also in our desire to control other people that we lose their respect.

The methods people use for control vary considerably. In "Means and Methods," we looked at how people developed methods for getting what they wanted. It should be realized that people who act weak and helpless to gain control may be no less controlling than more openly domineering people. They have simply developed different methods of exerting control. People playing the victim, who because of repetition have often come to believe they are victims, use sympathy to aid their agenda. The desire of control to get what a person wants can be very subtle, but it exists to various degrees in all of us.

It is difficult to resist the urge to control, especially for people living in a society where they are bombarded with the notion that "having things your way" brings happiness. We all need to stop and think before accepting the idea that control brings happiness. An example of how we fool ourselves about control can be visualized by understanding the dilemma of being a boss. Many of us would like to be the boss of a large company. We somehow believe that as boss, we would be in control. What needs to be realized is that the boss is really not in control. He actually has as many bosses as he has clients, and each client has demands that must be met despite how all the demands conflict.

I was a boss. I worked harder and more hours than anyone in the office to keep all my clients happy. I once missed a phone call from a good client because I was at my mother's funeral. The client was unhappy because he needed an answer from me immediately for a project under construction. We never had any additional work from his office. And I experienced another problem with being a boss of a small company. My employees were also my friends. That made letting people go much more difficult. I once went for ten months without income so I could pay my employees. Almost worse, I never had a true vacation. My work didn't go away when I did. Vacation just meant that I had to reallocate when I got things done. I often worked 70 hours or more the week before vacation and even more when I got back. The concept that control of the world around us brings happiness and personal peace is a delusion. It may bring material gain and pleasures, but not personal peace and inner happiness.

Control can bring inner happiness only if that control is limited to self-control. The desire to force one's control on others eventually brings loneliness. Our true friends are those who accept us as we are, not those who control us or tell us how to live. The perceived need to control can also lead to frustration, stress, anger, or worse. And it's not just the need to control the present that can be a problem. The thought reality that we should have controlled past events differently can lead to problems associated with self-judgment.

When things get beyond our control to the point that we wish we had more control, it is time to consider relinquishing control. It is time to understand and repeat the Serenity Prayer: "*God, grant me the serenity to accept the things I cannot change, the courage to change the things I can, and the wisdom to know the difference.*" The Serenity Prayer has been used by Alcoholics Anonymous for over 75 years.

Acceptance, rather than control, is most important in overcoming many difficult issues in life. We can influence others, but we cannot control them. We only have the ability to control ourselves from this moment onward. The past is now there for us to learn from. We should also be aware that the major step in recovery programs for addicts, and often from other mental problems, is to give up the need to be in control.

Our happiness is related to our limited thought reality. The thought reality that we need to be in control will almost always lead to frustration and unhappiness, as we eventually find we really cannot control what we want to control. Real happiness comes with the understanding and acceptance that we can only control ourselves.

In this book, I repeatedly point out the need to open our minds to the realization that most of what we know is only opinion. For that reason, I personally have a problem with individuals or even various institutions trying to control what others what should believe. A good example of institutional desire to control is the May 2016 ban of the Portland, Oregon Public Schools Board on any classroom materials that may cast any doubt on humans being the blame for present climate change. Although I agree that humanity is the most likely cause of the present rise of the earth's climate, I also believe that our minds need to be open to other possible causes.

There is good statistical data that supports the concept that the cause of the present change is the emission of greenhouse gases, as well as the destruction of forests, which at one time could balance out carbon emissions. But if we look at the history of Earth's climate, we find a record of consistent climate change when humanity could not have been the cause.

Between 8,000 and 5,000 years ago, in a period called the Holocene Climate Optimum, temperatures were significantly higher than today. The typical accepted temperature estimate is about one degree Celcius higher than today, although there are estimated of up to 4 degrees Celsius warmer than today. The actual rise above sea level today varies greatly because there has been no specific way to determine. Estimates vary from about half a meter to as much as 2 meters or more. The actual rise would have been dependent upon the amount of glacier melt. The real problem with the

Holocene period is that the last 7,000 years, with some ups and downs, have actually been a period of cooling. The fact that temperatures can drop, sometimes very quickly, in spite of glacial melting and increased greenhouse gasses, does not fit with present models on climate change. This needs to be considered. (51)

As reported by Dr. Christian Schluchter, professor emeritus at the University of Bern in Switzerland, the finding of 4,000-year-old wood in the face of retreating alpine glaciers indicate that the Alps were almost glacier free at the time and disproves the idea that these glaciers only began retreating in the 19th century.

As recently as 1,000 years ago, the temperature of the earth was as warm, or warmer than it is now. In between, there was what has been labeled a mini-ice age. Although the temperature rise in the last 50 years is said to be unprecedented in recorded history, that statement is now questionable, based on more recent research which shows a much greater variability in climate than previously thought within the past 2000 years. (52)

Many of us older folks can remember the downturn of temperatures in the 1970s, which caused dozens of scientists and major newspapers to declare a new ice age was coming, and air pollution was being blamed. (53)

One new thought on climate change is the effect of space weather on earth, which has not yet been seriously investigated. However, that is now beginning to be given more extensive consideration. (54) Space weather includes the variation in sun energy output, as well as the galactic cosmic rays, the effects of which are further altered by the weakening magnetic field around the earth. Space weather is a possible explanation for Earth's climate changes that happen without human influence and remain unexplained. Perhaps space weather is also particularly bad at this time. Although humanity certainly appears to be the major contributor to recent climate change, since there are other possibilities, it is still only a reasonable hypothesis—not established fact.

The Portland, Oregon school system, which places **all** the blame for climate change on humanity, is a good example of how educational and political leaders and even newspapers try to control the thinking of others. The object of education should be to open the mind, not to indoctrinate others with their beliefs. Global warming should be presented as an issue that is very important for humanity to understand and to do something about where possible. But to force the specific opinion of a school board on students is no different than a government forcing a religious belief on those it governs.

When people decide their views must be believed by all and outlaw dissenting opinion, humanity is in trouble. Be wary of people in authority who have all the answers.

I will believe something if I come to understand it or if it makes sense to me, not because I am told I must believe. Great leaders teach by opening the minds of people to the truth so they can come to understand and so believe. Even the noted Christian, St. Augustine, only accepted Christianity through reason, not because he was told what he had to believe.

Great leaders do not demand mental compliance. Control of what people believe produces mental zombies. It is minds open to new knowledge, even controversial knowledge, that produce creative solutions, as well people who can think for themselves.

The only real way to control the masses is to educate people on good reasons why they should control themselves. It is only when people cannot civilly control themselves that authoritative control is actually required. Teaching what is important for self-worth is critical because without self-worth, there may be no reason to develop self-control. The more people are educated in understanding what is important for self-worth and for a happy life, the more willing they will be to develop of self-control. Also, if all people believe that there are after-death consequences for how life is lived, people would be more likely to control themselves.

With my present understanding of life, I no longer feel a need to try to control the events and the people in my life, and I am happier and more content. Perhaps all this was taught to me years ago and it didn't get through then. I don't know. But I do know there are many people like me who are looking for something in life to believe in, which makes sense to them. Therefore, I urge everyone reading this book to look at the effect of personal desire for control, of others or of self, on their lives. Everyone needs to understand the detrimental effects of the vice of control and the reason giving up that desire is important.

The idea that we can actually control the world around us is an illusion. What is to be gained by control is based upon the assumption that how all people act can be controlled. That is an illusion even when few people are involved. It is also often an illusion in the construction industry. Construction company owners are not dumb, and when they take a project, they plan how the project will be controlled so they make a profit. If everything in the construction industry was really under control, there would be no reason for contractors to go bankrupt, which many do. A certain amount of control is important to getting things done. But full control is an illusion. I'm sure any classroom teacher would agree. Real control will exist only when people understand why and how to control themselves. Therefore, teaching should always include reasons for people to control themselves.

In *Human Understanding*, we realize that the desire to control other people and the world is probably the major source of the world's problems and unhappiness. It is a subtle vice that inhabits our thought realities. Like many other bad habits, the desire for control grows with repeated acts of selfishness, or maybe it causes selfishness to grow. Although control may help us in the material world, it will not help us find inner happiness. The only control that can lead to happiness is self-control. Self-control can lead to acceptance and happiness. The only way to effectively control others is to teach them to control themselves. People will only control themselves when they understand why they should. Look at the fixed basics of life and the reason becomes clear.

ADDICTION

This chapter recognizes that not all addictions are the result of personal choice. Forced addictions and drug addictions at birth are a reality. However, these are generally exceptions and are not addressed herein. It is also recognized that due to body chemistry, some people are more prone to physical addiction than other people. But in those cases, there is still a choice being made, and this chapter applies.

Here, we look at addictions as consequences of personal choices, based upon perceived values to be gained. The choices may be influenced by environment and genetics, but choices are made. The reason this chapter follows the chapter on Control is I contend that childhood desire for control can itself become a habit or even an addiction that negatively influences the ability to be objective when it comes to obtaining desired values. It especially affects young people or others to whom some form of control seems important but who have not learned its negative consequences. The desire to control others, to prove the ability to control, to escape the control of others or even of boredom, to escape physical or mental pain, or to mistakenly believe in self control they do not have forms the basis for most all substance addictions as well as other harmful addictions and behavioral problems. The greater a child perceives the value of control, the more likely an addiction and/or other behavioral problems will result.

Addiction takes other forms than substance abuse. As has been pointed out repeatedly, people can also become addicted to something as seemingly innocent as a way of thinking. However there is no such thing as innocent addictive thinking. Addictive thinking impedes the ability to think rationally and can enter the subconscious where it can also affect physical and emotional well-being. But regardless of form, addiction normally begins with a perceived value to be gained that is greater than perceived adverse consequences, if consequences are even thought about.

If initial trial of any thought, action, or substance accomplishes the value desired or establishes a new desired value, it will likely be repeated. When repeated without consideration or worry of consequences, it is a habit. And when the value of the action, thought, or substance overpowers the thought desire to stop the thought or action, it is an addiction. Addiction is compounded when substance intake affects body chemistry. Unfortunately, there is no clear line between where habit ends and addiction begins. In some cases, addiction can start almost with the first value trial.

In its *Important Facts* publication, the National Association for Children of Alcoholics and Children of Addicted Parents notes that children of addicted parents are the higher risk group of children to become alcohol and drug abusers due to both genetic and family environment factors. It also notes that adopted children of alcoholic parents continue to have an increased risk (2- to 9-fold) of developing alcoholism.

Poverty is sometimes linked to addiction. It is found that the unhappiness of poverty can lead people to drink to escape the loss of personal control, which can eventually lead to addiction and subsequent family addictions. The Adverse Childhood Experience (ACE) Study conducted by Kaiser Permanete of the Health Organization and Centers for Disease Control and Prevention studied 17,337 people regarding traumatic childhood experiences and the effects on their lives. They were all asked about ten types of childhood trauma. These included neglect (physical and emotional), abuse (physical, emotional, and sexual) violence, substance abuse, household mental illness, separation or divorce, and incarceration of family members.

People who had been exposed to at least four adverse experiences had a 7-fold increase in alcoholism over those who had no such adverse experiences. They also had a two-fold increase in cancer. People exposed to at least six such experiences had a 30-fold increase in eventual suicide. Genetics are one thing. But the effect on the thought reality of children exposed to traumatic environments appears to have a much larger impact on children and eventual addiction and health. The fact that adopted children of alcoholic parents still had a big incidence of developing alcoholism point out that the effects of exposure to bad experiences begin at a very young age, the age when children learn the most.

Although genetics are a factor, I contend that the biggest reason for addictions running in families is not genetic, but rather the desire for control of at least one parent getting passed down from generation to generation. Most children, and spouses, do not respond well to a demanding, controlling, and possibly violent parent(s) or spouse. But one response they will have is an inner desire for control of their own to escape being controlled or to prove their own control and the worse the environment the greater the desire for becomes. Unfortunately, they have poor examples of how to effectively escape.

Doing something counter to what is acceptable is one way of establishing a form of control. The more people desire control, at any age, the less likely they are to listen to rules and warnings, especially of the people controlling them. Children and spouses in those situations are less likely to have feelings of self-worth, in which case they may not care about what harm they may be doing to themselves. The concern is about establishing the self-image that they are in control of their lives.

The concept of a controlling parent(s) or spouse being a large factor in addiction relates well to the previous study mentioned if, as I also believe, traumatic events in families are mostly caused by controlling parent(s). I should also note that traumatic events become worse when controlling people do not have control of themselves.

Children who grow up with traumatic situations or just in situations where any one of a number of nurturing aspects of life are missing, will try to replace what they are missing with a surrogate value—control being a much desired value. Even adults who are lacking self-worth will seek to replace it with a surrogate value. As flawed humans, we do many strange and dangerous things to feel good in some way, especially if we do not worry about the consequences or if we do not think the consequences could make things any worse. One way some people seek to feel good about themselves is to prove they can control something, especially something they are told they cannot control.

Addictions can be socially acceptable. They can be just questionable, such as compulsive eating or compulsive neatness. Addictions can be sexual, as well as something innocent. Addictions can be debilitating such as dependency, low self-esteeming, or a compulsion, such as gambling. While some people consider the non-drug addictions as simply obsessive-compulsive disorders, they are still addictions that originate with a perceived value or importance to thought reality. Addictions can be materially rewarded, as in the case of a success-driven CEO workaholic. But even non-substance addictions can be destructive to individuals and to society. They can also impede improvements in society. It is the addictive mind is not open to consider new ideas or new realities, because of an addictive way of thinking, that hinders progress.

Something I do not think has gotten enough attention as a contributing cause of dangerous addiction and crime is the lessening of the idea of negative consequences after death. The lack of contemplating what happens after death may not make a difference for people who do not believe in a higher purpose for life. But for those who do believe in an afterlife or even the possibility of an afterlife, contemplating death and perceived consequences can make a difference in thoughts and actions.

As I have expressed, pain, or fear of pain, is the world's greatest motivator, I believe the fear of unknown consequences after death do affect how people think and act if they believe in an afterlife. This belief is backed up by the *Divergent Effects of Belief in Heaven or Hell on National Crime Rates* of June 18, 2012 (DOI: 10.1371/journal). This report points out that crime rates are substantially higher when people consider they will get to heaven because of a benevolent God than people who believe in the reality of hell. Fear of a period of torment has a greater effect on behavior than reward for good behavior.

When children grow up in families where there is no concept of an afterlife, they may not develop an overall purpose for being moral nor any reason to worry about civil consequences other than breaking civil laws, for which they may have no respect. Although the importance of love needs to be stressed, potential negative afterlife consequences also need to be stressed, especially as these seem to have a greater effect.

Although unlawful behavior is related to environment, letting unlawful offenses go without some type punishment, due to environment, is not helpful. Offenders make choices. They have free will. The concept that what people do is all based upon genetics and environment, rather than personal choice, seems to have invaded the judicial system. That bothered psychologist and brain researcher Dr. Jonathan Schooler (55) enough that he devised tests to determine the effect of deleting the concept of free will from conscious thinking. The result was that people subjected to the concept that there was no free will, substantially increased their tendency to cheat, over those people subjected to the concept of free will. The test points out bad choices can be viewed as good choices if there is no feeling of responsibility for choices made. When people are not held responsible for bad choices, this increases the probability of future bad choices.

Furthermore, being sympathetic to an addictive group or person will not help them. Sympathy will more likely intensify the condition that is the source of the addiction. Be aware that an addict quickly learns how playing the victim can gain something without work or payment. However, I do not advocate punishment without explaining why the punishment is in a person's the best interest and providing guidance for rehabilitation. Along with the punishment, there should be required education in understanding that self-worth is required for happiness and what is required to attain it. But since there is a difference of opinion about what life is about, important life lessons and after-life concerns are not being taught and morality seems to be fading into the background.

We see the relaxation of morality in modern society, which does not seem to worry about consequences. We have only to look at the examples of unrealistic worldly pleasures that are flashed in the faces of children and copied by many adults. But it's "okay" because the youth are told, "Don't look" or "Don't do it." And then we wonder why youth don't listen. We hold high famous sports heroes, even when they are bad examples. Our public schools do little to nothing to explain the need for self-worth, virtue, or even personal responsibility. In many ways, modern society promotes a double standard that impressionable youth may not be able to understand. As long as self-centered purpose and values are glorified by society or even by some family units, and promoted through examples, we should not be too surprised by many of the addictions observed.

We have looked at many reasons and contributing factors for addiction. It is unfortunate that these things exist and influence the choices people make. But, as adults, we make the choices as to how we live our lives. There is a point in life when each of us must decide whether we are going to remain children all our lives or if we are going to do what it takes to grow up. As long as people focus on self, addictions will continue to prevail. Worse yet, people who are addicted will likely remain addicted and lose the chance for self-worth, inner peace, and happiness, as most likely will their children. Blaming others will not change the situation. The chain has to end.

As I contend that most drug and alcohol and other dangerous addictions are directly or indirectly brought on by the desire to be in control, to escape control, to prove control, or the belief in being able to control things beyond self for reasons of personal value gain, the most important step in overcoming addiction is learning to accept life as it is. It is necessary to accept that as humans, we do not have the control over ourselves and others that we like to think we have, and that we need to avoid those things that can lead to addiction. This doesn't mean we shouldn't try to change the poor circumstances in our lives. That we should do. But real change involves change from controlling to accepting and that requires learning self-control. That will only happen when we repeatedly focus on the value of self-control and of poor consequences resulting from the desire for control of others.

Simple addictions may possibly be overcome with work on understanding of how we often let desire for control and worldly pleasure hurt our lives, and by working on new values, especially the values of acceptance and self-control. But such new values must be able to overpower addictive thought reality. That is more simply said than done. That is why addictions often require professional therapy and, in cases of physical addictions, medical attention. Overcoming any addiction requires sustained effort to constantly focus on replacement values and on the adverse consequences of not changing. It takes learning self-control and self-discipline.

In looking for new values to help overcome addiction, new material values will not likely help. The only new values that can overpower worldly values, on more than a temporary basis, are those that promote self-worth and inner happiness. In the chapter on Self-Worth, we saw that the only thing that truly brought self-worth was being able to actually do what we know in our hearts we should be doing. It involved doing for others. That can be difficult for people wrapped up in themselves. They need more than a desire to change thought reality. They need help, good advice, good examples, personal effort, and other people to let them know they matter and are loved.

A belief in a Higher Power of love and ultimate justice can help. Regardless of what science may say about the existence of a Higher Power, the acceptance of a Higher Power has proven to be a very important step in Alcoholic Anonymous for overcoming addiction. The acceptance of being powerless and acceptance that it is only a power greater than self that can help overcome the addiction are basically at the heart of the AA program. With that acceptance, addicts are open for change and the other program steps.

In *Human Understanding*, we realize that addiction begins with a thought reality that is in some way focused on controlling what is necessary to attain worldly values, one of which is control itself. There are a number of genetic and environmental conditions that can lead to addictions, the far greatest of which is a controlling parent(s) or guardian(s). Also, where love is lacking, the substitute is often some physical value that results in addiction.

Another contributing factor in addiction is a lack of fear of consequences, both in life and after-life. Overcoming addiction requires finding a value better than the mental and physical value of the addiction. Looking to other physical values will seldom be greater than the value of the addiction. Therefore, the best place to look for new values is beyond physical reality to love and acceptance.

JUDGMENT

udgments are mental convictions. All the evaluations we make in life are based upon our perceptions and upon our personal thought reality's concept and evaluation of right and wrong. When our evaluations are viewed as actual reality, rather than personal opinion, right or wrong, they become judgments. Regardless if a judgment is right or wrong, when a judgment is made regarding another person, it most often comes from a concious or subconcious desire to control other people in some way. The desire can be to blame or even congratulate as well as to influence (help control) what will happen in future similar situations.

Judgment can be meant to influence people not even involved in the situation precipitating the judgment. Judgments can be positive or negative. We usually think of positive judgments as good, but that is not necessarily so when they are incorrect. Negative judgments are more personally controlling and come from people who think they know more than or that they are nicer than the people they judge. Judgments have consequences for both the person judging, as well as for the person(s) judged.

As we reviewed with feelings and perceptions, when we encounter something we feel we need to understand, we combine the perception of what is encountered with our preconditioned notions and come up with a mental assessment of what we encounter and how to respond. With proper understanding, we should arrive at a good assessment. But, unless everything about what we are evaluating is known and fully understood, only an assessment is justified. And when it comes to an understanding of other people, a full understanding is virtually impossible. Even in court, unless the evidence is indisputable, the judgments handed out are based upon the opinions of juries and judges.

When a professional engineer testifies or writes a report, the engineer does not testify with a judgment. The engineer never says, "This is the way it happened." The engineer cannot provide a judgment, regardless of expertise. Instead, the engineer says, "It is my professional opinion ..." Even for experts, analysis is presented as an opinion based upon the evidence. If experts can only give opinions about their areas of expertise, it is something the rest of us need to think about, especially if we are judgmental.

Despite a limited amount of accuracy, preconditioned notions are necessary for humanity. As limited as they may be, they provide the basis for the assessments we need to make, as well as the judgments we should not make. Assessment opens the mind to new knowledge and understanding. Judgment closes the mind to growth in knowledge and understanding. If we expect to learn the truth about anything, we need to accept that we don't know it all. As Albert Einstein is noted for stating, "A true genius admits he/she knows little." If Einstein can say that, how can any of the rest of us think we know it all?

Sigmund Freud introduced the concept that being judgmental is the result of childhood experiences. That concept follows along with the "Means and Methods" section of how children develop their thought habits, including the thought habit of wanting control, which leads to judgments. But regardless of where judgment originates, once the need for judgment is initiated into thought reality, it can become a habit or even an addiction. However, a blessing of humanity is that people can change their habits, even bad ones.

The desire to judge is not entirely a constant, as is detailed in a research paper published in the *Annual Review of Psychology* (Vol. 66: 799-823, Jan. 2015), entitled "Emotions and Decision Making." Research has found that when people are in a happy state of mind, they are less judgmental. As will be seen in the chapter on Happiness, happiness is dependent on a mental decision to eliminate judgment and to appreciate *"what is"*. Thus, it is no surprise that happy people are less judgmental. Conversely, people need to consider they may be happier if they are less judgmental.

We have looked at how judgment comes about, but most of us don't realize how judgmental we are. And we often fail to recognize the adverse effects of our judgments on our lives. Let's be honest, we often do judge other people, even while most of us have trouble making proper value judgments about ourselves and what we do. People do not like being judged. Judgment often isolates judgmental people from having close friends and satisfying personal relationships. Judgment, which is a form of control, is a major cause of breakups in families and relationships. Where there is judgment, there is a lack of trust. And where there is a lack of trust, happiness and inner peace depart. Conversely, with trust, in spite of differences, we find friendship and personal peace. Consider the people you get along best with. They are not likely to be people who are judgmental about what you do and how you do it. You might want to consider how your judgments affect your relationships or even your neighbors.

A humorous example of judgment is that of Father Murphy, who was invited to the home of 86-year-old Mrs. O'Brian for dinner. During dinner, he excused himself to go to the bathroom. While walking past the piano on the way to the bathroom, he noticed a condom floating in a bowl of water on the piano. He was very upset with Mrs. O'Brian and told her so when he came back.

Father Murphy was most embarrassed when Mrs. O'Brian responded by saying: "I don't understand what's wrong. I found a little package on the sidewalk a few months ago. It said get wet, put on organ, prevents disease. I haven't been sick since."

This is just one example of how we can embarrass ourselves by judging without knowing the circumstances. Fiction though this is, it presents a humorous lesson about how preconceived notions of thought reality can be very misleading. All the facts need to be known before judging. Poor judgment can be very embarrassing. We do not have to like everything others do but personal peace requires that judgment of others must be left to courts and a Higher Power.

Another aspect of judgment that can be very detrimental is self-judgment. Unfortunately, people who judge themselves think they have all the correct information needed to judge their past actions. They fail to recognize that even when judging themselves they are evaluating based upon their limited and often misguided and biased thought reality opinions.

In 1957, Albert Ellis, PhD approached the American Association of Cognitive Behavioral Therapy with the concept that although self-judgments may result from childhood experiences, as Freud suggested, they actually exist because of an incorrect belief system. Dr. Ellis and Aaron Beck became two of the most important people in the development of Cognitive Behavioral Therapy (CBT). The object of CBT is to introduce those suffering from self-judgment to new thought habits. The importance of new thought habits should be no surprise to the readers of this book.

For those suffering from self-judgment, there are now a number of books available to help in changing self-judgment to self-compassion. Two that may be helpful are *Compassion and Self-Hate* by Theodor Isaac Rubin and *The Mindful Path to Self-Compassion* by Christopher Germer. As with all changes in thought reality, such change takes time and effort.

Another book I recommend with regard to self-judgment is *Biblical Blues* by Andre Papineau, (56) a priest and professor of homiletics (the art of preaching). It is a great book on looking at new ways to understand the set-ups and let-downs of life, based upon biblical stories, but it applies to life situations. Papineau points out how seemingly bad situations and decisions can be important to the greater good of individuals and the greater community. He also points out how bad situations seemed to have been preordained for the good that is to be derived from them. In reasoning things out from a different perspective, we realize how our personal judgments, including those of ourselves, can mislead us.

There is a line in the movie *The Imitation Game* given by the main woman in the movie to Alan Turing, the person most responsible for breaking the enigma code of the Germans during World War II. He was a homosexual and judged himself poorly. The woman basically told him that it was specifically because who he was that he was able to do what he did, and that is likely so. The estimate is that the war in Europe could have lasted years longer and perhaps another 14 million lives would have been lost if not for him. People might want to consider that maybe there is a higher-level reason for who they are and the events in their lives before judging themselves.

People who judge mistakes as failures do not open their minds to the lessons that mistakes and even failures provide. There are many successful business people who will say their success was built on learning from earlier mistakes. Henry Ford went bankrupt five times before becoming successful. If there is any type of self-judgment which could be justified, it is for judging self rather than learning from previous mistakes.

When something tragic happens, we tend to look for something or someone to blame, But before casting blame on anyone, including self, it would be wise to consider that are many, many, many bad decisions made every day that could, and possibly should, result in tragic events, but do not. It is likely that every one of us has made a number of bad decisions that could have resulted in tragedy, but fortunately nothing bad happened.

It seems some tragedies are related to fate or are the inevitable victims of the odds. One mother can take her eyes off a child for a whole day and nothing bad will happen to the child. Another very attentive mother can take her eyes off her child for one minute and find her child electrocuted or dead from some other cause. The father backing out of the driveway does not see his young son run out from the corner of the house. Should these parents be judged as negligent by self or by others?

As humans, we are not perfect and cannot always anticipate the outcomes of everything we do or don't do or what others do or don't do. Before casting blame on self or others, it is important to realize that bad things happen even to the most careful people. Why? We do not know. And it is specifically because we do not know that we have no right to judge such occurrences. Perhaps it is fate and there was nothing we could have done that would have changed the outcome or eventual outcome. Anyone who considers the possibility of a higher level of reality should also consider that possibility before casting judgment on self or others.

Fate seems to be involved in some way when there are people who walk away uninjured from horrific accidents, while others are killed in minor accidents. A favorite example of fate is that of Greek playwright, Aeschylus, famous for writing tragedies, who, as legend has it, was killed when an eagle or other bird dropped a tortoise onto his bald head, mistaking his head for a rock. I am to the point in my life that I have seen and read about enough to believe that there is more to fate than we accept in physical reality. I have also come to realized that every human event is affected by more than what one person does or does not do, whether in the past or immediately beforehand. We do not have the control of life events we may think we have.

A reality of life is that there is little that we fully understand and for that reason, we have almost no rational basis for our judgments of people, ourselves or others. And as we no full understanding, we should only be making assessments. We have an obligation to make assessments for ourselves and for those for whom we are in some way responsible. We can even assess what some people do as being evil. But we have no right to judge other people, or ourselves, as evil. Society may have the right to judge and prosecute within the laws of that society, but we as individuals do not. We must learn to separate actions, which we can judge based upon consequences, from people whom we should not judge.

There will always be differing amounts of fairness in this physical world, as well as differing amounts of perceived fairness. Unfortunately, that often leads to judgments, especially people who think they have come up short. It is time to realize, as Bill Gates is said to have stated: "Life in not fair. Get used to it. Judgment does nothing to make things better."

One way to avoid the desire to judge other people and events in life is to accept the reality of Higher Power and ultimate justice. Though there is a difference in the concept of how justice may be brought about, actual belief in such justice can help reduce the need to be judgmental.

In *Human Understanding*, we realize that when we come to a mental conviction of other people as good or bad in what they say or do, we are being judgmental. We realize that our mental notions perceptions are not always correct and that the ideas and beliefs of our thought reality are only personal assessments and not necessarily factual. We realize that even with accurate perception of events, we do not know enough about other people to correctly evaluate the reasons they do what they do. We also realize that although we can feel remorse for our misdeeds, we do not really know enough about fate or even about influencing factors in our lives to fully judge ourselves.

We can make assessments of ourselves and others and situations, and act upon them, as required for our own lives and those we are entrusted with. But we must leave the judgment of people up to civil authorities or a Higher Power. That is necessary for society to function and for our personal happiness. If we want to discover real inner happiness and peace and even experience real love, we need to let go of our judgments and appreciate that we have been given the gift of life. And, for those who believe in a Higher Power of love, there is no need to worry about human judgment.

ANGER

nother result of the desire to be in control in some way is
anger. As we have reviewed in "Feelings and Emotions,"
we react to our experiences both emotionally and mentally. Initial emotional anger is an instantaneous negative reaction to
something encountered, which results from body chemistry combined with subconscious preconceived notions that occur before
there is time for mental evaluation. Such emotional reactive anger
is not wrong. It is nature's way of letting us know we do not like
whatever it was that got us angry.

But as soon as the mind is aware of the circumstances that
cause emotional anger, we are supposed to combine our preconceived notions, which our senses perceive, and rationally evaluate
the situation and react rationally and appropriately. However, once
the mind is aware of an encounter, the way people react can vary
anywhere from complete control to the lack of rational thought.

When preconditioned notions include notions of control, such
as misunderstanding, judgment, retribution, revenge, or even elation, rational evaluation does not always take place. Even if some
rational evaluation takes place, negative mental notions can influence evaluation and result in anger. The intensity of the resulting
anger will be mainly a function of personal self-control, or lack
thereof, and how seriously a person feels affected or offended.
When resulting negative mental judgments overpower self-control,
the consequence is the feeling of anger, which results in unhappiness for all involved. The factors affecting the intensity of anger are
also a factor in how long anger is sustained.

I have repeatedly mentioned that the images we have and the things we constantly think about affect our thought reality. Thinking often about things negatively causes preconditioned notions to be negative. You might picture negative thinking as a virus that infects thought reality. It causes the mind to focus more on negative things, which in turn leads to judgment and results in anger. Negative thinking and anger go together hand in hand.

Anger robs us of much of the happiness we could be enjoying if we were focusing on positive images. The negative thinking involved with anger slowly gnaws away at our ability to appreciate life and restricts our ability to accept life with a happy and healthy attitude. And the longer anger lasts, the harder it will be to get rid of. Anger, as well as negative thinking, can overpower the importance of virtue and self-control in thought reality. Other people initiate many of our negative mental notions causing anger, but those notions are only as permanent as we allow them to be. Even viruses can be eliminated with the right counter program and proper installation.

When angry, it would be wise to think not only about possible consequences, but also about what anger is telling us about our controlling and judgmental thought reality. Sustained anger tells us that we have a problem. We need to realize that rash actions and sustained anger can hurt us as much or possibly more than the people we are angry with. Rash anger has been described as grabbing a hot coal to throw at someone. Not so smart.

If we get angry more than just occasionally, if we get very angry, or if we sustain our anger, there are some questions we all need to ask of ourselves. Have we looked at the long-term consequences of our anger? Does anger actually accomplish anything? Are we going to do anything about our anger? We make the choices about what mental notions are important to us. Do we intend to hold onto the notions that help create and sustain our anger and unhappiness? We might want to think about how anger, resulting from the desire to control, adversely affects ourselves and our relationships as well as our families, as was pointed out in the chapter on Addiction.

Dr. Don Colbert, author of *Deadly Emotions*, says that anger can profoundly damage our health, and backs up this contention with scientific evidence. According to Dr. Joseph Mercola website (www.mercola.com), the American Medical Association (AMA) states that 80 percent of all health problems are stress related, and even the conservative Center for Disease Control and Prevention (CDC) states that 85 percent of all disease appears to have an emotional element.

Anger also can set a bad example for children. In families where anger gets something for the angry person, anger will be imitated by children, even by one-year-olds. Anger can also cause resentment in children which reduces the ability to love and find personal peace.

Anger also adversely affects relationships. Where there is anger, there is lack of trust, which is critical to good relationships.

Since anger is a feeling related to thought reality notions, the way to reduce the feelings of anger is to find ways to change the thought notions that hold anger. The plan of attack on feeling problems is addressed in "Feelings and Emotions," along with some reference books that could be helpful. It is most important to be willing to look at what is causing anger from a new perspective, which could include a look at ourselves.

A good thought notion to have is that people generally, though not always, do what they think is best, based upon their thought reality and their resulting habits. When they do something that upsets us and we get angry, we may be angry with people who in their minds are trying to help us. Misunderstanding of the intentions of others is one of the greatest causes of anger. People often ruin relationships because they do not respect the right of other people to think differently.

Another notion to have is that most people respond much better to candidness than to anger. When what others do upsets you, explain it to them calmly and they will be more likely to respect your wishes. Anger can separate us from friends and family. It can also cost us our jobs, as well as the ability to appreciate *"what is"* and to enjoy positive thinking. It is always helpful to consider consequences before acting.

Another thought notion to have is that situations that can provoke anger can often be avoided. Many people are angry because of situations they should not even be involved with in the first place. Thought notion should be that, unless intervention is absolutely needed, other people should be responsible for their own problems.

When one of my sons was 16 and had a driver's license for only a short time, he told me he had gotten a speeding ticket. He was surprised when I did not get angry. To which I responded that I had no reason to be angry. He would have to pay the speeding ticket and the increase in insurance if he wanted to keep driving. I followed that up by telling him that if he was old enough to drive, he was old enough to be responsible for his actions. If I had gotten angry, he would have taken out his frustrations on me and upset me. The point here is that we may be able to neutralize some situations that could get us angry, if we let others take responsibility for their own actions instead of letting their problems become our problems. At the same time, we can help the other party learn to take responsibility for their own problems. This is especially true with children who need to learn lessons in responsibility.

The most important thought reality notion to have about anger is that it solves nothing and typically makes things worse. Problems are solved only with cool heads, even problems caused by others. Unfortunately, changing thought reality notions takes more that thinking occasionally about not getting angry. It takes a sustained effort and it doesn't happen all at once. New positive thought notions must be imaged or thought about so often that they eventually overpower the notions of control and revenge.

An interesting side note is that scientists at Harvard University, studying 670 men using the Cook-Medley Hostility Scale, determined that the men with the biggest hostility ratings had the worst lung capacity (57). Reduced lung capacity may not mean much at this point in the book. But, further on in this book, when we look at understanding some physical ramifications of smaller lung capacity, it will point to worsening health and a shrinking brain. Why is not yet understood, but it is something to consider before getting angry.

Eliminating anger from our lives is very important to overall happiness. Life is happier when thought notions are based upon positive thinking and appreciation. Another aspect of situations that create anger is that when anger is controlled, it can lead to constructive ways to reduce the cause of things that get us angry. According to the American Psychology Association's article from March 2003, *Monitor in Psychology*, anger can spur progressive change, as witnessed by the 1960s civil rights movement and the earlier women's suffrage movement. Although these are large-scale examples, anger can also work for individuals who are willing to direct their situational unhappiness toward something positive.

Anger can also be very detrimental to professional employment for more than one reason. In running a professional office, I considered relationships with clients, as well as with co-workers, to be very important. Anger does not work well in these situations. Sustained anger is also an indication that a person tends to have a fixed view of reality and is not open to new ways to perceive things. Professions like to hire people with open minds who can control their feelings.

In **Human Understanding**, we realize that instantaneous emotional anger is a natural, though undesirable, reaction. Anger that lingers is the result controlling and judgmental thought notions that negatively affect mental evaluation. And like other forms of control and judgment, anger has negative side-effects for self and others. We need to think of anger like other forms of mental pain which tell us we need to change how we think or things will only get worse. Sustained anger tells us *we* have a problem and that for our happiness, we need to learn how to control our anger.

If and when we get angry, we need to evaluate not only what got us angry, but also why we let ourselves get angry. In learning about how and why we react the way we do, we can work on changing the mental notions that result in anger and find some inner peace. In learning how to control our own thoughts, rather than trying to control other people, we not only can control our anger but we develop a sense of self-worth in just being able to control ourselves. It is also easier to control anger if we develop a thought reality that includes a just and loving Higher Power and belief in an ultimate justice.

STRESS

For the engineer, the definition of stress is, "The amount of pressure applied to various materials that strains or deforms them." For the structural engineer, it is most important to keep actual stress within the stress capacity of each material used. Some amount of stress is required for building materials to accomplish something. Stress is not the problem. The problem is overstress. Exceeding stress limits can result in structural failure.

The term "stress," as applied to humanity, is similar to "mental pressure," as there is always some amount of stress applied to the mind with every evaluation. Some stress can be positive, as well as negative. Mental stress itself is not a problem.

For us, stress is considered an internalized feeling. Like other feelings, it is not thought about, except when expectations, situations, or conditions are encountered that are perceived as not likely to end up as we would like. In those situations, the mind senses it is losing control and a feeling of stress results. The more the mind senses the loss of control, the greater the internalized stress. Also, the greater the mind imagines dire consequences for not being able to control the situation, the greater the internalized stress. When the mind cannot cope with the loss of control and the imagined consequences, it becomes overstressed, and problems result. Unfortunately, the terminology for "over-stress" is commonly just the word "stress."

People do many things to reduce negative stress in their lives. Some people think about such things as changing jobs, neighborhoods, churches, husbands or wives, and even ending their lives. And some people actually do those things to reduce stress.

Environmental changes may eliminate an immediate or perceived cause of stress and give a temporary illusion the problem is gone. But the main source of problem remains.

The direct source of negative stress is preconditioned thought notions and habits that do not know how to handle the problem encountered or how to face imagined negative consequences, which in many cases are mentally exaggerated.

Negative stress is a serious problem that has been growing in magnitude as society becomes more competitive and life becomes faster paced. The *National College Health Assessment* conducted in spring 2015 at the University of Wisconsin indicated that over half of the students reported overwhelming anxiety in a given year. Also, 10 percent of the UW student body seriously considered suicide and 1 percent actually attempted suicide.

Stress is a big problem, especially for young people learning how to cope with pressure. According to the *National Institute of Mental Health,* and published in *Time* Magazine, Nov. 7, 2016, about 30 percent of girls and 20 percent of boys—totaling 6.3 million teens—have had an anxiety disorder.

The greatest factor in how stress will affect a person relates to how much that person's thought reality feels controlled or worried by the pressure applied. The amount of worry or fear will depend upon personal background, education, maturity, genetics, and other factors. Research by Hardiness Institute founder Salvatore Maddi, professor of psychology and social sciences at the University of California, Irvine, and PhD Harvard graduate, indicates that the most positive response to stress appeared to be among those people who have had a lot of stress in their childhood. (58)

One of the possible reasons for the growth in negative stress is that children are being shielded from stressful situations when young and have no training in how to deal with them. Educators and parents, in trying to make all children feel good, rather than having to face stress early in life, may be actually contributing to the problem, as the research of Salavatore Maddi would seem to indicate.

Shielding children from stressful situations may not be in their best interest. However, the beneficial stressful situations referred to are not likely traumatic experiences. Stress will be magnified when people's health and welfare or even personal safety appear to be at stake. Stress is also magnified by the perfectionist thought reality, which says that what is to be accomplished must be flawless.

I would suggest other contributing causes for the growth of stress problems. The rapid increase in stress problems seem to be happening at the same time as the growth of electronic devices. Dependence on electronic devices for entertainment and communication may be having a negative effect on thought reality. Children playing electronic games don't have to worry about bad endings; they can play again and again until the outcome is satisfactory or they can quit one game and try another which they can master. Some children also play games in which they enter into a false reality. Repeatedly not having to worry about adverse consequences can have a bad effect on thought reality when it comes to facing consequences that cannot be avoided. The more such games are played, the more thought reality drifts from thinking it has to face actual reality, which it is then ill-equipped to do.

The advent of the cell phone and texting has also removed needed experience in dealing face to face with other people, which is important in the real business world. It also removes concern about not being able to call for help when needed, which can lead to lack of preparation for possible stressful situations.

Another factor could be materialism. As life becomes more and more focused on the material level, the importance of the spiritual level fades. When thought reality gets locked into the concept that material success is all-important, stress and even depression are almost inevitable for many people because most will not have the worldly success they want. Even personal thoughts that their wants will not be achievable can be very stressful.

At least when thought reality accepts a spiritual level, there is something to fall back on. I see the lack of recognizing, and even emphasizing, the existence of the spiritual level as contributing factor in the rise in stress. And as long as these factors, and others, remain or even grow, I see the situation getting worse, not better.

Problems resulting from stress are not just mental. Significant amounts of stress can have some bad effects on the brain and the body. Maia Szalavtiz, a neuroscience journalist for *Time* magazine and author, published an article, "How Stress Can Lead to Depression" (Aug. 3, 2011.) In the article, she notes research that says that chronic high stress kills neurons in the hippocampus of the brain and prevents the birth of new cells. A *Science Daily: Science News* article, "Emotional Stress Can Change Brain Function" is based on a research report of Iaroslav Savtchouk and Sigiong June Liu of the Louisiana State University Health Science Center published in the *Journal of Neuroscience* Jan 12, 2011.

When we let stress overpower us in one way, it can negatively affect us in many ways. It is similar to when too much stress is placed on one building structural member, it not only fails that member, but it can also cause stress redistribution of load, which can overstress other building members and cause further damage to the building.

The *Harvard Business Review*'s first step to controlling stress is to realize that stress is just a feeling. Stressful situations can be caused by others, or even by nature. But harmful stress is a thought reality feeling problem. And as has been repeatedly pointed out in this book, feeling problems are caused by perception and preconceived thought reality notions, which are not adequate for understanding how to cope with what is perceived. Because stress is a feeling, it can be reduced or overcome the same way as other unwanted or uncontrolled feelings as previously addressed in the chapter "Feelings and Emotions."

To develop new positive thought notions, the mind must be open to the fact that mental notions and mental perceptions can be far from reality. The mind that is open to new thought notions is also open to alternative mental evaluations that can reduce stress. Changing thought notions requires working on our beliefs, biases, ideas, values, and possibly purpose for living.

The intensity of stress is related to the value we place on our need to control the situation precipitating the stress. As a result, it is important to focus on those things that will reduce the importance of what is producing stress. For many people, that may mean accepting the fact they cannot control everything as they would like.

Most important for reducing stress is learning to give up the perceived thought notion that everything must be under control. For some people, that may mean a change in a controlling life style. For others, it may just mean giving up the notion that everything must be perfect, or that every occasion should have a happy ending.

When under stress, it is time to consider that not living up to self-expectations or to what others expect is not a personal failure. It is only a preconditioned self-judgment. It is time to open up thought reality to the notion that there is only so much you can do and that mistakes and bad experiences are a part of learning.

In some ways, stress is the opposite of happiness. Happiness is the appreciation of *"what is."* Stress is more the fear of *"what is."* Until you accept who you are, with all your limitations, you will experience various amounts of stress. Failure to live up to expectations, yours and those of others, could be a good option to consider. And in many stressful situations, letting go may be the best option. If you can admit you are a limited human being and ask for help, you might learn that the world can go on without you. Even though that thought might hurt the ego, it is a fact the ego needs to consider.

Something else to consider is that when working hard to fulfill a very stressful task, it might be best to ask for help. If you complete the task on your own, you will later likely be asked to perform similar or possibly more stressful tasks in the future. Ask for help and others will better understand your limits.

Another factor in reducing stress is the acceptance of a higher level of reality. I have suggested that a significant factor in stress and even depression is the lack of a belief in a spiritual level. Most people will inevitably fail in getting what they want out of life. When people concerned with material success lose control of getting their desired wants, they can become stressed. Acceptance of an inner consciousness and acceptance that failure to achieve worldly success is not that important will reduce stress. The thought notion at we are loved regardless of our limitations and mistakes can also reduce stress.

Meditation is also helpful in controlling feeling problems. Meditation teaches how to let go of conscious thought and it teaches self-control. It also adds new mental pathways for the brain to function. Learning to control our thought habits or changing the value of our thoughts is critical to controlling stress. Previously, Mark Waldman was quoted as saying that, "meditation is the most effective way to treat anxiety and depression." Meditation lessens the stress that leads to anxiety and depression.

When it comes to meditation, Saki Sanotorelli, executive director of the Center for Mind Fitness in Medicine, Health Care, and Society at the University of Massachusetts Medical School, said in his book, *Heal Thyself: Lessons on Mindfulness in Medicine*, "The mind is far more malleable than we previously thought. A good example can be found with the Buddhist monks. Their mental stability and calmness isn't mystical; it's biological. The brain can grow new cells and reshape itself, and meditation appears to encourage this process."

A 2015 study published in the journal *Neurobiology of Stress* looked at adverse changes in the brain, as well as the brain's plasticity. The study found that even for mature adults, "Development never ends." This article points out that although we can't change the past, with the right intervention, we can find ways to compensate and cope. It is never too late to change.

We normally think of stress as detrimental. However, if thought reality can control the feeling of anxiety and fear that results in negative stress, it can actually be motivational. According to the article "Turning Stress into an Asset" by Amy Gallo, published in the *Harvard Business Review* (June 28, 2011), research shows that stress can be bad or good depending on how you use it. When managed correctly, stress can actually have a positive impact on productivity and performance. If stressful situations are viewed as challenges, rather than something to fear, they can actually increase creativity and productivity. But that again goes back to how thought reality notions view challenges.

Another interesting fact about stress was mentioned in *Nature* (2011; 474(7352): 498). An international study showed that being born and raised in a major urban area is associated with greater risk of anxiety and mood disorder. For those who suffer from stress, getting back to nature and away from the fast pace of urban life could be a good thing.

In **Human Understanding**, we come to realize that negative stress is a feeling problem that occurs when thought reality is faced with situations for which there is no perceived satisfactory solution. The degree of negative stress is related to the perceived consequences of not being able to cope with the situation. Negative stress is exaggerated by a thought reality belief of personal responsibility to control the situation, especially where responsibility for, or to, others is involved.

Stressful situations can be bad for our sanity and our physical health. For that reason, it is important to let go of the mental notion that you must be in control, and accept you are human, that you can only do so much, and ask for help when needed.

Daily stress can be reduced, as with other feeling problems, by changing the preconditioned notions that result in stress. Consider physical exercise for stress release. Meditation or even the acceptance of a Higher Power of love is another way to release stress. But when stress cannot be controlled by self, seek professional help. We all need thought reality that appreciates *"what is,"* rather than a thought reality that worries about *"what is."* The more thought reality focuses on appreciation, the less stress will be a problem.

ACCEPTANCE

I often use the word "acceptance" in this book. Like the word love, acceptance is also thought of in myriad ways. For many reasons, I consider acceptance to be the opposite of control, the negative results of which we have just explored. To some people, acceptance is recognition of and resignation to the will of others. But acceptance is much more than how we accept other people and what they do or what they want us to do.

In the *New World Dictionary*, acceptance is defined as "the act of being accepted, as approval, as belief in, or as an expressed or implied act by which one accepts an obligation." In this book, although the act of acceptance is a function of the mind, acceptance itself could be considered a virtue. That is because it is an intangible character of inner consciousness that accepts a spiritual purpose to life and also accepts all the responsibilities that come with that acceptance.

A spiritual acceptance of a purpose for life helps us to understand that virtue leads to order and happiness and vice leads to chaos and unhappiness. That is a basic we must accept to find true self-worth and inner happiness.

Acceptance helps us to realize that unless ideas are derived from fixed basics, they are just opinions. Acceptance also helps in accepting the responsibilities that come with that understanding Acceptance does not actually require belief in a god. A Buddhist is an example. Acceptance does not even require a religion. However, without some idealistic higher purpose normally associated with religion or spirituality, there is no purpose for acceptance and it will not likely exist. With a mature understanding of what acceptance involves comes the realization that personal serenity and joy come from within self, not from the physical world. Acceptance as a virtue leads to the understanding we are connected to a higher level of reality through the virtue of love.

In pointing out that acceptance can be thought of as a virtue, it would be good to reflect on the value of virtue. Pelin Kesebir and Ed Diener present a very good picture of the relationship between virtue and happiness in their book, *The Virtuous Cycle: The Relationship between Happiness and Virtue*. It is an in-depth study that goes back to Aristotle, who saw happiness as the result of cultivating one's virtues and living in accordance with them. Besides the more technical aspects of the manuscript, I like several of the quotes and words of wisdom, such as George Washington's Inaugural Address in 1789: "… an indissoluble union between virtue and happiness."

Happiness is related to virtue. But happiness is not possible without the acceptance of virtue. It is in acceptance of virtue that we can begin to understand love and the disharmony wrought by the desire to control.

On her website, www.mcguinesscounseling.com, therapist Ellen McGuiness, MA, LPC, says about acceptance, "Acceptance is the acknowledgment of what is. Acceptance forgoes judgment on circumstances. It is a mindset that lets you let go of frustration and disappointment, stress, and anger, regret, and false hopes. It is the practice of recognizing the limits of your control."

Acceptance does not require that we approve of what is. It is only an assent to the reality of what is. The reality of life is that we are not really in control and we need to acknowledge that fact. We could be dead tomorrow or even sooner. The virtue of acceptance is centered about the responsibility to control only what we can control—ourselves. A saying which reflects that thought, is a saying of Jesuit priest and psychotherapist Anthony de Mello in his book *One Minute of Wisdom*, "If it is peace you seek, change yourself, not other people. It is easier to protect your feet with slippers than to carpet the whole of the world."

Acceptance also means accepting things that may initially seem unjust. Things may not be as unjust as we think. I like to think of the occasions, my children would come home and complain that their teacher blamed them for something they did not do. My response was, "I also went to school and I know how many more times I got away with something than the number of times I got caught. Consider it make-up for just one of the times you got away with something." Acceptance can tolerate what seems unjust because it accepts that there is a bigger picture than what we see at any moment or that we may ever see.

Some people imagine an accepting life as devoid of worldly excitement and rewards. And while an accepting life may not be centered on worldly excitement and rewards, it does not exclude them. It also presents a means to inner peace, and self-worth, as well as inner excitement that the world cannot provide. Acceptance is not weak. It may not require physical strength and power, but the personal obligations and the consequences of acceptance require much self-control and strength of conviction.

Acceptance does not always mean letting oneself get beaten or always turning the other cheek. It also doesn't mean liking or being satisfied with the way things are. Acceptance requires taking responsibility for what one is entrusted with. That responsibility not only relates to actions, but it also requires growth in knowledge and understanding. Acceptance requires actively pursuing a caring and loving way of living. This may mean actively defending what is necessary to defend. The first choice is always to promote peace through methods that are caring and loving. If that is not possible in a passive manner, it may involve physically defending a caring and loving world.

Acceptance also requires the utilization of talents that will enable humanity to preserve and promote the concept of a higher purpose. We do not know in what way our talents may be needed. But it is an obligation to use them in the way we believe best promotes overall peace. Acceptance also requires appreciation of the good things in life, as long as they are used appropriately. Acceptance requires that we accept ourselves as we are and other people as they are, which includes accepting their shortcomings.

Let me share a story about a man who is told to evacuate his house because the rising river is about to flood the town. He said that he truly accepted God and that God would save him, so he stayed. The river rose and a man in a boat came to the house to rescue him. From the second-floor window, he said that his acceptance of God would cause God to save him. When he was on the roof, a helicopter team tried to rescue him, but his response was the same. The river rose higher and he drowned.

At the gate to heaven, he asked God why he hadn't been saved. The response was: "I sent a man to warn you, a boat, and a helicopter to rescue you. What more did you expect?" Acceptance does not expect a return for being accepting. It requires that we appreciate and utilize the gifts and opportunities we are given.

Acceptance requires living in the present, not as being controlled by the past. The expression "Don't cry over spilled milk" is appropriate. The past is not there to worry about; it is there to learn from. It provides information from which to fashion better future thoughts and actions. To grow in knowledge and happiness, we must move forward in life. Acceptance also requires we learn from our mistakes, not dwell on them.

Real acceptance is rewarding, for it instills wisdom and allows us to see beyond what our eyes perceive — the beauty of all creation. It allows us to see beyond anger and anxiety. Real acceptance believes that love given, in some way, results in love gained. Acceptance does not guarantee a peaceful life. But people of acceptance are people of self-worth who are proud of who they are, because in their hearts, they know they are doing what they should be doing in life. It is unfortunate that the virtue of acceptance is not well pursued.

In *Human Understanding*, we realize that acceptance is a virtue that lifts the veil of judgment and unhappiness of worldly existence by helping us to understand that physical life exists for a higher purpose. With acceptance, we realize that happiness is of the inner self, not the world. Acceptance is counter to the vice of control that permeates the physical world, and as such acceptance can be difficult to maintain. It carries the responsibility of being in control of one's self, the responsibility to grow in knowledge, and the responsibility to make the world a more loving place by virtue of the talents entrusted to us.

Humility

A nother virtue that springs from acceptance is humility. Perhaps the best definition of humility I have come across is, "Humility is accepting the truth of who you are," though I was unable to find its origins. Humility recognizes that one's talents and possessions are a gift. Humility responds to that recognition by sharing those talents and possessions with others. Humility is also defined as acting humble. And humble is defined by *Merriam Webster Learner's Dictionary* as, "not proud: not thinking of yourself as better than other people."

What is it that you have really earned totally by yourself? Even a billionaire is indebted to the people who brought about the circumstances that enabled that person to become a billionaire. The good things we have today are the direct or indirect gifts of our parents and of all those who came before us that have made our life possible. We are even blessed enough to have bad examples that show us what results from selfishness and evil.

It is not realistic to think we should be unhappy when others have given us so much. The civilization, the comforts, and the freedoms we have, come from the effort and the lives of other people—millions of other people. Humility understands this and for those reasons the humble are always thankful rather than proud.

One important and appreciated personality aspect of humble people is they do no try to control the situation or conversation. Humble people are enjoyable to be around. They do not judge others. They can laugh at themselves. The humble will forgive and ask to be forgiven. Humble people understand that each person has his or her own talents and limitations and that we all make mistakes.

Additionally, the humble realize that even mistakes are important to the growth of knowledge. It took many people, in many fields of endeavor, many ages and many mistakes to bring about the good things we have today.

The humble understand that we are all part of a bigger picture in which everyone needs to work together—each with our own strengths and weaknesses—if the world is to move forward. The humble will therefore not be afraid to admit mistakes and to ask for help or to render help when needed.

It is good that we, as individuals, work hard and feel good about what we are achieving. But it is very important to realize that our achievements also belong to all who have given of themselves to us, in some manner from which we have benefited, whether an hour ago or a thousand years ago. It is also important to recognize that for what we are given, we must give back. Therefore, humility requires that just as we have been given much by those who came before us, we have a responsibility to use our talents for the good of those who will come after us.

I have reviewed a number of articles that relate to happiness. Evangelist and bestselling author of *The Purpose-Driven Life: What am I here For*, Rick Warren says that happiness comes from harmony and that harmony comes from humility. A quote from his book "Humility is not thinking less of yourself. It's about thinking of yourself less." The quote is actually a derivation of C. S. Lewis quote in the book, *Mere Christianity*, "The truly humble man will not be thinking about humility. He will not be thinking about himself at all."

The Association for Psychological Science says humility is important to good relationships because humility strengthens social bonds. That is because humility recognizes and fairly evaluates everyone. With humility, situations are accepted at face value.

Leadership expert Jim Collins labels humility the secret ingredient that allows people to compete at high levels without breaking down relations. In a 2012 issue of the *Journal of Psychology and*

Theology, "Religious Involvement, Humility, and Change in Self-rated Health over Time," Neal Krause of the University of Michigan Center on the Demography of Aging found that older adults who were humble rated their health more favorably.

It is important to realize that happiness is greatly dependent upon relationships, and relationships are influenced by humility.

Humility is a virtue that comes with the realization that that life is not about self but about a person's ability to see where he or she belongs in the world for the betterment of the world. The virtue of humility does not just happen. As with other virtues, it requires thinking about what humility is and how it can help improve life for self and others often enough that it becomes incorporated as a value in thought reality.

The humble person does not claim to know all the answers to life. But in living a virtuous life, humble people become the examples of love and caring the world needs to progress rather than to regress.

In **Human Understanding**, people of humility recognize that what they have in life is the direct or indirect result of the efforts of other people—whether yesterday or five thousand years ago. They also understand that the efforts of those people resulted from their accepting and utilizing the gifts given to them. The humble therefore realize that it is their responsibility to give back for all they have received and to make the world better for those who will come after.

Pride makes us artificial. Humility makes us real.
—Thomas Merton, OCSO (59)

HAPPINESS AND JOY

HAPPINESS

We all want happiness and joy in our lives. Therefore, it is important to understand what brings about happiness and joy. What do happiness and joy mean to you? And what brings them about? Happiness, like stress, anger, fear, worry, and anxiety, is a feeling that is based upon our perceptions and preconditioned mental notions of thought reality. It is important to realize that what we repeatedly think about affects our mental notions and even perception. Thinking happy thoughts provides positive preconceived mental notions that lead to happy feelings. Because acceptance helps remove negative thinking, it is also important to happiness.

We all want to be happy. But it seems that many of us think happiness should just happen and that if it doesn't, it is someone else's fault. Maybe some people are instinctively happy. But because happiness is a feeling, it is affected mostly by our reality of thought. In a world that seems centered on worldly wants, many people look to worldly things, worldly pleasures, and even worldly acceptance for happiness.

Dependence on the worldly acceptance of others for happiness is well indicated by the numbers of people who join groups or even gangs to feel accepted. The feeling of being accepted is so important that some people will lie, steal, or even kill to get or maintain acceptance or at least some accepted notoriety. In some respect, they have the right idea, because without a feeling of acceptance, there is emptiness rather than happiness. But the acceptance that truly matters is acceptance of self.

Real happiness (happiness that lasts) begins with self-worth. We need to like and respect ourselves, or as we reviewed in self-worth, there will always be an inner feeling of dissatisfaction and unhappiness. Real happiness requires the effort needed to feel good about self. Self-worth and happiness come with doing what inner consciousness says is the right thing to do. And the more self-worth we have, the more we will be respected, though not necessarily accepted, by others.

Happiness is a state of mind. It is dependent upon thought reality, not upon what others think or say. When happiness is missing in life, it is time to focus the mind on new, positive thought notions of what happiness really is and what brings it about.

A most interesting insight into happiness can be found in the country of Bhutan. It is a country that is considered to have the happiest people in the world. The strange thing is these people attribute their happiness to thinking about death, often five times a day. This topic is addressed by Karen M. Wyatt, author of the award-winning book, *What Really Matters: Seven Lessons for Living from the Stories of the Dead.*

In 2007, a study was conducted by psychologists Nathan DeWall and Roy Baumeister to determine the negative or positive effect about contemplating death, as compared to contemplating other less traumatic life events. Their findings comments were published in *Psychological Science,* and again in the October 30, 2007 edition of *Time* magazine, under the title, "Are We Happier Facing Death?" The result of the research led to the conclusion that "death is a psychologically threating fact, but when people contemplate death, it apparently triggers an automatic system that begins to search for happiness." This has been a surprising discovery in that contemplating death has in the past been thought to be associated with traumatization.

Additional studies on happiness and contemplating death have been conducted as by Immo Fritsche of the University of Leipzig,

Germany, and another by Matthew Gailliot and colleagues that appeared in a 2008 *Personality and Social Psychology* bulletin. The results were similar.

Since the initial investigations, controversy on contemplating death has produced new research and publications. The May 20th, 2014, *Huffington Post* provided more insight into the subject in the article, "How Contemplating Your Death Can Help You Truly Live."

Research is still being conducted on this topic. However, it is not all that surprising that contemplating death repeatedly will affect thought notions about what is important in life. In contemplating death, the awareness of personal vulnerability entices people to enjoy what time they have rather than trying to accumulate things they may never live to enjoy. In affluent societies, people seldom think of death. There is always tomorrow. In affluent societies, happiness is for tomorrow because "today I need to get something else done." People seem to have forgotten—or never learned—how to take the time to enjoy each day. Death is something to think about because tomorrow may never come.

I very recently attended the funeral of a 90-year-old woman who, at 15 years of age, was taken from her home in Hungary by the Russians and forced to work in a coal mine every day for five years, with little more than a loaf of bread a day to live on. She didn't have a bed to sleep on and once had to go a year without a bath. She also suffered the indignity of being sterilized. Even after she was let go, it took another five years before she was somehow reunited with her family. Yet, after all that, she was one of the most positive and kind persons you could ever meet. After what she had been through, she had a choice. She could choose to be bitter for all that was taken from her or she could appreciate her life after her agony. She chose to appreciate and lived a difficult but happy life thereafter. She was a happy person who appreciated each day and all that she did have. Her happiness was based upon the choice to appreciate rather than dwell on what was taken from her. If ever there are stories recorded about happiness being a choice, hers is one for the books.

In an article that appeared in *Psychology Today* excerpted from *The Pursuit of Happiness: Who is Happy and Why*, David G. Meyers, PhD, explains that telling people to act and talk positively will make them happier sounds phony. But he also tells us, that in the new role of imagining things to be happier, the phoniness gradually subsides.

In playing the part, we open ourselves up to new reactions from others and even ourselves. Even pretending opens our minds to new thought notions. It is through the repetition of positive attitudes and images that new thoughts impact our thought notions and can help thought reality overcome old thought habits that restrict our happiness. Something to consider is that if thinking positive thoughts can actually make you happier, thinking negative thoughts can only make things worse. As previously mentioned, the images we concentrate on greatly influence our lives.

We are happy when we laugh. We are happy when things seem to go our way. We are happy when we accomplish something difficult, when we make someone smile, even when some event beyond our control happens as we wish. If we think deeply about happiness, we will realize that happiness appears to be a wonderful feeling that is a natural response to a good situation. But periods of happiness always seem to come to an end. So, what is it that will bring more than a few fleeting moments of happiness?

Consider happiness from a worldly perspective. Power and wealth, for the few who achieve these, bring temporary periods of self-satisfaction and varying amounts of physical pleasure, but they do not bring the feeling of self-worth that is required for real happiness and inner peace. Even the greatest physical pleasure, repeated often enough, becomes boring. Therefore, what can keep us happy when there is nothing exciting, nothing funny, or nothing to distract our thoughts away from ourselves? How can worldly, material things free our minds of all our cares and worries?

With money, power, and material things also comes worry about the possible loss of those things. No earthly things are secure. Where there are humans and material things, there is always the possibility of decay, dishonesty, betrayal, or death. Most people begin to worry about dying long before they die, especially if they have wealth and power. The more that is possessed, the more there is to worry about.

The most important thing to realize about happiness is that it is not something we can achieve. Real happiness simply results from personal decisions to appreciate what is happening. Happiness springs from a state of mind. It is a state of mind free, at least for that moment, from worry or fear, which opens it to the pleasant acceptance of what is going on at that moment.

When a funny joke is told or good news is heard our minds are, at that moment, free from judgments and other habitual controls of the thought process. Then, at least temporarily, we can laugh and enjoy life as it is. When we return to our normal habits of thought reality, the moments of happiness are often gone. Taken to an exaggerated level, should we decide to mentally free ourselves of all our wants and desire for control and instead appreciate all that we come in contact with, we would theoretically be continuously happy. With that understanding, my personal definition of happiness is the appreciation of *"what is"*.

Mother Teresa, in spite of all she suffered, appreciated everything in her life enough to give of herself almost entirely. If she had not, how could she have endured? She said: "Only in heaven will we see how much we owe the poor for helping us love God better because of them." She had mental notions that appreciated the poor and the opportunity to help them. It is the decision to appreciate the things in our lives, rather than to judge them, which will lead to personal happiness and inner peace.

The real beauty of happiness is that it is free for those who surrender their judgments and desires and adopt acceptance and appreciation of *"what is."* People who learn to appreciate *what is* can be content and thankful, even when things seem to go badly. They realize that things could actually be worse. Their happiness is based upon appreciation of all the gifts they have received, rather than thinking about what they haven't received. Happiness is available to all people if they learn to give up the notion of control and learn to appreciate *"what is."*

Happiness is fully appreciating a child's graduation even though that child had the talent to graduate much higher in the class ranking. Happiness is appreciation of a new grandchild even if the child was born out of wedlock or perhaps handicapped. Happiness is being able to appreciate someone's assistance even when that assistance is actually a detriment.

Acceptance that results in happiness is not influenced by expectations or judgment of what we think should be or should not be. When expectations and judgment decide the conditions of happiness, real happiness is severely limited. When we express happiness or appreciation with what other people do, regardless of we might have expected, we also promote a feeling of satisfaction and happiness in them. This pays off big time because the more the people around us are happy, the happier we will be.

If we want to feel a more stable inner happiness, we must open our minds to the importance of acceptance and love. With our choices, we determine, to various degrees, the happiness, sadness, or even anger in our lives. Overall happiness and conversely overall sadness is a choice. If we decide to appreciate what happens to us in life, we will be happy people. If we choose to be dissatisfied with our lives, we will end up unhappy people.

JOY

Joy, like happiness, requires the mind to be accepting of what is. But joy is different and more profound than happiness. We can experience happiness and satisfaction by ourselves and as a result of our physical experiences. But we cannot experience joy without others. Joy springs from love and the acceptance and appreciation of what happens to others. Real joy is selfless, which is beyond the ego. The most interesting thing about joy is that it is not a momentary thing. It is more fulfilling than happiness because it can last for a lifetime. We can feel joy with every accomplishment of the people dear to us. Joy is an intense appreciation of the good fortune of others or an intense appreciation of what others do for us.

In *Human Understanding*, we come to realize that happiness is an appreciation of what is. The more intense the appreciation, the more intense the happiness will be. Joy is similar to happiness. It is the selfless appreciation of the accomplishments and the happiness of others. If we want to experience real happiness and joy, we must let go of judgment and dissatisfaction and appreciate all that we have. We choose the degree of our happiness or unhappiness in our lives by how we choose to appreciate what is. Happiness is a choice. Joy requires an appreciation of the existance and accomplishments of others.

FORGIVENESS

Something that is important to real happiness and joy is forgiveness. Acceptance of *"what is"* is required for real happiness. Judgment of others infringes on the acceptance of *"what is"* and upon our inner happiness. Judgment is of control and opposite the acceptance needed for inner happiness and peace of mind. Where there is judgment, the way to inner happiness, and even better health, is forgiveness.

Dr. Everett L Worthington Jr., PhD, professor and chair person in the Department of Psychology at Virginia Commonwealth University, has spent much of his career studying forgiveness. One of the tests that Dr. Worthington was involved with was researching the relationship of people who rated their relationships as terrible or terrific. He found those people who had bad relationships also scored poorly on their willingness to forgive. The people with happy relationships seem to keep their stress levels in a normal range with the ability to forgive their partners faults, according to his Sept. 1, 2004 article in the *Greater Good Magazine* entitled "The New Science of Forgiveness."

Another study mentioned by Dr. Worthington in the article is a test of 1,500 Americans by Loren Toussaint, a psychologist at Luther College in Iowa. Toussaint, along with David Williams, Marc Musick, and Susan Everson conducted a study regarding the degree to which each person practiced and experienced forgiveness. They found that older and middle-aged people forgave more often and felt more forgiven by God. They also found a significant relationship between forgiving others and physical health. People who forgave others reported greater satisfaction with life and were less likely to report symptoms of psychological distress.

Forgiveness research has entered into neurological research, for example, *Investigating the Functional Anatomy of Sympathy and Forgiveness* by T.F. Farrow et al, and "How the Brain Heals Wounds: The Functional Neuroanatomy of Forgiveness," an article published in *Neuroscience* (09 Dec. 2013 https://doi.org/10.3389/fnhum.2013.00839). Although why the brain reacts as it does is not known, looking at the source of anger from the offenders perspective as well as sympathy and empathy were important in effecting that part of the brain involved with anger.

The research of Charlotte Witvliet of Hope College indicates that the moral response of sincere forgiveness lowers heart rate, blood pressure, and sweat activity to normal, as well as a lessening of frown lines of the face. But for forgiveness to be more than momentary negative notions cannot just try to be pushed down. Rather it is important to feel positive emotions toward the offender and seeing that person as needing help, empathizing with that person. Nathaniel Wade and Jack Berry show that when people learn to feel positive emotions toward perceived transgressors, there are changes in physiology, including lowered blood pressure, and heart rate, according to *The Joy of Forgiveness* (https://blogs.hope.edu/stories-of-hope/social-sciences/the joy of forgiveness).

Anger is a feeling and as the previous articles, as well as the chapter on feelings, point out that to change feelings it is necessary to change the thought notions that control thought reality. We need to look at anger from a new perspective. The first step in forgiveness is to realize how unfair our judgments can be. People do some loving things, some mean things, and even strange things for purposes we have no way of understanding. While we may judge an incident as unjust and even mean, which it may be, we have no way of knowing what was in the mind of the offender or all the background circumstances leading to what happened, or even if fate played a part. What other people do to us may be the result of what was unjustly done to them. We need to understand not only how unfair our judgments can be, but also how selfish and controlling they can be.

Forgiveness is more than uttering a pardon for past harm. Real forgiveness is something that comes from the heart, not just the lips. Real forgiveness actually requires letting go of whatever incident initiated the need for forgiveness. Real forgiveness realizes that people who harm others actually need help. That understanding releases thought reality from feelings of resentment, hostility, or anger toward the perceived transgressor, and frees the mind to accept and appreciate *"what is."* Real forgiveness releases lingering negative feelings that have a negative effect on the thought reality as well as the health of a person holding anger.

The person owed the apology should also ask the transgressor for forgiveness if there was a harboring of anger related to what happened. When we judge other people, instead of their actions, we also need forgiveness for our judgmental thinking. True forgiveness recognizes that some of the greatest harm we do to others is to be examples of selfish thinking rather than examples of acceptance and love.

Forgiveness does not condone the wrongs of others. Forgiveness does not mean that wrongs do not have to be atoned for. But forgiveness recognizes that those people who act in seemingly unloving ways are often people who need to be shown an example of love. Forgiveness sees not only that which got us angry, but also recognizes all the good things the offending person or group may have done for us or others in the past.

If we do not forgive others, how can we forgive ourselves or ever expect to be forgiven for our transgressions? In the act of true forgiveness, we can come to realize what real love is all about. Without the ability to forgive, we will never understand the concept of love. It is not about who is right or who is wrong. It is about accepting that all people are worthy of love, although what they do may not be. Personal inner peace with self cannot be attained without the ability to forgive and to ask for forgiveness. With sincere forgiveness, we open ourselves up to the experience of real love and inner peace.

Forgiveness is also a word used in structural engineering. Not all structural materials are brittle and snap when overstressed. Some materials, such as steel, will stretch when highly stressed rather than snap and collapse. This yielding of materials is sometimes called "material forgiveness," and provides safety against immediate building failure when a building is overstressed. In life, as in structural engineering, forgiveness, rather than a brittle and opinionated way of thinking, can reduce the adverse results of over-stress.

In *Human Understanding*, we come to realize that to find inner peace and happiness we must learn to give up trying to control or judge others. That is not possible without forgiveness. Only in forgiveness will we be forgiven for our transgressions. It is forgiveness that frees our minds from judgments and allows them to be free to experience the inner contentment that only real love (the accepting of all others and giving of self for others) can bring.

TOUGH LOVE

"Tough love" is a term used to describe treating others sternly or harshly with the intent to help them in the long run. It is actually meant to cause a transition from the desire to have what is wanted to acceptance of what is. It is called "tough" because those being treated are being treated sternly, although the treatment is supposedly given out of love and concern.

Coaches are often hardest on the potentially best players when they are concerned those players are not utilizing their talents. The British sometimes use the term "tough love" for an authoritarian way of raising very young children, up to five years of age. It is believed to be in the best interest of the children.

As was reviewed in the chapter "A Reason for Pain," when everything is going well, there is no reason to change things. There always needs to be a reason to change or to improve or to even mature. Hopefully maturity can be reached by learning the importance of effort, obedience, and other aspects of maturing with little or no pain. However, sometimes significant pain is required to get people's attention, especially when they are not willing to listen.

Tough love, as used for intervention with addiction, is to deny an addict any direct or indirect source of support, situations, or substances that prolong the addiction. The intent of tough love is to force a change in the addict's addicted habits of thought.

Addictions take many forms. When addiction is mentioned, we normally think about drug or alcohol addiction. But there are many other dependency addictions; some are more serious than others. A mild form of addiction would be adult children who continue to take their dirty clothes to their mothers to have them washed.

Some people may view the concept of withholding those things or services on which an addict has become dependent as cruel and unloving. Others will view it as the only loving thing to do. There will always be misconceptions about the proper employment of tough love if it is not understood. To comprehend the need for tough love, let us consider how the mind of a hardened drug addict functions.

Sustaining a drug addiction can actually become the main purpose of thought processing. The physical craving of the body can cause that to happen. Therefore, responsibility and rational thought will seldom, if ever, occur with an intense physical addiction. An addict usually finds a way to work the system or specific people to get what he or she wants without having to earn it or give it back. Lying, stealing, begging, crying, and threats are but some of the forms of manipulation used to get what the addict wants. We may feel sorry for a person seemingly so pitiful.

But no matter how much generosity is extended, it will be of no help to the addict unless it is something of more value to the addicted thought reality. Giving into the wishes of the addict only entrenches the addiction. Even in less severe addictions, the manipulative practices of the addict may be less, but they will also be there.

In removing the addict's ability to take and take without consequence, hopefully the addict will not only be removed from the addiction source, but also feel enough physical or mental pain to cause him or her to reevaluate the value of the addictive habit. Without some form of pain, there is no reason for an addict to change. At this point comes much responsibility on those enforcing the tough love. Withholding sources for addictive substances does nothing to direct an addict on how to change for the better.

The drug addict who hits bottom may for the moment lose all sense of value, including that of life itself. If there is no support, no positive new purpose, or no new values significant enough and near enough to turn to, the addict may commit suicide or just change the form of addiction. More than anything else, the addict needs the support and examples of love in the critical time when he or she is truly searching for new values and purpose and willing to work for it. The addict needs to know he or she is loved, even though the addiction is totally unacceptable. Tough love requires loving responsibility from those employing it to provide love and a new feeling of worthiness to the addict.

It took a good friend a divorce and the loss of his job as the manager of the construction portion of a large business to finally seek help. It took those losses, as well as friendship losses and the realization there was nothing in life for him if he continued drinking, before he finally allowed himself to get help. With medical help, friends, and his faithfully attending AA meetings, he eventually recovered and was back at his old job in about a year. He had a new life, later a new wife, and many happy alcohol-free years thereafter. Without taking away his job, which was his real happiness and social friendships, I doubt that he would ever have quit drinking.

Those who feel that tough love is an unloving act should consider how the love of the Higher Power is extended to humanity. We are given a free choice. If we choose worldly wants over virtue, the Higher Power will not stop us. We get to suffer the consequences. It is the gift of pain that follows selfish acts, which can cause people to rethink what they are doing to themselves.

Because we are loved enough to be given a free will, we are also free to hurt ourselves. The pain we suffer, we suffer because of our lack of acceptance of virtue and reliance on material values. But the pain that results from our addictions could be the gift that causes us to abandon those addictions. It may help turn purpose in life to something beyond worldly wants.

In *Human Understanding*, we recognize that tough love is one way, and may be the only way, to change the thought process of the truly addicted. Although tough love may at first be seen to be unloving, it seems to have originated with the Higher Power.

RELATIONSHIPS

Relationships are an important part of human development and happiness. The relationships we have in many ways influence who we are. They help form our thought reality. As social beings, we are dependent on one another in many ways. Our initial relationships were ones of dependency, not only for physical needs but also for mental development, as well as for learning a reason to live and for the development of self-worth. But as we grow, we develop a personal desire to be happy.

As social beings, we cannot achieve either the self-worth or the happiness we desire without other people. So we all look for relationships in which we feel loved or to at least make us feel better about ourselves. Even priests, monks, sisters, and hermits look for relationships, though theirs are with a Higher Power.

Relationships can also be a critical part of business development. Most business ideas come from individuals. But ideas usually turn into successful business ventures through relationships. In the business community, relationships can be every bit as important as money in getting businesses started. Although it may not seem fair at times, advancement in professions can be based as much on the ability to develop relationships as it is on other talents. Being able to foster relationships is itself an important talent. An understanding of relationships is as important for successful businesses as it is for personal life.

How we relate to family members is important to our personal development. But relationships outside the family are particularly important to people who do not find love or acceptance within the family or within the class structure in which they live. People who feel unloved often latch onto whatever relationships make them feel accepted. This is why gangs can become the family for children from difficult and broken homes (regardless of financial class) or for young people who have no other perceived way to feel acceptable.

Relationships are easier and more rewarding where love exists. Some of happiest and most accepting people live in some of the poorest places in the world. Where worldly wants are replaced by love and acceptance, there is little to no judgment and relationships can flourish.

Relationships can vary anywhere from those necessary for survival, to those that bring happiness, joy, and love, to those that bring stress and anger. Relationships will typically have an impact on our self-worth and happiness. That it is not only because of what we gain directly from others, but also because of what we gain by sharing with and giving to others.

On an adult level, people relate in many ways. We relate to each other with words and with actions. We relate by what we do and by what we choose not to do. When there is fear, guilt, distrust, or unfamiliarity, we may relate by avoidance. But we willingly relate well with those people whom we trust, people who are cheerful, people who we admire, people who are nice to us, people who give us a feeling of worth, and people with whom we have common interests. For the most part, except for parents or guardians, we choose those people with whom we relate and those who we avoid. There will always be situations, particularly family or cultural or even environmental, where choice may be restricted. But even in those situations, choices are made when possible.

There is a vast number of factors influencing relationships. Personal values, physical attraction, local customs, feelings, circumstances, morality, and personal goals are just some of them. There are also different degrees of importance for various relationships. The least important is between two people who have just met, have nothing in common, and may not meet again. Relationships generally, but not necessarily, grow in importance with the frequency of interaction.

However, more important than frequency are the feelings that result from relationships, as well as the time and effort put into the interaction. It might seem natural that the closest relationships would be with those with whom we interrelate most, such as family members. But the closest relationships are actually with those people we consciously or subconsciously believe will best satisfy our perceived sense of fulfillment or those who make us feel the best. As that feeling may not occur with people we know well, close relationships need not be with people we see often.

The depth of personal relationships is based upon perceived happiness and fulfillment, rather than the amount of familiarity. The concept of happiness and fulfillment will vary with different people as people differ in their personal thought reality. It may include love and acceptance. But it may also be thought of in terms of companionship, sex, intelligence, compassion, faithfulness, wealth, power, dependency, humor, and other traits. For many personal reasons, we choose those with whom we would like a relationship. And for similar or other reasons, we are chosen for a relationship. The caretaker is attracted to the needy while the needy are attracted to the caretaker.

The mutual attraction of desirable traits forms the basis of all two-way relationships. This is true even in a relationship between a charming middle-aged swindler and a wealthy older woman. He is attracted to her money and she is attracted to his charm. As long as these desirable traits remain the prominent values in the relationship, it will continue, regardless of what others may think of it. When the critical, desirable values that formed the relationship are no longer important, problems arise in a relationship.

The example of the relationship between the swindler and the wealthy older woman may seem a little extreme. But it is symptomatic of so many other types of relationships that are based upon expectations of something to be gained. This is true for both the giver and the receiver. The giver most often likes the feeling of importance and having control. The taker likes someone else assuming his or her responsibilities. But a dependent relationship gives only a temporary illusion of happiness. The greater the dependency, the smaller is the chance for long-term happiness and feeling of fulfillment.

What most people do not understand is that real satisfying and lasting relationships are based on mutual giving, not from what somebody else can provide.

Two of the most basic values in a good relationship are acceptance and respect. Acceptance and respect tell us that we mean something, that we are worthwhile, that we are lovable, and that we are of value. Where acceptance and respect are missing, the basic stabilizing factors in a relationship are missing as well. Where acceptance and respect are missing, negative expectations and feelings of non-acceptance will set in.

Where feelings of non-acceptance exist, in a close relationship, someone is usually blamed and the tendency is to look elsewhere for acceptance. Feelings of non-acceptance are not necessarily the fault of the party being blamed. If Mary criticizes her husband David when her physical or social expectations are not met, it isn't necessarily David's fault. If high expectations are initially placed on the relationship, what was expected may never come about.

The best relationships exist between people who do not expect to gain anything from the relationship. Rather, their desire is to give and to share. Where there are no expectations, there are also no disappointments. There are only surprises and most of them are happy. Acceptance and respect of the other person, just as that person is—without any expectations—will most likely result in a stable relationship. Respect and acceptance are the backbone of all happy relationships.

Respect in a relationship has nothing to do with authority. It has everything to do with accepting the other person as a person with feelings, desires, rights, and needs. Respect is manifested in many subtle ways. Respect is in accepting that each person has as much right to his/her opinion as the other. Respect is listening to what the other person has to say, regardless of one's personal feelings.

Respect does not say, "I'm right." Respect does not need to know what the other person thought about, is thinking of, or is planning to do. Respect is accepting that the other person is doing what he or she is able to do with where the person is in life. Respect lets go of expectations of the other person. Respect makes requests rather than demands. And respect accepts either a positive or negative response without judgment. Respect appreciates and applauds the accomplishments of the other.

Mutual respect and appreciation subtly encourage each person in a relationship to improve who they are. This respect and appreciation makes a relationship fulfilling and sustains it. Respect also understands that there can be large differences of opinion between well-intentioned people and accepts the differences as part of being human.

For instance, Jane may want Jim to say the words she wants to hear while Jim, poor at expressing feelings, tries to say it with flowers. Respect also understands and accepts that one person may approach everything rationally, while the other person bases his or her approach to what is important on feelings, and with that understanding, respect finds a way to compromise.

However, when people have different interests and personal wants and are not willing to share in the interests and wants of the other person, long-term relationships are difficult or doomed. This could be thought of as self-centered indifference. It is a condition that seems to grow with affluence. Some lessons are learned the hard way.

COMMUNICATION IN RELATIONSHIPS

Communication is the means by which we express our respect, our acceptance, and our recognition of the importance of others. Absence of communication may even express a lack of acceptance. Communication can be verbal or nonverbal. Hugs, smiles, kisses, a disapproving glance, just being there, or not being there, sarcasm, and so on are all methods of communication.

Regardless of the type of communication, trust and acceptance are important for effective communication. Proper trust and acceptance in communication respects that people communicate differently, not by design, but by the fact that they are different people. Some people have trouble expressing their feelings and intentions. Other people do not recognize what they should or should not do or say. Therefore patience, understanding, and acceptance are also necessary in good communication.

Proper communication requires that all parties listen and calmly discuss personal differences to arrive at something that is mutually acceptable. In the case of flowers verses words, Jane can come to understand that flowers are words that Jim cannot verbally express, while Jim can come to understand that he has to work on better verbal expression of his love. Regardless of how emotional or unemotional people can be, good relationships require that problems be discussed and mutually resolved. That will only happen when all parties accept and respect the differences in how people communicate and are willing to listen and to find ways to compromise.

Different family backgrounds can make communication difficult. I grew up in a family where people were expected to solve their own problems, at least from my perspective. I felt I needed to solve my own problems and should not ask for or expect help or even praise unless I asked for it. That led to my thinking people would ask for help if they needed it and didn't need help if they did not ask.

I also expected that if someone needed something or wanted to discuss something, we would speak up and rationally discuss the issue. Although a strictly rational approach to solving problems is great in business, it doesn't always work well with people who are emotional, and it didn't always go over well with some of the people in my life. I should have tried harder to understand the emotional needs of others. But it also would have helped if others had just verbally expressed their needs to a non-emotional me who was waiting for them to say what they wanted.

Even well-intentioned thought habits by two parties can create a communication problem if they are not willing to compromise on their means and methods of communication. It takes effort and increases vulnerability. But effort and accepting vulnerability is necessary for a solid relationship. Another lesson learned the hard way.

Another detriment to effective communication is disloyalty. When a person cheats on a friend or partner and then says, "Let's talk about it," it is not likely what he or she has to say will be believed. Truthfulness and loyalty build trust. Meaningful communication requires that each party remains trustworthy. With trust and acceptance, there is no end to the limits of communication and the rewards of a good relationship. Without trust, faithfulness, and acceptance, no relationship can be productive or rewarding.

Relationships can be just friendly. Friends can listen, share, empathize, hug, joke, just be there, offer advice, and provide many other comforts. A good friendship can be more fulfilling than a physical relationship.

Dear friends are those people whose perceptions of fulfillment are based on how they can help each other rather than on what they can get out of the relationship. That doesn't normally happen in a physical-based relationship. In good relationships, focus extends beyond self. The strength of a relationship really comes down to the unselfishness or selfishness of the participants. If selfish values or personal wants become more important than the value of the relationship, this needs to change or the relationship will fall apart.

Close personal relationships can be wonderful. They can also devastate us when they go wrong. Therefore, it is important to understand what can go wrong before getting involved in one. In a close relationship, it should be understood that the good qualities you initially see in a person will likely be the best you will ever see. At the onset of a desired relationship, most people try to communicate their best qualities so as to make themselves appear in the best light they can. So they should not be expected to improve from that point on.

Be aware that after infatuation wears off, the participants do not usually work as hard as before to remain physically attractive and are not as careful with regard to habits that might not be desirable. Undesirable traits can be covered up in new relationships, so it is important to know each other well before making any commitment to a long-term relationship. The appropriate story here is the one about little Johnny who, upon hearing about arranged marriages, asks his dad if people actually get married without knowing each other. The father's sarcastic reply was, "Son, it happens all the time."

THE PHYSICAL SIDE OF RELATIONSHIPS

Relationships would be much less complex if our physical nature were left out of the relationship equation. However, the fundamental drive for sexual involvement is strong. It often becomes a part, or even the biggest part, of perceived fulfillment in a relationship. The drive of body chemistry, mixed with the desire to be loved and totally accepted, can be a powerful influence on people's thoughts and actions.

The initial emotional effect is called "infatuation." Infatuation is great while it lasts, but it doesn't last forever. That is because infatuation is related to the physical senses rather than rational thought. Infatuation will typically overlook initial problems and personal shortcomings, particularly by the emotionally inexperienced or emotionally insecure. Hence the expression "love is blind." The expression should really be, "infatuation is blind."

Relationships are blind when people allow themselves to become infatuated before making a common-sense evaluation of the other party's character. It is very important to realize that infatuation will fade, even between two compatible people. It will fade as everyday responsibilities, including children, force more practical values to the forefront of the thought process. Even when responsibilities do not cause the end of infatuation, it will normally fade within two years.

When infatuation fades and when the expectations of the relationship are not met, the nonphysical portion, and even the physical portion, of the relationship can get difficult. Old habits that were once overlooked become annoying. The cute comments that were once laughed at are now often disliked. The little signs of recognition and affection now seem to be missing. The self-assurance of the other person that was once so attractive is now domineering. What once was valued so highly in the other person, no longer seems important. Faithfulness and responsibility and even effort may be questioned.

When infatuation fades, the true characters of the participants are revealed. Once the feelings of acceptance and respect are questioned within a relationship, it becomes easy to think about dissolving the relationship. This is particularly true with judgmental people who do not see how they themselves and their judgments may be the source of the dissatisfaction. In many cases, the biggest complainer within a relationship will be the greatest source for discord. It is that person who is typically least accepting and who expects the other party to do most of the changing.

The evolution from high expectations to the more practical realization of everyday responsibilities and disappointments occurs to a greater or lesser degree in all relationships that have an obligatory bond—whether real or imagined. Relationships involving intimacy or other forms of deep personal investment bring more intense feelings. Problems within these relationships become more intense as a result. How relationships evolve after problems begin is dependent upon the maturity of the people involved.

The ideal marital relationship would be between two emotionally mature individuals who choose to live together out of love and the desire to share of themselves. They would be people who could laugh at themselves and accept each other with no expectations. The reality is that today such a marriage would be a rarity for newlyweds. When and where old tribal customs required a man to prove he was mature and a capable provider prior to marriage, couples were more mature. Today, there are seldom any requirements for maturity and responsibility, man or woman, prior to marriage. The result is many poor marriages, and even worse is the resulting children who suffer and do not learn how to think and act maturely.

There was a reason tribal customs required responsibility before marriage. In modern society, a person's freedom to act sexually irresponsibly is more protected than the welfare of any child who may be conceived. It might be time to require that to receive child welfare, both parents be rendered incapable of having other children. There needs to be pain or the immature do not learn. For those people who have not emotionally matured, marriage can be the most maturing of all life experiences, if worked on with love and acceptance. But marriage can and does also expose personal immaturity.

There are many immature ways to try to solve problems that arise within a relationship. One way is to quickly dissolve the relationship. Some people try to spice things up with physical or material pleasures. Still others will use their manipulative practices of weakness, power, lying, or bribing, to get their wants met while pretending they still care about the relationship. Some people maintain the relationship in appearance, but let unhappy feelings fester and get worse. Some people even do mean things to get even for what they see as unfair. And there are some people who will try anything to make things better.

A humorous and exaggerated example is Jethro, who wasn't the brightest firefly in the woods. When discovered by a neighbor in his barn, undressed, dancing lewdly in front of a tractor, Jethro explained that his wife had been ignoring him and a psychiatrist had suggested doing something sexy to attract her. I probably should have left that one out, but then again humor is supposed to make reading more enjoyable.

Humor can also help relationships because it is enjoyable. But even humor cannot solve relationship problems, because it is only a temporary distraction from reality. Relationship problems require new notions in thought reality of what is important to a relationship, as well as focus on those thoughts. The essential focus should be on acceptance and love, which result in maturity and eventual harmony.

The mature way to solve relationship problems is to put aside personal wants and concentrate on what must be done to resolve the problems. The decision to go beyond personal feelings and to focus on acceptance of each other, can return respect and comfort to the relationship. For this to happen, both parties in the relationship must work together on acceptance and on personal responsibility. When problems occur within a relationship, there is a need to understand that there was a reason the relationship blossomed initially and that reason still exists if the basic purpose and values of both parties have remained the same.

When the purpose and values of one or both parties have changed, the situation is more difficult. But it might still be a great relationship if both people are willing to work at acceptance. Arranged marriages have not always been successful, but a surprisingly large number of them have. When it is absolutely necessary to solve a problem, rather than run from it, even people of different backgrounds can work surprisingly well together to solve their relationship problems.

In close relationships, there is a need to understand that dissatisfaction often originates from unrealistic expectations and upon misunderstandings, rather than what the other person did or didn't do. But it can also arise when one person feels unimportant and feels his or her wants are unimportant and ignored. The success of a great relationship is not in meeting the right person. The success in a relationship is brought about by two people committing themselves to acceptance of each other, to sharing with each other, and to unselfishness. Fulfillment in a relationship is based upon the amount of love and acceptance that is mutually invested.

There are successful relationships that began on a computer. But relationships that begin online can also be a potential disaster. Many people allow themselves to get involved at an emotional level, with just words, without truly knowing anything certain about the other person, sometimes without ever meeting them. This probably would not happen to the mature person. But, for the emotionally naïve, the perceived value of a relationship may cause that person to ignore all common sense and reveal personal information and invest intimate feelings prior to really knowing the other party. For the insecure, being told they are beautiful and worthy of being loved can bring a feeling of worth they have not previously experienced and they may respond accordingly. This can end up creating emotional ties, and sometimes infatuation, prior to having information on which to make a sound assessment. At this point, common sense is already out the window and rational decision-making is difficult.

The computer example was used as it is easy to visualize getting involved without adequate knowledge of the other person. Any time personal trust is extended without real knowledge of the other person, there are potential pitfalls. This does not mean we have to know everything about the people we associate with. Reality is we may never know as much as we possibly should. But just from a safety point, it is important to know if the other person can control his or her emotions and tempers.

According to Michael Gottfredson and Travis Hirschi, authors of *A General Theory of Crime*, people who do not develop a sense of self-control, act impulsively and without thought of consequences. Be sure self-control exists before getting involved.

In the chapter "Addictions," it was pointed out that people who desire control, but have little self-control, are the primary cause of trauma within families. Such trauma can result in addictions, domestic abuse, and even suicide. Self-control is most critical to happy relationships. Self-control is needed for respect and trust to exist and is essential to a stable relationship.

Please think about the other person's desire for self-control and actual self-control before allowing emotional feelings to take hold. Remember that initial meetings with another person will not necessarily reveal much about the other person's real character. If there is any chance of a relationship becoming close and personal, be sure to have real knowledge of the other person's character and self-control before allowing infatuation or even "feelings" to begin.

When feelings are generated in a relationship (particularly sexual feelings) before people really know each other, it is almost impossible to be objective. If there is anything I wish a young, single person would get out of this chapter, it is an understanding of this paragraph. Their long-term happiness depends on it. I would like them to understand that where self-control is poor and selfishness is apparent, long-term relationships are doomed.

In *Human Understanding*, we realize that as social creatures, relationships are important to us and to our happiness. Therefore, understanding how relationships function can be important to developing positive relationships and avoiding negative ones. Successful relationships are based upon love, acceptance, sharing, and trust. These are the backbone of successful relationships. Relationships based upon love bring not only happiness, but also joy.

HEALTH CONSIDERATIONS

PRAYER

Prayer is not normally thought of as a health issue, but for inner consciousness health, it is the most important. Prayer is not something we need to go to church to do. Prayer can be conveyed in thought, in words, in actions, or even in the absence of conscious thought. Prayer can be public or private. Prayer can range from a personal request, to a means of worship, to a thank you, to prayer solely for the sake of praying. There is only one prerequisite to prayer. That prerequisite is the acceptance of a Higher Power of some nature.

Just as our bodies and minds need nourishment and exercise to remain healthy, it would then make sense that our inner consciousness also needs some form of nourishment and exercise to remain healthy. Some people look to the words of the holy books and religious duties for spiritual nourishment and exercise. We can read and listen to what is preached to us and follow that up with appropriate deeds. But we often overlook a means of direct communication with the spiritual level that provides spiritual nourishment and exercise. That means is prayer.

Prayer accepts the Higher Power and connects us, through that acceptance, to the Higher Power. Even the Buddhists, who do not believe in a god, believe that it is necessary to connect consciousness to a higher level through meditative prayer.

There are many reasons people pray such as grieving, celebrating, requesting, contrition, gratitude, intercession, celebration, and so on. There are also different levels of prayer. Prayer should not be just a 911 call when we need help. The lowest level would be considered prayers of personal request. As prayer becomes more compassionate, the level of prayer increases. The more the prayer is directed beyond self and aligns itself with the spirit of love, the higher the level of prayer. Totally selfless prayer of the prophets, mystics, saints, and other people that is aligned with, or coherent with, the love of the Higher Power or Supreme Consciousness can result in unnatural physical occurrences, such as cures, levitation, states of ecstasy, and other miracles, some of which have been previously described. These people have shown the rest of us that loving, selfless prayer can draw power of a higher level into our material world.

If we understand that prayer is a form of communication, we should also understand that real communication goes two ways. And just because we do not seem to get a response to our prayers of request does not mean prayer is useless. If we accept a higher power, we should also accept our prayers are heard. And we need to accept that the good things of the Higher Power are related to virtue and are not necessarily what we are praying for. We need to visualize that prayers that ask for worldly things are like a child asking for candy to cure a tummy ache. We do not always know what is good for us and for those we love.

If prayers for specific wants are not answered as desired, they may be answered in ways we do not recognize for our spiritual needs. If we only look for what we want, we will not likely perceive any response. We need to realize that our prayers may be answered in ways we do not expect.

A good prayer does not expect. A good prayer lets go of wants and worries. In his book *Merton's Place of Nowhere,* James Finley points out how Thomas Merton compared letting go to that of a green apple on a tree. The apple does not grow and get red by squirming, pushing, worrying, or by insisting that the sun shine. No, the apple waits attentively while it remains open to receive the juice from the roots and the warmth of the sun's radiance to transform it. Where there is a belief in a Higher Power, there should also be an acceptance that the Higher Power will provide what is needed at the appropriate time, which may not be what we want or at the time we want.

I have had very poor luck investing in stocks that were highly recommended. With the last big investment, I prayed and watched as it went down the drain. In the time since that happened, I have come to realize that if things always went the way I had wanted, I probably would have been too wrapped up in my success to think about much other than my success and how to physically enjoy it. I certainly would not have developed the perspective on life I now have, and probably not have written this book, at least not in the way it is now written.

Looking back at what has happened in my life, I can now accept that maybe my prayers were answered, just not in the way I envisioned they should have been. As we often do not know what is best for ourselves and others, our prayers may be answered in ways we may not want.

Sometimes responses to prayer are attributed to other causes. In 1877, the Governor of Minnesota declared April 26, 1877 a day of prayer to ask for relief from a locust plague called Albert's Swarm. The swarm, which started in 1873, grew to cover 196,000 square miles of the Great Plains states. The swarm in 1875 is now considered to be the largest swarm of locusts in the history of humankind. (60)

As the plague affected much of the country's food supply, people from all over the country prayed. The day of prayer, April 26, was warm and sunny, with the same weather predicted for the 27th. But as midnight approached, the wind shifted and a cold rain began and turned to sleet and snow. The freakish very late-season storm in mid-America killed most of the hatching locusts. And in July and August, those locusts remaining inexplicably flew away.

Was prayer a contributing factor? Non-believers say no, prayer had nothing to do with it. Which reminds me of a story about an Irishman trying to find a parking space anywhere near a specific downtown building in which he had an important meeting and dared not be late. After five times around the block, he decided to resort to prayer. He promised to go to church each day for a year if God would quickly provide him a parking place. Just after he finished the prayer, he turned the corner and there was a parking place. Upon seeing a spot to park, he said "You can forget what I said God, I found one by myself." We may want to consider that good fortune may be more than just luck.

Randolph Byrd, MD, a cardiologist at the University of California at the San Francisco School of Medicine, tested the impact of prayer from a distance, recording its effects on 393 patients who all had severe chest pains and/or heart attacks. Half were prayed for, and half were not. The patients had no knowledge of being prayed for. The prayed-for group required fewer antibiotics (3 in the prayed-for group, compared to 17 in the group not prayed for), had less need for mechanical respirators (zero as compared to 12), required fewer diuretics (5 compare to 15), suffered less congestive heart failure (8 compared to 20), experienced less cardiopulmonary arrest (3 compared to 14) and fell ill with pneumonia less often (3 compared to 13). This research was published in a 1988 study titled, "Positive Therapeutic Effects of Intercessory Prayer on a Coronary Care Unit Population" by *Southern Medical Journal*.

Other research on the effect of distance prayer on AIDS patients was conducted by Elisabeth Trag, MD, clinical director of Psychosocial Oncology at California Pacific Medical Center in San Francisco in 1995. That study followed that up in 1998 in, "A Randomized Double-Blind Study of the Effects of Distant Healing in a Population with Advanced AIDS" by Fred Sicher, MA, Elisabeth Trag MD, Dan Morrell, PhD, and Helene S. Smith, PhD. The study showed that those patients prayed for performed in statistically significantly more benign course.

In all relationships, some type of communication is necessary to keep the relationship going. The more sincere the communication, the stronger the relationship is. Prayer seems to be no different in that the more often we pray, the more often we think about the Higher Power. The farther we drift from prayer, the farther we drift from our relationship with the Higher Power and with the belief in prayer.

The problem is that the higher Power will hear all prayers, even those of non-believers, though they would not be meaningful without a belief. it is confusing to some people.

Prayer needs to be practiced often. The more the prayer is practiced, for selfless, loving reasons, the more effective the prayer. Another story I heard from Dr. Margret Schlientz concerned a Mother Superior who asked her advice about what to do with one of the sisters who was not praying anymore. Dr. Schlientz recommended that the Mother Superior, every night after everyone else was asleep, place her hand on the sister's door and pray for her for ten minutes. Dr. Schlientz said that a few years later, she met the Mother Superior again.

As it turned out, after some months of the Mother Superior's praying outside the sister's door, the sister attended communal prayer again. When the Mother Superior asked what had brought about the change, the sister said, "Because you changed."

Making a repeated sincere and caring effort to help others through prayer can have a positive effect on the persons praying that they do not even recognize.

Another form of prayer that is beneficial to both mind and body is meditative prayer. It is generally considered a type of eastern Buddhist prayer, but it has been practiced by people of many religions. Meditation is a good way of emptying our minds of worldly thoughts. It is important to free our minds of our worldly distractions and to open our spiritual consciousness to spiritual inspiration. Please realize that mental distractions during prayer are normal. The important thing to do with distractions is to let them go as soon as they are realized. Regardless of the type of prayer we employ, prayer opens the mind and inner consciousness to the Higher Power of love.

Prayer is beneficial not only on the spiritual level. It is also there for us when we need help on a physical and/or mental level, if we believe in prayer. Prayer can provide hope when we're distressed. Every time we pray with our hearts, we reinforce our humility and decrease egotism. For in praying and in meditation, we learn to give up control. The more we give up control, the more we learn acceptance and reduce stress.

It is important that parents pray with their children so that children will understand that prayer is a key part of life. It is comforting to the thought process of a child to develop a belief that, no matter how bad things in life may be, there is a Higher Power that can make all things right. This belief is best instilled by the open and active prayer life of parents.

If you ever wonder how to pray for yourself in a selfless way, pray that you may do the will of the Higher Power or pray that you may be a good example for the people around you. Regardless of how you pray, pray often.

Praying may sound like a simple thing to do. But it runs counter to modern culture. Also, the existence of evil will work hard to keep a person from contact with love. It takes self-discipline to pray. Yet, when we do what we know we should be doing, in spite of difficulty, we end up feeling much better about ourselves.

We normally think of prayer as something intangible. But is it completely intangible? The research of Boguslaw Lipinski, who studies bioelectric phenomena, indicates prayer can produce effects that can be recorded. In 1985 in Medugorje, Yugoslavia, the site of supposed apparitions of the Blessed Mary, Dr. Lipinski recorded some unusual electrical energy readings that occurred during Mass and prayer. (61) On March 15, 1985, the measured ion concentration rose to 100,000 per cubic centimeter and the instrument to detect nuclear radiation reached 100,000 millirads per hour. That dosage of nuclear radiation would normally be lethal within eight hours. But no one suffered any ill effects.

So, what caused the nuclear radiation measured? It should be noted that normal ion concentration outside is typically below 1000 per cu cm. although it can get somewhat higher indoors. The readings increased with the beginning of prayer and with the size of the group praying. Conscious prayer, although intangible to us, may actually produce something more than what is intangible. With many people mentally coherent in prayer, could it possibly be affecting something at the quantum level? In the chapter "The Reality of Independent Consciousness," we looked at the possibility that mental coherence with that of the Higher Power could affect changes at the quantum level.

That possibility is backed up by a scientific study on the effects of coherence meditation to reduce crime in Washington D.C. The study, which was conducted between June 7th and July 20th, 1993, involved a group of TM-Sedhas meditators, whose numbers increased from 800 to 4000 over the period. At the same time, the violent crime numbers steadily dropped by 23.3 percent. The drop seemed to be related to the number of people meditating. (62) When the meditation stopped, the crime rate rose back to normal. Information on the study is available through the World Peace Group at http://worldpeacegroup.org/washington_crime_study.html. The article is "Washington Crime Reduced by 23 percent."

A similar, but longer, study occurred in the Merseyside area of Liverpool, England, which at the time had the third highest crime rate in the ten largest districts in England. In this 1988 study, the crime rate dropped 13.4 percent in the next five years, while the national crime rate soared by 45 percent. Information on the study is available through on the World Peace Group website (http://worldpeacegroup.org/liverpool_crime_study.html).

Back in the chapter "The Reality of an Independent Consciousness," we looked at the idea of collective consciousness affecting the world about us. As we look at some of the examples of the effect of prayer and meditation, it would appear that there is truth to this concept. The condition of the overall consciousness of humanity could affect the harmony of the world itself. We all need to understand that fact. It would be interesting to see what would happen if everyone would pray at least once a day for world peace.

We all have the ability to help the world if we decide we would like to. The ability to pray is something that cannot be taken away as long as consciousness exists. Old age, prison, or even paralysis cannot take away the ability to pray. Praying is something positive we can always do. The people of Nineveh listened to Johnna and changed their ways and the city was saved. Is humanity ready to listen to the message of the need for prayer and love?

In *Human Understanding*, we realize that prayer keeps us connected to the Higher Power. Prayer also helps us realize that we are not in control. Prayer is not about getting worldly wants. Although it is often employed for material wants, it is about asking for help for what we and others need for spiritual well-being. Becoming selfless for the good of others is the most loving prayer and likely produces the most significant results, possibly because the more loving it is the more it is connected to the power of the Higher Power.

As Mark Robert Waldman points out, focusing on prayer or spiritual meditation is important in times of difficulty. It can help us face problems in our lives and result in self-worth and inner peace. Prayer on an everyday basis can help us face life's daily trials. Even scientific studies point out the positive statistical effects of prayer, as well as some unexpected and unexplained energy effects.

NUTRITION

A healthy body and mind are important to happy and rewarding life. We all know that nutrition is essential for staying alive. Food and drink and oxygen make up the fuels that feed the engines of our bodies. As with any fuel, the ingredients can have a positive or negative effect on an engine. Too much or too little may also affect how smooth the engine runs. Too much of the wrong stuff and the engine may sputter or shut down. The human body is an organic machine that needs proper fuel to run smoothly. It is unfortunate that not all people have an adequate source of proper nutrition. However, this chapter only addresses the nutritional needs of the body, not its scarcity or abundance.

There is much information available on proper nutrition. We even have catch phrases to remind us to eat healthy. This information is important for keeping our bodies properly tuned. Despite nutritional needs being listed under recommended daily allowances, nutritional needs are really not the same for all people.

Most of our ancestors lived in a general geographic area for hundreds or thousands of years at a time when only the fittest survived. Over time, their bodies adapted, to some degree, to the nutrients available to them. Those needs have been genetically passed on. As a result, nutritional needs can vary between races, nationalities, and even people from localized areas within specific countries. They can vary within a family that includes different ancestral backgrounds. Even if we eat the same foods as our ancestors, the nutrient value may be different due to different soils or if the foods are grown soils depleted of important trace elements. Also the nutrient value of products such as meat, fish, eggs, and milk are affected by changes in the natural diets of the creatures from which these products come.

Besides differences in nutritional needs due to ancestry, nutritional needs also change with age and gender. The pharmaceutical industry has found that drugs do not work the same for all people, especially for men and women. This should lead us to understand that the engine in each body is unique and that each body needs to be tuned a little differently.

In general, most basic nutritional needs of the young people in developed countries are met with the vitamins and minerals added to processed foods and drinks, although most nutritionists would say it's better to get one's vitamins and minerals from natural foods. But that does not mean they cover everyone's needs, particularly those of older people and people with food allergies. It may be a good idea to observe and record how we and those we are responsible for react to specific foods and food supplements.

If there is any question about how well the engine of the body is running, be sure to check the fuel, as well as the engine. Older body engines may need some additives to keep them running smoothly. Once the body's engine stops, it is difficult to restart. To further view the similarity between the body's motor and a mechanical engine, we need to realize that both can be restarted with a surge of electricity. When we want a car to run smoothly, we change oil regularly and do not put diesel fuel in a gas tank. Yet we will eat just about anything that tastes good, regardless of how it affects our bodies. And then we wonder why we grow fat and our bodies do not function properly. It's about time we treat our bodies as well as we treat our cars.

Because nutrition is so important to feeling well, vitamin dealers today are flooding the market with nutritional supplements. They claim to help with almost every bodily function—from better mental focus to better sleep, from irritable bowel syndrome to better sex, from bigger, stronger bodies to weight loss, and with any other symptom people may worry about.

With vitamins, there is no work involved. Just pop the pill. The vitamin industry caters to pride, fear, convenience, and even ignorance. It is a multi-billion-dollar business and many companies are trying to get a piece of the monetary pie. Maybe a good percentage of these supplements have merit, or even some substantial merit. But that doesn't mean they will necessarily help you or even be good for you.

Before jumping on the supplement bandwagon, there are many things to consider. You should realize that herbal supplements do not have to be backed by scientific studies (although some are) and may not accomplish what they are advertised to accomplish. It would also help to get a nutritionist's opinion before taking supplements. Supplements, by definition, are not a cure for anything. Supplements may or may not help you. If you try a supplement, monitor if there is any noticeable difference, positive or negative. Be objective in that observation. If you take many different drugs or even supplements together with medication, there could be unhealthy side effects. Additives can be helpful, but be careful how they are mixed.

Something that everybody should be aware of is that supplements and drugs taken for some period of time can cause the body to become dependent upon them, like a crutch. Use crutches long enough and the leg muscles wither. We do not know the long-term effects of most drugs on normal bodily functions. For the elderly, the effect may be worth the risk. However, for younger people, drugs and supplements could have long-term impacts and, worse yet, could even adversely affect any children that they may conceive.

Realize that drugs and supplements are poorly tested for long-term effects and hereditary effects, if tested at all for these effects. Because of drug-addicted newborns, we know that the drugs mothers ingest have an effect on their children. It would be wise to consider how the drug thalidomide affected newborns.

Thalidomide is a drug first used in Germany in 1957 as an over-the-counter remedy. It was advertised as safe for everyone. By 1960, it was marketed in 40 countries. In 1960, Australian Obstetrician William McBride found it alleviated morning sickness in pregnant women and became used by pregnant women. In 1961, many babies were being born with major limb deformations which were traced back to thalidomide. Thousands of babies were affected. Thalidomide also restricted blood vessels which had additional negative effects. Actually, the deformation of babies began not long after the drug was introduced but the cause did not become clear until pregnant women started using thalidomide.

It would also be wise to consider the effects of food additives on health and the digestive system. Just one example is aspartame, which is a widely used artificial sweetener in diet soda and numerous other products. Aspartame contains wood alcohol, which is a poison, as well as DKP, which is known to cause the growth of tumors. For actual recorded effects, we just need to look at the result of studies on people who consume diet sodas.

The article "Diet Drink Consumption and the Risk of Cardiovascular Events: A Report from the Woman's Health Initiative" on approximately 60,000 women found that women who consumed two or more diet sodas a day are over 30 percent more likely to experience a cardiovascular event and 50 percent were more likely to die from a related disease. (63)

Our digestive systems did not develop to handle chemical additives. Worse yet, chemical substitutes often do not do what then are intended to do. A study published in the March 17, 2015 *Journal of the American Geriatrics Society* of people over 65 found that people who drank diet soda gained almost triple the abdominal body fat over nine years as those who didn't drink diet soda.

But supplements and additives are not the only questionable things we ingest. Most people in the United States also consume genetically modified (GM) foods. Over 80 percent of the corn, soybean and cotton acreage in the U.S. is genetically modified.

Many other crops are also genetically modified. Recently approval was given by the FDA for genetically modified apples and potatoes. According to the web site of the US Library of Medicine National Institute of Health (www.ncbi.nlm.hil.gov/imc/articles/pmc3639326/) the main concerns are related to the possibility of a transfer of allergens into the new food, the gene transfer from GM foods to human cells or to bacteria in the gastrointestinal tract, and the mixing of GM crops with wild species, with conventional crops, or with other GM crops, all of which could have an undesired effect on food and food safety.

Unfortunately, we really do not know exactly how safe genetically modified produce is. Testing on the effects of GM food is based upon relatively short periods of time, during which there appear to be no significant observable negative effects. The reality of new chemical compounds and /or molecules is that they can have long-term, negative effects on the human body or on heredity that are not recognized in a short testing period. The result is the public becomes the major test sample and suffers any adverse consequences.

Over the past two decades, we have seen a rapid rise in gluten-related disorders, as well as a significant rise in autism and other physical, mental and emotional problems. The rise has paralleled the introduction of GM (genetically modified) farm products such as corn, soybean, wheat, and cotton. The Institute for Responsible Technology published the article, "Genetically Engineered Food May Cause Rising Food Allergies." It points out that in 1999 researchers at York Laboratory discovered the incidence of soy allergies in the United kingdom had increased 50 percent from the previous year. (64) GM soy had recently been introduced into the United Kingdom from the US.

There is also much discussion about the Bt toxin, introduced into plants for pest control, having a bad effect on human intestines. That is not a surprise because many of these GM crops produce toxins to kill insects. *Bacillus thuringiensis* (Bt) is a bacterium that produces proteins that are toxic to insects, and is in the same family of bacteria as *B. anthracis*, which causes anthrax, and *B. cereus*, which causes food poisoning. Bt is the most widely used biological pesticide in the world. And we eat these crops.

A press advisory May 19, 2009 from the American Academy of Environmental Medicine (AAEM) released its position on GM foods, stating that "GM foods pose a serious health risk" and calling for a moratorium on GM foods. Citing several animal studies, the AAEM concludes "there is more than a casual association between GM foods and adverse health effects" and that "GM foods pose a serious health risk in the areas of toxicology, allergy and immune function, reproductive health, and metabolic, physiologic, and genetic health." In 2015, the Lyme-Induced Autism Foundation (LAF) urged doctors to prescribe diets free of GM foods. (www.shareguide.com).

The UK's Institute of Science in Society's report is titled "BT Kills Human Kidney Cells." There are many other recent studies that indicate dangers with GM products. Yet most Americans consume GM products and are not even aware of that fact.

The FDA issued a disclaimer that GM foods can create unpredictable, hard-to-detect, side effects. Despite potential adverse side effects, there is no disclaimer of warning on food that contains GM products. It seems the FDA is more sympathetic to the well-being of business than to people's well-being.

If you want more controversy on this issue, check out how many important positions at the FDA are filled by past employees of Monsanto, the company that supplies most of the seed for the GM products. Additional investigation should also have applied to the injection of rBST (also called BGH, bovine growth hormone) into cows to increase the production of milk. Based on further testing, it has been banned in all countries of the European Union, Canada, Japan, Australia, and in other countries. This is but one substance ingested in the US but banned in most developed nations as mentioned in a June 26, 2013 ABC News release by Susanna Kim titled "11 Food Ingredients Banned outside the US that We Eat."

To eat healthy, it would be wise to do some research on GM food and on food additives. As this book talks about opening our minds to controversial issues and new realities, we should also open our minds to the fact that GM crops may have the long-term consequences of which we know almost nothing.

While on the Food and Drug Administration, we might want to look at natural substances that have been demonstrated to kill viruses without side effects, but are not use-approved by the FDA. As Irving Stone wrote, "It takes more than logic and clear-cut demonstrations to overcome the inertia and dogma of established thought." (65)

As early as the 1940s, the use of high doses of intravenous vitamin C was being pioneered by Dr. Frederick Klenner and found sucessful in the treatment of many different infections and diseases. (66) A study of high-dosage intravenous vitamin C published in 1950 reported that 327 out of 327 cases of shingles were cured within 72 hours. (67)

The 327-test-case result is also mentioned in an article of the Riordan Clinic titled "High-dose Intravenous Vitamin C as a Successful Treatment of Viral Infections" (www.riordanclinic.org). The best book on the benefits of vitamin C is *Primal Panacea* by Thomas E. Levy, MD, JD. This book not only mentions the complete resolution of 327 cases of the shingles, it also mentions that on June 10, 1949, Dr. Klenner presented a summarization of his work with polio, in which he cured 60 out of 60 cases of polio to the annual session of the American Medical Association. In addition, Dr. Levy mentions that, Robert Cathcart MD, based upon his experience, asserted that any AIDS patient could be put into remission if enough vitamin C were taken to neutralize the toxicity produced by the virus and adequately treat any secondary infections as published in *Medical Hypotheses*, "Vitamin C in the Treatment of

Aquired Immune Deficiency Syndrome (AIDS) in 1984. The ability of vitamin C to kill viruses has been known for generations, but it is still not approved as a cure, even when there are no known side effects.

Vitamin C has even been demonstrated to kill cancer cells. In 1968, Dr. Linus Pauling, two-time Nobel Prize winner, conducted a scientific study that showed that high doses of vitamin C given intravenously could extend the life of advanced cancer patients six-fold. There are many other cases where vitamin C has been shown to cure acute sickness, yet it is not accepted for medical use.

Another natural element that has been proven to kill viruses and cancer cells is oxygen in a triple molecule form called ozone. Why is ozone being used in extensively in Europe as a treatment for cancer but not in the United States? Could it be because these treatments are not patentable and profitable to big business?

After having been diagnosed twice for cancer I am concerned with preventing cancer, as well as approval of proven treatments for cancer and other diseases, in the United States. I am especially concerned since the American Cancer Society (ACS), whose mission statement focus is to eliminate cancer as a problem by preventing cancer, now appears to be more interested in the finding the right drugs for treating cancer. I am even wondering on whose behalf the ACS functions.

That question is brought about by ACS's repeated statement that cell phone towers do little to increase the probability of cancer, when actual tests of people who have lived within 1/3 mile of a cell phone tower for ten years or more, show a cancer rate 4 to 5 times higher than people not living close to a cell phone tower.

Published information on the cancer around cell phone towers includes, "Increased Incidence of Cancer Near a Transmitter Station" published by the *International Journal of Cancer Prevention*, which showed a 4.15-time increase. Be aware that the only specific testing on the effects of cell phones on people was relatively short-term testing in the 1990s by the cell phone industry itself. That report suggested that the industry inform the public of the dangers and warn users to use precautionary steps until more research could be done. The public was not informed and little to no additional research has been done. It should be noted that one of the items in the report is that the rate of neuroma, a benign tumor of the auditory nerve, was 50 percent higher in people who repeatedly used cell phones for six years of more. It would be in everybody's best interest if the long-term effects of cell phones use be researched before thinking they are harmless.

Of all the things we consume, the most important is oxygen. Oxygen intake is the primary fuel that keeps our bodies running. Doctors William B. Kannel and Helen Hubert, both from the Boston School of Medicine, have been involved with the decades of data from the Framingham Heart Study. They have concluded that our lungs are the number-one predictor of death. This study began in 1948 with 5,209 people between the ages of 30 to 62, and has continued through a number of generations. In the follow-up testing, research included other physiological conditions, including dementia.

Among other things, more modern testing has included magnetic resonance imaging of the brain, as well as of the heart. Brain imaging indicates that those people who perform poorly on the treadmill have smaller brains. The article "Sedentary Lifestyle Linked to Smaller Brain Later in Life" on www.GoodTherapy. org by Zawn Villines summarizes the testing and the results, involved with the Farmington Study. It involved people, without any dementia or heart disease, who were tested at 40 years old and 20 years later. (68)

Tests on over 1,000 people after 20 years showed that the people with the greatest increase in heart rate and the most brain shrinkage had the lowest VO2 max. (VO2 max indicates how efficiently the body uses oxygen.) Your lungs, like other parts of the body, lose effectiveness if not properly exercised. The heart is not the only thing that suffers the consequences. The brain needs oxygen-rich blood to function properly. The study found that brain aging is associated with the "Cardiac Index". Your ability to function mentally is also associated with your ability to breathe oxygen effectively. And as we will see in the next chapter, it is exercise, especially high-intensity exercise, that can increase lung function.

Most people are not aware that the percentage of oxygen in the air we breathe has been slowly declining. The decline is only estimated to be 0.7 percent in the last 800,000 years, as stated in an article in *Forbes*, "Earth's Oxygen Levels are Declining and Scientists Don't Know Why."

Comprising between 20 and 21 percent of air, oxygen is only down slightly from more recent historical levels. However, according to the science journal *Nature*, it has dropped 2 percent in the last five decades in pristine areas. But it has dropped to 15 percent or even 12 percent in some big cities. Anything less than 7 percent oxygen is not able to support life.

The reduction in oxygen has a negative effect on our oxygen intake and consequently overall health. There is much new information now available on the importance of oxygen to overall health. When thinking of nutrition, do not forget the importance of oxygen and breathing properly.

In **Human Understanding**, we eat and breathe, and hopefully we do both well. But we also realize that we need to be careful about what we eat and breathe to be able to live for a higher purpose other than just nourishment or enjoyment.

Exercise

Humankind did not evolve into the present physical form by sitting at desks, watching television, and riding in cars. Humankind's form evolved through walking and running, lifting and throwing, hunting and farming. Most of us do little of that work in our modern environment so our bodies have not yet evolved to where our present-day jobs keep us physically fit. Therefore, we need to exercise to stay physically fit.

But it is not just the body that needs exercise; the brain does as well. We don't do that by just watching television. And we don't exercise our minds when we accept everything we're told without trying to understand what it is that we are being told and why.

We have all heard enough about physical exercise to realize it is important to physical health. There are many studies that show that is true. Yet, in spite of the realization, many of us find it difficult to start or maintain an exercise program. Why? The answer goes back to the thought reality. Unless the value of an exercise program is more important to thought reality than other things we presently value, we won't make the effort to exercise. If we are comfortable with the way things are, why exert ourselves?

If it were a matter of life or death, we would likely undertake such a program because the value would increase sufficiently to warrant a change. To start an exercise program and maintain it requires focus on the value to be received. If we can visualize an important value to be gained by exercise, we may be able to start and maintain an exercise program. It is also helpful to have encouragement. Once such a program is started and maintained, the value will become more obvious and easier to sustain.

There are those of us who will excuse ourselves from exercise because we think we do not have the time. That is actually not a good excuse anymore. New, high-intensity exercise routines (HIT) or (HIIT) substantially reduce the time needed for effective exercise. There are a number of HIT programs. The typical program will include up to 30 seconds of intense exercise followed by a rest period, generally a little longer than the exercise time. The total time involved can be 12 to 20 minutes 3 days a week or 12 minutes 4 times a week depending upon the program. The Tabata Method requires 20 seconds of drop dead exertion followed by 10 seconds or more of rest repeated 8 times 4 times a week, which comes to as little as 16 minutes a week, according to the *Journal of Physiology online* (2012 Jan 30 doi.10.1113/physiology 2011.224725).

A good source for information on HIT exercise is Dr. Joseph Mercola. Besides being a *New York Times* bestselling author, Dr Mercola was named top ultimate game-changer in 2009 by the *Huffington Post*. Initially, exercise can be exhausting. However, according to Dr. Michael J. Breus, PhD, the "Sleep Doctor," when a good exercise program is maintained, it will reduce fatigue, reduce stress and anxiety, increase the quality of sleep, and help with insomnia and other sleep disorders. (http://thesleepdoctor.com)

At the minimum, good exercise will result in a gain of expendable energy. When my wife's first husband died, as badly as she felt, she would still reluctantly drag herself to an exercise class. She dreaded the start of each session. But once the exercise class got going, she would always feel better. She found herself going to exercise class to feel better. The body that is exercised feels better and has more reserve energy. For people faithful to an exercise program, the benefits are not just physical. These people also feel an increase in self-worth because they realize they are doing what they know is good for them.

A good exercise program increases both self-discipline and self-worth. All that is required is a consistent effort. It can even be done at home with little to no expense. Yet, most of us do not maintain a good exercise program. What this points out is how locked we are into our habits and values, even when we know we should change them.

And if we do not make an effort to improve ourselves on the physical level, is it any wonder many of us neglect our mental and spiritual health as well? It might make sense to not only exercise regularly, but to also offer the exercise up as a form of prayer. That way, we can accomplish two things at once.

As to the important aspects of a good exercise program, it would be helpful to keep up with what research is finding out about different types of exercise. Exercising our respiratory function is very important to our health. Our lungs need to be exercised as much as, or possibly more than, other parts of our bodies. If we do not breathe heavily enough, the capacity of the lungs diminishes and so does our all-important oxygen intake. The trend in exercise programs today is short, high-intensity training (HIT), which increases lung capacity and lung health. Healthy lungs are every bit as critical, or more critical, to life as a healthy heart. That is because the heart health is dependent on lung health.

Al Sears, MD, (69) in his book *P.A.C.E: The 12-Minute Fitness Revolution*, summarized the results of a 16-week study of different exercise programs on identical 18-year-old twins. One twin jogged ten miles straight each day with no breaks. Her sister's exercise was sprinting six exercise sets. Each set had a 50-yard intense exertion interval, followed by a 30-second recovery period. The twin jogging ten miles lost 5 percent in body fat (8 pounds), but also lost two pounds of muscle. Her twin sister lost 14.5 percent body fat (18 pounds) and gained nine pounds of muscle.

The book also quotes John Defendis, former Mr. USA, who said, "The key is not to do cardio, because you'll lose muscle. The idea is to increase lean muscle. To do that effectively, you must intensify and be progressive in workouts." The most important type of exercise is exercise that increases lung capacity and results in better breathing and more oxygen intake. According to Dr. Sears, by the time you are 80, your lung power may decrease by 60 percent. This is of special concern to the heart and brain. But Dr. Sears also points out that with proper exercise, lung capacity can be increased.

The value of high-intensity training was confirmed by scientists at McMaster University in Hamilton, Ontario, Canada, who found that 12 minutes of exercise that include 3 to 20 seconds of all-out effort, followed by 30 seconds of rest achieved as much result as 45 minutes of moderate exercise. *Pillar 3: Exercise and Brain Aerobics* of the Alzheimer's Research & Prevention Foundation states: "Regular physical exercise can reduce your risk for developing Alzheimer's disease by up to a stunning 50 percent." (http:// alzheimersprevention.org). The same organization also said this about yoga meditation exercise: "This non-religious practice can be adapted for several lengths, but practicing it for just 12 minutes a day has been shown to reduce stress and increase activity in areas of the brain that are central to memory." These are things to consider.

While most exercise programs concentrate on the physical, don't forget mental exercise. The brain needs to be exercised or, like an unused machine, it will be difficult to keep in working condition. The expression "use it or lose it" applies to our brains, as well as the rest of our bodies. One way we can exercise the brain is by challenging it. We can challenge it by trying to better understand the facts about issues we previously accepted without question. Often-suggested ways to challenge the brain are solving puzzles or learning a new language, but there are other methods. All you have to do is to challenge your mind.

Brain studies have also shown that meditation can be an important exercise for the brain. The coherence of brain waves attained though transcendental mental meditation has been found to be a large factor in the communication between the left and right hemispheres of the brain. According to quantum physicist and educator John Hagelin, PhD, (70) coherence that can be attained through meditation is responsible for intelligence, creativity, and psychological and emotional stability. Information is presented in video and written format at www.meditationplex.com.

The functionality of the brain normally begins to decrease about the age of 30. But with coherence of brain functions, the abilities of the brain will continue to grow. It is interesting to realize that Einstein's brain when he died was not like that of a normal older person. His brain had an unusually high amount of fibers connecting the two cerebral hemispheres (left and right sides) of the brain, which can be augmented by meditation. The study, "The Corpus Callosum of Einstein's Brain: Another Clue to his Intelligence" published in the journal *Brain*, addresses the connection between the hemispheres of Einstein's brain. The video of John Hagelin mentioned above addresses how meditation increases the connection.

The effects of meditation have been researched by over a hundred universities and research institutions. Just a few of the findings:

• 47 percent reduction in the risk of cardiovascular-related mortality (*Circulation: Cardiovascular Quality and Outcome* 5: 750- 758, 2012);

• 40 percent reduction in psychological distress, including stress, anxiety, and depression (*American Journal of Hypertension* 22 (12): 1326-1331, 2009);

• 10 percent improvement in test scores and GPA (*Education* 131:556-565, 2011);

• Reduced ADHD symptoms and other learning disorders (*Mind and Brain*: (1): 78-81, 2011).

Anyone interested in holding onto, or actually improving their physical well-being, as well as their mental abilities, should seriously consider meditation as a form of exercise.

In *Human Understanding,* we realize that the condition of the body is important to our health and how we function physically and mentally. For that reason, it is important to exercise to keep physically fit. However, human fitness for the sake of fitness alone will always come to an end. Being physically and mentally fit to serve a higher purpose will benefit more than just our bodies.

SUMMARY OF PART III

Part III covers a number of considerations; the most important being the presentation of logical reasons to accept the concept that there is a Higher Power of love, the nature of which is unknown. That is followed with an understanding of the importance of the images to thought reality. Our mental images have an effect on our behavior. A society that images a loving Higher Power will be more loving than a society with an image of a judgmental higher power or any society with no higher image of love. Where there is no positive image to follow, people will do whatever they have been conditioned to do or do as they please.

The importance of love is difficult for humanity to comprehend. Love is a virtue, not a feeling. Love is like an unconscious commitment to give of self without any selfish reason. Real love never asks why. It does not want for self, yet it results in humanity's most fulfilling feeling. Love is difficult for humans to understanding because physical minds are conditioned to think on the physical level of reality. Love is of a higher reality of fulfillment. Humans need to understand that the ideal fulfillment they seek is fulfillment of their spiritual inner consciousness.

In the chapters on religion, I present the concept that the general morality of the various civilizations was initiated mostly from a fearful image of a Higher Power and from an image of afterlife consequences. Although many people act out of love, I believe—and research has shown—a bigger factor in how most humans act is fear. Fear was important for the initiation of religion and morality, but later religion and morality became internalized and the importance of love came to be understood. Although religions now have specific beliefs, what is important in religion is how religion can effectively deliver the message of the importance of love. True religion must be about love. The concept of fear of the Lord should actually be fear of what will happen should we turn from love to selfishness.

It is important to understand that it is not religion that provides salvation or paradise or oneness of consciousness. Religion is what humans have put together to help humanity to that end. Religions are like human families in which the parents are trying to do their best for their children. But because religious parents are human, they also make mistakes. That is most apparent in the conflicts between various religions, as well as conflicts in what is considered inspired scripture and resulting doctrine.

So as not to be misled by the errors in what humans have put together, it is important to make sure that what is accepted of what is preached or taught, within the religion of choice, is based upon love. A loving religion can help to lead people and the world to salvation through teaching and example. But even the most loving religion means nothing if people do not take to heart the message of love and forgiveness. It is love that is most important aspect of religion, as it is in any family. Lose the message and the example of love and the world is lost.

I have pointed out that idealism is important to retain, even though we will be more practical in how we actually live. Without the ideal, there is nothing to strive for. Practicality is for daily living. Idealism is of wisdom, for it looks beyond the here and now. Intelligence is good but overrated. It is wisdom that helps us to look beyond the sometimes shortsighted, intelligent solutions to today's problems and to perceive what will actually result in inner peace and happiness. It is wisdom that tells us to open our minds to values that will last, not just to worldly values.

The desire for control is considered, in this book, the most subtle and divisive vice that exists. It throws a veil over the voice of inner consciousness and amplifies the selfishness of ego consciousness, which focuses on worldly wants. In focusing on material desires, the ego can be successful in worldly terms, but the cost can be disharmony with the inner consciousness self, which is concerned with the intangibles of virtue. I have described negative thinking as similar to a virus. But even a worse virus like vice is the desire for control. I see the desire for control as the great virus (sin) of humanity, which gets handed down from generation to generation. It is the desire to control that leads away for inner happiness to addiction, judgment, anger, stress, and other forms of mental unhappiness

To overcome the devastating consequences of control, it is important to introduce new ideas and images into thought reality that allow the mind to see through the shortsightedness of the ego. Acceptance is the opposite of control. It allows humanity to listen to more than the ego. Acceptance lifts the veil over the human mind that interferes with the acceptance of the voice of inner consciousness. It allows us to understand the reality of virtue and vice, that life is lived for a higher purpose, and that final existence in love is the culmination of living a virtuous life.

A testament to the importance of acceptance is the success of Alcoholics Anonymous, in which the first steps are acceptance of being powerless to stop feeding the addiction and then turning personal control over to a higher power. Where real happiness is desired, people need to learn acceptance. That is because happiness comes from within, not with what can be controlled beyond self.

When it comes to what is encountered in life, acceptance does not have to approve of *what is*. Rather, it requires the acceptance of the reality of *what is*. In life, we are limited in what we know and have only a limited amount of control. For that reason, we should be humble. Humility reminds us that we understand little about life. As Einstein said; "A true genius admits he/she knows nothing." We need to open our minds to new thoughts of acceptance and love that emanate from our inner consciousness.

Another important aspect of acceptance is that it allows us to open our minds to appreciating rather than judging. And it is in appreciation that we really find happiness. The definition of happiness in this book is that happiness is the acceptance and appreciation of *"what is."* When we try to control or judge what we encounter rather than accept, we ruin our potential happiness. Until the vice of control is abandoned, people will not know how to appreciate *"what is"* and how to increase happiness.

Relationships are a necessary part of finding worthiness in life. Relationships that are beneficial are those based upon acceptance, respect, trust, and good communication. We may not realize it, but the relationships we choose are with those people we perceive have a common interest and especially those we perceive make us happy to be with. A big factor in intimate relationships is infatuation. But without enough wisdom to consider what will happen when infatuation ends, people tend to get intimately involved and often overlook the faults of the other party. When infatuation does end and faults become irritable, or even before it ends, the maturity of the individuals will be tested.

Before allowing oneself to become infatuated with another person, there are some things to strongly consider. The first thing, for personal safety, is to know if the other person is respectful or even has self-control. The other thing is to realize that in initial meetings between people who are attracted to each other; both will likely be at their best behavior. Before getting involved further, please understand that what is seen initially is likely the best you will ever see. People sometimes change when facing a crisis, but do not count on it being in your favor.

With regard to health issues, think of the body as a vehicle that is there for the purpose of taking inner consciousness on a journey to fulfillment, and think of ego consciousness as the vehicle driver. The vehicle (the body) needs to be properly fueled, as unhealthy fuel will cause the vehicle to slow down or stop. Unfortunately, there are many unhealthy fuels that are very appealing or highly touted and some easy to get without much effort, so care is needed in the selection of fuel. Even when the vehicle is properly fueled, the parts need to be kept in good condition (through exercise).

That said, the big issue on the journey is the destination. Inner consciousness and ego can have different ideas on the final destination. If the ego assumes control, it will take whatever road looks most promising to ego's desires. The right road and proper destination will only be reached if the ego accepts the instruction of inner consciousness to stay on the road of virtue. But if inner consciousness does not make the effort to understand the road map of virtue, the road of virtue will be confusing, even to inner consciousness.

It is through prayer and acts of virtue, which provide self-worth, that inner consciousness knows the right road. The more prayer and acts of loving kindness are repeated, the better the focus on the road. Prayer can help the health of inner consciousness and of the vehicle, as well as help keep the vehicle on the right road.

PART IV

THE PATH TO FULFILLMENT

UNDERSTANDING

When life is confusing or we seem to have lost our way to what we hoped to be a happy and fulfilling life, we need answers to questions about life. What is it that truly brings satisfying happiness? What is it that causes anger and anxiety? What will make us feel better about self? There are so many questions about life and many answers given. There are, however, only a few basics that need to be understood to answer those questions.

Perhaps most important to understand is that our thought reality, formed by our beliefs and values, greatly determines the degree of happiness in life. If thought reality believes we are happy, we will be happy. But a happy thought reality does not just happen. Therefore, it is important for thought reality to know what will result in a happy thought reality.

For that reason, it is time to realize that happiness and joy are not a physical science. No scientific rationalizations have been able to provide a path to happiness and joy. That is because science continues to overlook purpose in life beyond physical reality. Thought reality, based upon physical science, overlooks the non-physical intangibles of virtue and vice, and the fact that the virtue of love is required for real inner happiness and joy.

It is virtue that brings order, joy and love, while vice brings chaos and eventual despair. The main choices we make in life are between virtue and selfishness (which leads to vice). The right choice is more apparent when that fact is understood.

Also important to thought reality's search for happiness and joy is an understanding of the need for acceptance. As was explained in this book, happiness, for thought reality, is dependent upon the acceptance of *"what is,"* although we do not have to like the reality of *"what is."*

Acceptance is the opposite of control. Thought reality focused on control and worldly success will always include some amount of worry and often disappointment.

Should we suffer from the mental pain of such things as anxiety, depression, fear, loss of hope, or loss of self-worth, we need to realize that mental pain itself is a message to us. Most often, it is telling us we are thinking in ways that are not healthy to inner consciousness and to happiness. It is letting us know that we need to better understand what it is that will relieve the pain and bring a feeling of self-worth to our thought reality.

Something else to understand is that having a purpose and living for a purpose is important for personal happiness and satisfaction. And if you believe there is a higher purpose for human life, or even believe that there is just a chance of a higher purpose, it would also be important to understand that there would likely be consequences after death for how life is lived in relationship to that higher purpose. But even if you do not now believe in a higher purpose for life, you should think about what you may have accomplished toward whatever your purpose in life may be.

In business, the item most critical to success is the bottom line. Most of us do not look toward the bottom line when it comes to the business of life. Each of us should ask ourself: "What will I have netted when my live comes to an end?" The answer will be different depending upon the acceptance or non-acceptance of life after death. For those who do not believe in an afterlife, the bottom line is often considered personal accomplishments which, in some way, will have a good effect on the world. And it is a good bottom line. But even that does not happen unless there is an effort to go beyond self. It does not come with selfishness. It comes with love and giving.

For those people who believe in an afterlife, the bottom line can be thought of as what has been accomplished in life for a higher purpose of some nature. It may be that the purpose was to help the world in some way. But, the bottom line for the independent consciousness of the higher level is what it has gained or lost with regard to the intangibles of virtue and vice. The interesting thing about this view is that even those people who do not believe in an afterlife, in working for the good of others, are also working on the value of virtue in their lives. Even if they are unaware, their inner consciousness is also working on increasing their acceptance of virtue.

Whether or not there is a belief in an afterlife, the bottom line that nets something worthy and allows people to feel good about their lives is living virtuously. Should any afterlife exist, it will be affected by the intangibles we take with us after physical death. If that is the case, all who live virtuously will be positively affected in the afterlife, Conversely, those who do not live virtuously will likely have a negative bottom line.

The basic understanding of life is: Virtue brings order and love. Vice brings chaos and despair. That is a basic we need to understand with all the choices we make in life. We need to remind ourselves of this simple understanding as often as we can, so it becomes part of everyday thinking.

In *Human Understanding*, we realize that real inner happiness and self-worth in this life, and any afterlife that may exist, will be based upon virtue, especially the virtue of love. The other option in life is vice, which begets chaos. We get to choose.

ACCEPTANCE AND DECISION

For some of us, there may come a time in our lives when we realize we are hurting others and ourselves due to our selfishness. With the understanding that we are the primary cause of our personal pain we may, with enough personal pain and realization of the pain we cause others, admit to having a problem. But understanding the problem and admitting that we have a problem will still not solve the problem. We must go beyond just admitting we have a problem. We must decide to make changes in our lives.

Please realize that if we make a decision to change things in our lives based just on how badly we feel, it is just another selfish decision. How many times has "I'm sorry" been said, and meant nothing in terms of real change? As long as selfish values remain in control, no real change will occur, no matter how great the pain. No change will occur as long as we worry about our feelings. And no significant change will occur until we learn to forgive others and ourselves. No real change is possible until we accept that we are the source of our problems. We are selfish, controlling, judgmental, and self-indulgent. But even acceptance of that fact means nothing unless it is followed by a decision to undertake whatever effort is required for real change.

The only real change that will be more than superficial is to change the value of personal thought reality from control and selfishness to acceptance and love. And the only way that can be accomplished is with a sincere commitment to a program that focuses purpose in life away from selfishness to love and acceptance.

Hopefully, when you are personally hurting in some way, causing hurt, or just want to be a happier person, you will remember some of what is written here. The path to personal peace begins with an acceptance and personal admission that you are the most significant cause of your own happiness or unhappiness, and that you are the only person who can change your level of happiness.

In *Human Understanding*, we realize that happiness in life requires accepting that we cannot control what happens to us in life. When we admit that we are not in control, we have the opportunity to improve happiness in our lives. But at that point, we need to make the decision to learn how to control ourselves. Until we do what it takes to gain self-control, real happiness will remain elusive. Should we make a decision to change thought reality from control and selfishness to virtue and love, it will only happen if we commit to doing what it takes to change. We get to decide what is most important to us.

COMMITMENT TO A PROGRAM

When we decide we want to accomplish something, it is still just a decision. Regardless of the seriousness of the decision and the motivation that others can give, success will only come if we are committed to do whatever it takes to follow through with that decision.

If we should decide to make significant changes in our lives, it will take more than just a promise. Any effort to change what we believe to be important to us will severely test our will power. The security of our present thought reality will not want to change. It will tell us to hold onto what we have come to believe and value. Friends and family members, who retain our old beliefs and values, may ridicule us. Therefore, when the time comes that we want to make changes in what we value and in our beliefs, it is important to have a plan for how we are going to accomplish the change.

The success of any major endeavor is generally based on a plan and the proper execution of that plan. Buildings have plans, businesses have plans, sports training programs have plans, generals have plans, and even successful thieves have plans. A successful plan is based upon proper understanding of the problems that will be encountered in achieving the goal. The plan then addresses the best way to overcome these problems and, along with practice and proper execution, makes the goal achievable.

The combination of proper planning, practice, and execution is called a program. When we face a difficult challenge in life, it is important to have a good program available to help us. The more difficult the goal, the more important it will be to have a well-thought-out program. When we desire to change a thought reality from the one of control to one of acceptance, it will be almost impossible to develop an effective program by ourselves.

To think we can do it on our own is our pride trying to remain in control. We only need to look honestly at what we have done for ourselves previously to realize we need help. We can blame others for our poor situations in life, but most of our personal troubles are the result of our poor understanding and our poor choices. If we are serious about changing our lives, we need to find a good program that is geared to what we want to accomplish and will provide positive motivation to guide us and we need to commit ourselves to that program.

I do not intend to present any specific program, although I make some suggestions that could be helpful, if not already included in the many programs available. Any additional suggestions I make are based upon the rational analysis of an engineer, not a psychiatrist. But the suggestions I make have been important to me and may be helpful to others. Perhaps the most important suggestion I can make is that it is important to image and contemplate on the importance of the desired change many times a day. Hopefully, the notion of the importance of imaging and repetition has been repeated often enough to become embedded in your thought reality. Major changes in purpose for life will only succeed with a commitment to constantly focus on the new purpose in life and values to be gained.

For many centuries, most people relied on religion and religious advice for thinking beyond personal wants. The help they were provided was likely as successful as the commitment, knowledge, and love of the leaders involved. Religious and lay programs and leaders have had both positive and negative effects on individuals and on society. The AA program is sometimes considered a religious program, but it is a spiritual program and not associated with any religion.

Today, there is greater understanding of human nature and what creates positive mental growth and change. This understanding exists in both religious and lay-administered programs. But the success of even modern programs depends on how they are administered. Mental wellness programs should empower participants to control themselves, rather than attempt to control the participants. Care should be taken in choosing a program. Whether mental wellness programs are religious or lay-administered, if the leaders do not help focus on acceptance and love, you might be wise to look elsewhere. There is a need for care in the choice of any wellness program.

The people who run mental wellness programs should be examples of love, caring, and encouragement. If a program is grounded in a loving purpose, but specific leaders are judgmental or selfish, it may be best to try groups where the leaders are less concerned about themselves. There is no need for more examples of judgment or control in our lives. Be careful not to confuse strict and caring leaders with selfish leaders who may not demand as much personal responsibility and effort.

Strict programs and leaders are not necessarily unloving. They may actually be more loving. They may just demand more personal effort. The greater the desire for control, the greater will be the effort needed to overcome it. If we don't want to make the effort required of the program, maybe we are not really committed to the program.

A good example of what a strict program, along with personal commitment, can do for a person is the TV show, *The Biggest Loser*. The tremendous loss of weight is obvious, but so is the effort required. A good program can help us do what we could not do for ourselves and make us feel good about ourselves. It can help the mind and the body and lead to self-worth and inner peace.

If not included in the program, I recommend meditation. Meditation can be helpful in times of inner conflict. Meditation has been shown to create structural and functional changes in the brain that could be helpful in restructuring how we think. However, meditation may be difficult to undertake, as the mind will not want to relax when the desire for control remains or when fear is present. Proper meditation normally requires lessons and practice to be successful. Should meditation be undertaken, it should still be only a part of an overall program.

Another suggestion is to record thoughts that seem important at the time (written or captured in a recording device) to better understand how thought reality will play mind games with our perceptions and our memories to hold on to, or even exaggerate existing beliefs and values. This becomes more obvious when we review specific thoughts a week, a month, six months, and even a year or two later. When we actually grasp the controlling and addictive nature of thought reality, we will be more willing to open our minds to new thought concepts.

Very important to effective change is volunteer work that requires giving of self. Although it is likely all successful improvement programs require it, volunteer work is so important I bring it up just to remind people how critical it is. Change has to actually start somewhere. Volunteering for the betterment of others is where change from selfishness to giving begins. In volunteering, we can begin to think and feel beyond feeling sorry for ourselves, which opens the mind to feelings of self-worth and of joy. Feelings of self-worth arrive with the appreciation of those people whom we have helped. In volunteering, we can also expose ourselves to the hardships and handicaps of so many people in the world around us and learn how lucky we really are.

When my first wife asked for a divorce, I was devastated. I felt sorry for myself and was confused about life as I had visualized it. I thought I had been a good husband and father. After a time of self-pity, I decided I had to get away from my thoughts about self. I committed myself to attending religious services each day and volunteering on Sunday at a home for elderly and handicapped people. It wasn't easy to begin, as it involved giving up watching the Packers on Sundays during the football season.

Fortunately, after eight years some of my prayers were answered and my volunteer time was changed. So I got to watch the Packers again. Growing up on logic rather than feelings, I really never thought much about the feelings and thought processes of other people and actually preferred not to deal with them. In volunteering in the nursing home, I was exposed to some real suffering and physical pain. I learned much about how other people feel and why. I also learned a lot about myself.

Among other things, I learned how good I really had it. I could walk. I could talk. And I could still think cognitively. But more importantly, I began to learn that many people function more on feelings rather than on logic. Only then did I begin to understand some of the patients' cares, fears, and frustrations, as well as their pleasures. I began to see other people's feelings as something important to be concerned about. And I began to understand why, even though great at engineering logic, I was poor in relationships.

I also learned I could get a good feeling by helping others. And I observed something that scared me. I observed how the virtues and vices of people's lifetimes are magnified in their old age. It made me think twice about my life. I am still the rationalist and still have a difficult time conversing with people whose thought processing centers on feelings. But I am now a better and happier person because of what I learned from volunteering.

Volunteering can bring about changes in what thought reality considers valuable. However, do not assume that just because you are doing volunteer work, you are changing. It may be that you are doing it to convince yourself you are changing while nothing else really changes. Real change needs to manifest itself in all you do in life.

In the process of change, there will be so many distractions. Thus, each of us needs to develop a method to effectively focus on any new purpose for which we are now living. We need to develop mental tools we can use a number of times each day and at times of severe temptation. Think of the example you want to be to others, especially those close to you. Focus on the personal satisfaction that comes with being able to control yourself. Focus on those you love and on what they should be able to expect of you. Focus on the concept that all you do is observable by your departed relatives who are now in the spiritual dimension watching you.

Focus on a mental image of the happiness you intend to bring to others by proper choices in life. Focus on the concept that our crosses, though difficult, are not as difficult as those people who willingly gave their lives so that we could have the good things we have today. People who believe in Christianity ought to focus on the cross. Whatever the focus is on, focus on it again and again and again and again every day. With a proper focus, new values can become habits of thought reality.

Another suggestion is to find a memento of sacrifice (personal, religious, family, or some other memento) and focus on it for 10 minutes a day, no less than two minutes at a time. At the same time mentally or orally slowly repeat: "I need to think more about other people and less about myself." Or repeat: "Help me to think more about others and less about myself." This can be considered a form of meditation. It would also be helpful to have a memento small enough to carry with you so that, in times of contemplation or temptation, you can look at it before coming to a decision.

A religion that stresses love, acceptance, forgiveness, and personal responsibility can function as a program for change for a person willing to follow the love and acceptance of the religion and actively give of self. It can also be a secondary wellness program that augments a lay-administered program. But realize that real commitment to a religious program requires more than attending services once a week. It requires that spirituality, which religion is supposed to lead us to, becomes part of daily life. In that quest, prayer will be helpful. The more we pray, the more thought reality will understand the importance of replacing selfishness with virtue.

Remember that help programs will not be perfect. Fallible people run recovery programs. The success of any recovery program, lay or religious, will be influenced by the example and enthusiasm of its leaders. But the actual cause of success or failure will be determined by the personal commitment to do whatever it takes to change. When we consider fasting, horsehair shirts, self-flagellation, and other forms of self-discipline, humans have used over the centuries to control themselves, what is normally required in help programs today may seem quite tame. However, real commitment may require mental decisions and abstentions that can be as difficult as physical torture. That commitment will only be possible with imaging new purpose and values that make the commitment worth the effort. Real change is not possible with a partial commitment. It must be total.

In *Human Understanding*, we realize that a significant change in life requires a commitment to a program focused on an intended outcome. Programs that will be most successful are programs that focus on learning to give up control of others and instead focus on self-control and on the need for acceptance, love, and self-discipline. Typically, we will not be able to set up and follow such a program without help. We need to seek programs appropriate for the changes we desire in our lives. Whether such a program is sponsored by AA, a church, a medical group, a doctor, or some other group, be sure that it focuses on love and on personal responsibility. Regardless of the program, change requires focus, focus, and more focus on what is to be achieved.

SELF-DISCIPLINE

The desire to change some everyday habits is easy to come by; doing it is difficult. To change thought habits, even temporarily, infringes on the security and values of present thought reality. Should we attempt to make major changes in our lives, we are fortunate if we have the support of other people to direct us and encourage us. But there are times we will be alone. If not alone physically, we will be alone in thought. Also, any attempt at change in what we value may also hindered by people with whom we normally associate, who do not approve of the change.

Major changes in how we live life are typically personal battles between our worldly wants and desire for self-worth and inner peace. The concept of how to successfully prepare one's self for a battle has been perfected through centuries of personal and civil warfare. It has produced saints, warriors, and even great empires. It is practiced to have control of self—mind and body. It is self-discipline.

Self-discipline is training in self-control. Discipline is not aimless. It exists for a purpose. The discipline of armies, as well as their leaders, has been the foundation of all successful empires. Self-control has always been important to those people we today refer to as great people, be they generals or saints or even master criminals. Even more important than observable success, self-control, established through self-discipline, increases self-worth.

When we have the self-discipline needed to do whatever we know we should be doing, regardless of how we feel, we believe in ourselves. When we believe in ourselves, we do not have to worry about what other people think. The point is that to win out against our difficulties, including our selfishness and insecurity, we need self-discipline. We must be able to deny those feelings and cravings that are destructive to us and to our goals and be able to do those things that are important for us.

A major problem with modern societies is that people have little reason to develop self-discipline. They have laws that protect people from themselves and from others, as well as conveniences that reduce the effort needed to accomplish something. There is no reason to exert oneself if there are easy ways to get what one wants. Why walk behind a lawn mower if you can ride on one? Why walk the golf course if you can ride? Yet looking at the people riding these pieces of leisure, it is obvious that many should probably be walking.

There is no reason for children to develop self-discipline if parents don't have any, or if parents or society do not make children take responsibility for their actions or inactions. The resulting lack of self-discipline shows up in many ways: the smaller number of people who will go out of their way for someone else, the fact that just saying yes or no can be an effort, the desire for instant gratification, and the number of people who live by the motto, "If it feels good, do it."

We even look to pills to lose weight rather than exercising or eating healthy. People today do not seem to realize that to personally mature, they need to be able to practice control over their desires and feelings so they will be able face and overcome major difficulties and challenges that occur in life. Be aware that self-discipline tends to fade with affluence and with reduced consequences for incorrect decisions. The easier life is for a person, the more that person needs to practice self-discipline or it will be lost when actually needed.

The quest to develop or maintain self-discipline should start by introducing it into daily life. Each day, do a number of things you do not like to do, but which you know you should. The best place to start is where you can immediately see and feel the benefits. Start with something reasonable and slowly proceed to something bigger and more loving. Start when you start the day. Make the bed each morning. Take some time to exercise each day, preferably at a fixed time. Take some time to pray a number of times each day.

In doing the minor things you don't like to do, little by little, you can begin doing other things you should be doing, rather than just satisfying your selfish wants. Forgo that extra snack you would like but really do not need. Lend a helping hand when an opportunity arises even if inconvenient. Do a little extra something each day that you do not feel like doing, but you know would be good to do. Practice holding positive thoughts rather than negative thoughts. Smile at people you do not know. Be cheerful even in tough times. Be careful not to litter. Volunteer for some worthy cause. Practice fasting if for no other reason than to practice self-control. Go to church to pray at least once a week even if you do not feel religious. Say some nice things about other people even if you don't have to. There are many opportunities to practice self-discipline if you really want to.

The more we work on self-discipline faithfully every day, the more it will become a habit. It is in developing habits we would like to have but haven't practiced, that we like ourselves more. We are in control of ourselves. We can say yes, or even no, when we know we should. Without self-discipline, we will not be able to say no to improper thoughts, wants, and feelings and we lose our self-respect and our self-worth.

Without self-discipline, we are much more likely to become addicted to something than if we had the self-discipline to say no. We need to make sure we control who we are in both thought and deed. The ability to curb unhealthy desires and to do what you know to be right is essential to self-worth and inner peace. Self-discipline cannot be gained by listening or with knowledge. It can only be gained through personal effort.

We can help teach the value of self-discipline through the examples of doing the right thing in spite of difficulty. We can also require those for whom we are responsible to do chores they don't want to do, but should. They need their own reasons to develop self-discipline. Learning to do what has to be done, in spite of feelings, will give those people a step up on others who have never developed any self-discipline.

My personal experience with self-discipline has been a difficult one. I found that people, including myself, tend to think they can replace self-discipline with knowledge of what they should do in every situation. The problem is knowledge does not always increase the ability to do what should be done. I had it good growing up, and affluence does not promote self-discipline. My life changed for the better when I committed to doing things for others to escape personal wants. I also committed to daily exercise. Until that time, I did not realize how important self-discipline was to feeling good about self. Unfortunately, old habits die slowly. But, the important thing is that in working on self-discipline, I am much more at peace with myself.

We can delude ourselves by believing that we can change habits and values at will. But most of us are locked into a thought process that limits our ability to go beyond our everyday comfort level. Without self-discipline, we become slaves to our worldly wants.

In *Human Understanding*, we realize it is our ability to do what we know is right—regardless of how we feel—that causes us to feel good about ourselves. That only happens when we put self-discipline into our lives. We need to work on self-discipline daily if we really what to be in control of ourselves and feel good about ourselves.

RESPONSIBILITY

I define responsibility as fulfilling obligations. The concept of love and acceptance teaches us that we must take responsibility for what we can do and for what we can affect. Yet, how often do we hear the words: "Why do any more than you have to" or "Let someone else worry about it"? Too many people feel their responsibility is limited only to what they have agreed to be accountable for.

There are different types of responsibility. Certainly, we must be responsible for that which we have agreed to. There is also an unstated responsibility to maintain all the good things we have been given, including intangibles such as freedoms and other rights. There is the responsibility to those people who depend on us. Another personal responsibility is to understand the purpose of our lives and living up to what we come to understand.

How often do we forget the price of the blessings we have in life? Everything we have is directly or indirectly related to other people, including our knowledge. Our education, our labor-saving appliances, and even our available opportunities are the result of the dedication, the sacrifices, the ingenuity, and the work of others. We have been given much. With being given much comes much responsibility.

The price we must pay is whatever is necessary to pass on to others what we have received and to hopefully improve upon it in some way. We fulfill this obligation by taking responsibility for our lives and for the lives of those with whom we are entrusted. That includes future generations. Too often today the attitude is that we are just here to enjoy what all those before us worked so hard for.

We cannot allow that feeling into our lives if we want to feel inner peace and self-worth.

Responsibility accepts that there is no such thing as a free ride. When we take without paying, we end up taking what really belongs to others. When we unfairly manipulate people to get things without properly working for them, we take from the goods, time, and effort of these people. When we abuse our power over other people for our own comfort, we are not much more than legal robbers. And if we are subsidized by the wealthy without the commitment to give back the best we can through personal effort, we are no better than the selfish rich.

When we demand an education but do not study, we are taking from the time and effort of those who financed us, as well as from those who were displaced in class. When we have children we are not prepared to handle, we take from those children and from their children. Responsibility requires that we work for what we want and what we get.

It would be helpful to visualize the concept that there will be ultimate justice. A friend doesn't play the lottery. He just isn't sure he wants to win as he feels that, should he win, there will be a price he will eventually have to pay, whether in this life or in some other. He believes that all things even out in the end. He may be out of his ever-loving mind. But then again, who knows?

What do you believe? Do you believe in an ultimate justice? Will there be a price to pay for what we receive in this life if we don't use our talents and opportunities responsibly? We might want to think about ultimate justice before taking much and giving little. We pay the price for what we are given by appreciation for and responsible use of our talents.

It is not that people shouldn't be rich. I believe rich people are required for a prosperous society. However, people need to earn their wealth through their own ingenuity and hard work, not through the hard work and ingenuity of others. That said, the need to earn your keep also applies to all people, not just the wealthy. Another responsibility of the wealthy is to realize that there are many people responsible for their good fortune, including all the people who directly or indirectly have monetarily contributed to their wealth, and to respond accordingly to those people rather than hoard wealth.

I present another controversy to think about. Which is the more responsible economic system, capitalism or socialism? I personally believe that if all people were responsible to the system, either system would work. The problem with economic systems is flawed human nature. In socialism, even though many people will be responsible, personal laziness, jealousy, and even greed of leaders ensure its eventual downfall. Capitalism eventually fails when the more industrious, creative, opportunistic, or even lucky people do not realize how blessed they are and look down on others as less deserving and do not take responsibility to help provide for the people that contribute to their wealth. Regardless of the type of economic structure, when a significant percent of the population considers self before overall responsibility, it will eventually lead to some form of social unrest. In any social environment, all members of the society must be responsible if that environment is to remain stable. It is moral responsibility for the good of all, not laws, that keeps governments functioning.

I might mention that capitalism could work better if the concept of trickle-down economics actually existed. The problem with capitalism is not that there are rich people. The main problem with capitalism is that the rich generally hoard the wealth and there is less and less for the remainder of an expanding population. The cry of the poor is to tax the rich more. While that may help the government income, it generally doesn't help money trickle down to the less wealthy. A creative solution to the problem would be responsible compromise. The wealthy get a reasonable tax rate and get to spend or donate what they earn. However, they would be surtaxed heavily on what they do not spend on domestic goods and services or do not donate. The surtax rate should be high enough that spending will occur and to keep a proper balance of wealth between the rich and others. It would also reduce the need for tariffs for more expensive items. Politicians need to open their minds to new responsible solutions to economic problems before it is too late.

In *Human Understanding*, we realize that one of the most responsible things we can do is to work on understanding true purpose in life. A better understanding of life comes with the realization we would be nothing without what has been given to us, including life itself. With that realization comes an understanding of responsibility to provide the best we can for those who are with us and those who will come after us. This includes knowledge and opportunity. If we follow through with this responsibility, we will find that acceptance and love, not selfishness and control, are the keys not only to our happiness but also the happiness of other people including future generations. The world moves forward only when people are responsible enough to give of themselves, rather than take for themselves.

Communication Challenges

People can be difficult. Even family members and people we think are our friends can be difficult when we do or say things they do not agree with. People can help bring about changes in life, but they can also make it more difficult, especially if they are people relied upon for survival or basic feelings of worth. Hopefully, if we try to make changes in our lives, we will have the support of family members and friends. But there will always be times that we will have to face difficult people. Therefore, it is important to understand how to deal with difficult people.

In communicating with difficult people, it is most important to understand why you may be treated rudely when making a change in values or even when trying just to make a point other people disagree with. To opinionated people, your choices and opinions may be considered a challenge to their view of what is important. When an opinionated person's beliefs, values, or purpose (thought reality) are perceived as being challenged, there is generally little middle ground for discussion. The closer you are to them, the greater they are challenged by you. Other people may subconsciously fear what you represent. And you must respect that fact rather than fight it. To argue your view is a waste of time and effort and even worse. It lowers you to a judgment level. Any argument may be viewed as a personal attack and likely worsen the situation.

In dealing with difficult (close-minded) people, it is important to recognize and respect that other people have a right to their own opinions, as much as you have to yours. You cannot expect other people to respect you if you do not respect them. Should you get involved in a discussion of views, be sure your points of discussion are offered as an opinion only—not fact, and listen to opposing opinions. No meaningful discussion can take place where differing absolutes exist.

By offering opinion only and listening, you allow room for discussion. Hopefully others will follow your lead. You can use such phrases as, "That may be, but I see things differently" or "I may be crazy but that's my opinion." For there to be a real discussion, there can't be anyone directly or indirectly saying, "I'm right and you're wrong." Discussion is an exchange of knowledge. Argument is an exchange of ignorance. This statement is attributed to Robert Quillen (American humorist 1867-1948) and quoted in *The School Day Begins: A Guide to Opening Exercises, Grades Kindergarten–12* by Agnes Krarup.

I have mentioned that I have had a difficult time with people who get wrapped up with their opinions and feelings to a point they are not open to calm, rational discussion. But I learned that by accepting that they cannot open their minds to another way of looking at things, I need no longer worry about getting my point across. And since I have begun to force myself to listen, I find that I still have some things to learn.

We normally think of communication in terms of speaking or writing. But speech or writing do not guarantee communication. We have all experienced talk that does not get through to us. Children do not listen to parents who do not live as they tell their children to live or who do not follow through on threats. We experience it with manipulative people or organizations which want something from us. We tune them out. Likewise, we tune out people who give promises we know will not be kept. What is said may be heard, but if it is not trusted, it will not be truly communicated. As Peter Drucker said; "The most important thing in communication is hearing what isn't said." (www.sourcesofinsight.com)

We all seem to hear better when we have reason to believe what is being communicated. Evil people are believed when they threaten, if they have shown they are evil enough to do what they threaten to do. Goodness is believed when the communicator has shown that he or she is a good person. Good communication requires that people be trusted as true to their word.

In addition, people who communicate enthusiastically are much more believable than people without enthusiasm. Enthusiasm presents the communicator as a person who believes in what he or she is saying. Enthusiasm also suggests that what is attempting to be communicated is of significant value. With enthusiasm, those being communicated with will more likely perceive there is something of value to be learned. In our example and our enthusiasm, we communicate to the world who we are and what we believe. When we communicate with honesty, goodness, enthusiasm, and fairness, we are trusted for what we say. If we are not sincere, about what we say, our words are likely wasted.

When people ridicule us for changes in our lives, or even for whatever life style or opinions we may have, we find out if we believe in ourselves. We do something important and profound if we communicate our acceptance of what we believe in the face of ridicule. We become an example of what we believe in. We actually communicate that our beliefs are important to us, even if other people are not listening by ear.

Sincerity and honesty in the face of ridicule will most often have some effect on the thought reality of those who ridicule us. Such acceptance may not help our situation directly, but it will always have a good effect somewhere in time. When we stay true to our beliefs and values in the face of ridicule, it will also increase our self-worth because we know we are doing the right thing. It will also increase the respect of others even if what we say is not respected or accepted.

In *Human Understanding*, we realize that not all decisions we make about our purpose and values in life will be applauded, because other people will often have different beliefs and values. We realize that in such situations, no argument will win approval. But we also realize we can make a case for what we believe by remaining true to our new or established values. Purpose in life is not something to be argued about. It is something to be lived. In living for a specific purpose we believe in, we communicate the value of what we believe, which will increase inner peace and self-worth.

Putting It All Together

E ach of us needs to take time to make sense of our lives. Why do we exist? What will make us truly happy? Are we just further-evolved animals? Is there life beyond death? There are an almost unlimited number of questions we can ask about life. The major question we need to ask ourselves is: Am I willing to open my mind to the possibility of a consciousness independent of physical consciousness, or will I choose to close my mind to facts and evidence that do not support my present thought reality?

In this book, we explore who we are, including how we function, how we learn, and what makes sense about consciousness. It is not intended to follow conventional scientific thinking about life because such thinking ignores that which it cannot explain. As an engineer, I need to look for a rational explanation about life that covers all issues, including those that science cannot explain.

If we open our minds to the concept of higher realities, there is an explanation for the otherwise unexplainable.

Science looks at the mind as a computer brain, but has no explanation for consciousness, especially consciousness that can choose to give up life for the benefit of others. If we look beyond what science says there is an explanation for consciousness and self-sacrifice. The explanation is that the brain does function as a computer as science proposes, but the brain is only one part of the human mind. In looking at the mind as having an independent inner consciousness as belonging to a higher reality of love, we have an explanation for such things as virtue and self-sacrifice. Inner consciousness can look at the value of intangibles of virtue such as love and realize there is more to life than physical existence.

A problem for the brain is that its basis for understanding relies on the correctness of personal thought reality. And personal thought reality relies on a limited amount of perceived information and the correctness of that information. The result is that human evaluations are more opinions that actual reality. To an engineer, opinions are not good enough. What is needed is fixed basics upon which brings about an understanding of life.

Effective knowledge is based upon understanding fixed basic principles. And, as I have stated, I also believe that all reality, including physical reality, has fixed basics and I have given much thought to understanding the fixed basics of human reality. Because an independent consciousness would be of a higher level of reality, a higher reality of love provides an explanation that answers the otherwise inexplicable—they are incorporated into the basics. The fixed basic principles I have listed herein are based upon the hypothesis that there is a Higher Level of love and that humans have an independent consciousness.

There are fixed basics applicable to physical reality as well as fixed basics that apply to all levels of reality. Those applicable to all realities I refer to as universal fixed basics.

The basic fixed principles I have come to accept hold regardless of the age of the earth, regardless of whether or not the preexistence of souls or reincarnation exists, regardless of religion, regardless of intelligence or education, regardless of any existence of more intelligent aliens, regardless of wealth, regardless of handicaps, and regardless of so many other controversial issues.

There are two fixed universal basics of reality. The first basic of universal fixed reality is the existence of a Higher Power of some nature, of which there is no human way to understand. I do not try to define the Higher Power, although I associate the Higher Power with the culmination of all virtue, which is love. The Higher Power is responsible for the existence of humanity and inner consciousness as well as all other levels of reality that may exist.

The second basic of universal fixed reality is the existence of virtue and vice. I believe, as did Aristotle, that virtue and vice are not relative, they are objective. And where there is virtue, there is always the possibility of vice. Virtue is responsible for order and joy and culminates in the highest reality that can exist—love. Vice is responsible for chaos and eventual despair. It is in the full acceptance of virtue that consciousness unites with the oneness of the Higher Power of love. It is the acceptance of vice that consciousness unites with despair. This universal fixed fundamental exists in all dimensions and all levels of conscious reality.

The third basic is that all living creatures are governed by a brain that operates much like a sophisticated computer. It searches for values which it learns with life experiences. With these experiences and any genetically passed on information, it forms the basic "thought reality" that governs how each creature evaluates and functions. Decisions of the brain are typically habitual and based upon perceived values and notions of thought reality. The thought reality of physical creatures is normally confined to physical values. However, where "thought reality" comes to incorporate an independent higher level consciousness, it also incorporates an understanding of the higher intangibles of virtue and vice, the decisions of thought reality can deviate from the values of the physical world.

The fourth fixed basic is that humans, and possibly many other intelligent creatures, have an independent consciousness of a higher level than physical reality. It is independent inner consciousness that can possess the intangibles of virtue and vice and introduces them to normal physical thought reality. It is inner consciousness that enables all creatures, which possess it, to make choices and to value what is beyond physical reality. Although inner consciousness is of a higher level, its awareness is through the physical reality and is influenced by the values and traumas of physical reality. But it is still in the higher level choices of virtue (what is loving) or vice (what is unloving) that inner consciousness influences whether we are selfish, unselfish, or somewhere between.

A fifth basic of understanding is that all creatures with consciousness have free will to do as they choose. Free-will choices are those that affect personal purpose and values for living, especially the choice between virtue and vice. The fundamental choice in life is between the fixed realities of virtue and vice—between love and selfishness.

The final fixed basic of human existence is that creatures who possess inner consciousness do take something when their physical existence ends. Surviving inner consciousness takes with it what it has gained or lost related of the fixed universal realities of virtue and vice. These exist beyond physical reality. Just as the body can accumulate things at the physical level, inner consciousness can accumulate things that exist beyond the physical level.

To simplify things further, we can develop a short, one-size-fits-all fixed thought reality basic. That which is loving and caring is good and will make us feel good about ourselves and bring inner happiness. That which is not loving and caring (selfish) is not good and will eventually result in unhappiness. Although this is an idealistic simplification, it is something that we should consider in all we do. The same simplification was given to humanity long ago in the form of the Great Commandments: "Thou shall love the Lord thy God with thy whole heart and thy whole soul, and thy whole strength, and thy whole mind. Thou shall love thy neighbor as thyself." The choices we make have consequences. It is the choice of love over selfishness that will result in fulfillment.

There is some additional understanding required for a happy and fulfilling life. These are not necessarily fixed basics, but come close. The first is a feeling of self-worth. For self-worth, it is necessary to do the right and most loving thing so often that it comes naturally. The second is learning acceptance. We need to accept and to appreciate *"what is,"* rather than to judge. The third is that we need to take care of ourselves physically and mentally as well as we can, while still accepting a higher purpose in life.

Although the simplified understanding of life presented in this book is based on logic and much research and can be helpful in happiness with life, it is in fact the opinion of one engineer. It should not be taken as a definitive understanding of life. Rather it should be considered a basis for thought for each person in deciding purpose and principles in their lives. It remains the responsibility of each person to decide for themselves their purpose in life and the principles they are going to live by. Hopefully and understanding of what is presented in the book will be valuable in that decision.

Once we have decided upon purpose in life and the basic principles we should live by, the next step is learning how to apply whatever principles we decide upon to our lives. As a friend said to me, "When it's all said and done, let's hope there is more done than said." This will not happen without personal responsibility and self-discipline.

If our choice in life is the reality of love, we will need help in focusing on the importance of love over selfishness--on spirituality. We need something to remind us of the importance of thinking and acting in unselfish ways. About the only thing in the world that keeps the reminding the world of the need for spirituality and love is the voice and morality of religion that is focused on love.

Religion is important to humanity. It is religion that establishes morality. Religion can also be very helpful to anyone wanting to improve their spirituality; that is if the focus of the religion is on love.

For those who accept a Higher Power, and even for the Buddhists who do not believe in a God, prayer is important. As pointed out in this book, prayer has power that we do not understand. But even without what prayer can accomplish, prayer keeps us in contact with the essences of love and encourages us to love. The more we pray, the more our minds focus on purpose beyond self, which is most important for personal happiness and peace.

Acceptance of the spiritual level of reality is important to us, not only because it exists and because it helps humanity to focus to purpose beyond self, but because it provides hope.

The path to understanding I have presented in this book is idealistic. Realistically few, if any, of us can reach total acceptance and unconditional love in this lifetime. We can only strive to be accepting and loving within our abilities and our situations, and with our limiting thought realities. Developing a thought reality based upon the concept on a Higher Power of love does not mean we should all put down our tools and hug one another. It does not mean we must calmly accept the fateful events in our lives. It does not mean we should not enjoy life and have fun.

Realistically speaking, we will continue to have old feelings and desires, some of which may be rewarding and some of which may bring grief. Because we are human, there is only so much we can actually change in our lives. But it is our obligation to try. I will be the first to admit that I cannot achieve the ideal I would like to achieve. I try, but at times I revert to old habits. Yet because I believe life is about learning, I believe spiritual growth is a process and that I, as a human, am expected to make mistakes in that process. Perhaps the biggest impact my new belief has had on my life is that I have learned acceptance and to appreciate *"what is."* Despite the difficulties in my life, I find myself happy and upbeat.

Life not about having worldly success and pleasure. Life is about learning to love and to forgive. In learning that love is about giving to others and forgiving others, we accept the love and the fulfillment offered by the Higher Power of love.

In *Human Understanding*, we realize the purpose for life is to accept love into who we are. Love is the most important reality of life. It is not important that we are great achievers in this world. What is important is that we make the effort to be as loving and accepting and forgiving as we can. The path to personal self-worth and happiness is love, acceptance, and forgiveness. The child is loved who continually makes the effort to improve. The greater the child's effort, the greater will be the admiration of the parent. Imagine oneself as a child of the Highest Power—a child who is loved. What a wonderful thought reality to have. It is a thought reality open to all humanity.

A Tree and Me
by R. J. Brust

I once looked at a tree and that's all I saw
I didn't notice how big or small.
I knew it lost its leaves in fall.
But it was just a tree, and that was all.

The concerns of my mind were all I could see,
Not this creation of God and all its beauty.
I was blind to the lesson of that tree,
As it spread forth a semblance of me.

We both started from others, yet gifts from our God,
I in a womb, the tree in a pod.
We are both dependent on all those around,
On the nearness of water, on the goodness of ground.

The light and the shadows that others give
Form us and shape us as long as they live.
But they do not control us. We can be free.
We can each have our own personality.

We can refuse to bud or produce sour seeds.
Or we can bear fruit to help other's needs.
Our limbs will grow big if we but reach out.
If we keep to ourselves, tiny limbs will we sprout.

We both have storms to weather in life,
And the further we reach the more we chance strife.
Yet the further we stretch, the more beauty we give.
To all those that within sight and shadow live.

With leaves or with smiles we can bestow
Comfort and beauty as further we grow.
And the further we reach, the more we have sight
As onward we grow toward the heavenly light.

I once looked at a tree. But what did I see?
Was it small? Was it like me?
As leaves change colors with the autumn time,
I now see the beauty that could have been mine.

But late though it may be, and though I am small,
I can still have my beauty. I still can stand tall.
I can stretch out and let smiles appear.
For as with the tree, there is a New Year.

ENDNOTES

(1) The actual methods that have been used for dating the earth's age have been found to be faulty. The majority of age analysis is performed using the potassium-argon (K-Ar) method. After Jonckheere and Wapnur published information on fission tracks that questioned the method, Naeser and Fleischer of Harvard calibrated that the method could be off by a factor of 60 or more.

As far as the K-Ar method of testing goes, it is based upon the assumption that 40Ar has escaped and is at zero. But that is not necessarily so. K-Ar tests on rock samples from the dome of Mt. Saint Helen conducted at Geochron Laboratories in Cambridge MA. gave ages of from 340,000 to 2,800,000 years

Geologists Davidson, Charlier, Hora, and Perloth in their article "Minerals, Osochorns, and Isotopic Fingerprinting: Pitfalls and Promise" (*Geology* 2005 Vol 33 No 1) noted that testing of crystalline portions of rock can be meaningless if the initial conditions of formation are not known.

Also according to Thomas Krogh and Donald David (Earth Science Dept./ Royal Ontario Museum) the isotopic composition of leachable material depends more on the cooling history and the annealing temperature of each host material than it does on their geologic ages. These are not known.

(2) The scientific accepted age has been mainly based upon measurement of radioactive decay expressed in terms of half-life. Robert V. Gentry noted that if radiometric methods were used to determine the earth's age, science fails to explain the small radiohalos in various minerals, which can only be explained by almost instantaneous hardening of rock rather than the millennia accepted by geologists. Geologists have no good explanation. The only good explanation for the small radiohalos is a much shorter existence.

(3) The London Hammer was found in 1936 in Texas. It consisted of a hammer with an iron head and a wooden handle and could be mistaken for a modern hammer except that it was found embedded in rock that is supposed to be 400 million years old by scientific dating and the iron in the hammer head contained no traces of carbon. All iron made in modern times has some amount of carbon in it. The hammer remains embedded in the rock. The handle has partially turned to coal.

(4) Sir Kenneth Robinson, English author, speaker, and international advisor on education. Also Professor Emeritus at University of Warwick .

(5) Dr. George Land Ph.D. Dr. Land was elected as senior fellow at Univ. of Minnesota and a fellow at New York Academy of Sciences for his outstanding contribution to science. In 1989, Dr. Land received the Outstanding Creative Achievement Award from the Creative Education Association.

(6) Solomon Eliot Asch (1907–1996)–Polish Gestalt psychologist and pioneer in social psychology in the United States. In 2002 Asch was ranked as the 41st most cited psychologist of the 20th century.

(7) Adolf Eichmann – German Nazi SS Lieutenant Colonel and Chief of the Jewish Office of the Gestapo during World War II. He was one of the major organizers of the Holocaust.

(8) Richard Leider, Founder of Inventure–The Purpose Company. Richard is recognized as one of America's preeminent executive life coaches. He is a senior fellow at the Univ. of Minnesota's Center for Spirituality and Healing. Richard is a National Certified Counselor and a National Certified Master Career Counselor. He is also chief curator of AARP's Life Reimagined Institute.

(9) Margarett Schlientz, Ph.D. in Psychiatric Nursing. Stories presented in a workshop on healing Feb. 1990 at Gesu Church on Marquette University Campus, Milwaukee WI.

(10) Dr. Ian Stevenson (1918 – 2007) - Former head of the Dept. of Psychiatry at the Univ. of Virginia and Director of the Division of Personality Studies at the Univ. of Virginia. Dr. Stevenson traveled extensively to investigate over 3000 cases of children remembering past lives. Though his investigations were ignored by the scientific community, the scientific community had no way to explain the cases in which birthmarks existed on children that mimicked the wounds that caused the death of the people they remembered being. The most interesting case being that of a child who remembered being a man named Maha Ram had multiple birth marks that mimicked the police photos pf a man named Maha Ram that was shot in the chest with a shotgun.

(11) Entanglement: A phenomenon in which the quantum states of two or more objects interact with reference to each other, even though the objects may be spatially separated.

(12) Dr. Helen Wambach (1925-1986) - Licensed psychologist noted for her demographic studies of past lives by hypnosis. She originally set out to disprove reincarnation exists.

(13) Dr. Eben Alexander - Academic neurosurgeon for 25 years including 15 years at Brigham & Women's Hospital and Harvard School of Medicine who had no belief in actual out-of-body experiences until he had one himself in 2008.

(14) PMH Atwater MD. LHD. PhD. (Honorary) - Researcher of nearly 7000 near-death experiences over 43 years. Among other award was a Lifetime Achievement Award from the National Association of Transpersonal Hypnotherapists. She stated "Every near-death incident I know had elements in it unknowable to the NDE that was verified and checked."

(15) As recently as 2014, and documented by the Discovery Channel, a teenage Buddhist named Rom Bahadur Bonjon sat still in the hollow of a tree without food or water for ten months. After that, he moved the location of his 6-year fast due to the publicity.

Theresa Neumann, who died in 1962, and who was under 24-hour surveillance for extended periods, ate nothing but a communion wafer once a day for the last 36 years of her life. She also had the stigmata and lost 6 to 8 pounds whenever she experienced the passion of Christ. But a week later, she would be back to her normal 121 pounds without having eaten anything. She said that her existence was to prove that man can live by the invisible light of God.

There are other Buddhist and Hindu people who have claimed they have not eaten or drunken anything for years. Prahlad Jani claims to have not eaten nor drunken anything for 70 years. He was recently tested for a period of 30 days without any sign of weakness and without any bodily discharge.

(16) Quote from James Finley while discussing his book *Merton's Place of Nowhere* about the life of Thomas Merton in a seminar at Sacred Heart Seminary, Hales Corners, Wisconsin in 1991.

(17) Dr. Athena Staik - Relationship consultant, author, educator& licensed marriage and family therapist.

(18) The story of the Prodigal Son comes from Luke 15: 11-32 in the Christian Bible. A short version of the story follows. A son asks for his inheritance before his father dies. He then wastes it in dissolute living and ends up feeding swine to survive, which was worse than his father treated his hired help. Realizing this he decides to return home and says to his father "I have sinned

against heaven and against thee. I am not worthy to be called your son." He was willing to be a lowly servant.

During his absence, his fatther continued to love him and often went out to a location where he can see a long distance down the road in hopes of seeing his son. When he does see him from afar he runs out to hug him and calls for a feast to celebrate for his son who was dead had come back to life; he was lost and was now found.

(19) Taoism - Belief originating in China based upon the *Tao Te Ching*. The *Tao Te Ching* is a classic Chinese text written thousands of years ago. One translation of *Tao Te Ching* means "The Classics of the Virtuous Way."

(20) J. Achterberg, K. Cooke, T. Richards, L. Standish, L. Kozak, and J. Lake, "Evidence for Correlations Between Distant Intentionality and Brain Function in Recipients: A Functional Magnetic Resonance Imaging Analysis."

(21) Information from Plato's *The Republic* (translation by William Scott and Richard Sterling).

(22) Origen of Alexandria (185-254) - Origen is considered a Doctor of the Church. and the person who introduced the concept of the Trinity. In his work *First Principles*, he presented the concept of the preexistence preexistence of souls, multiple age and the transmigration of souls, and the eventual restoration of all souls to a state of dynamic perfection in proximity to the Godhead. He was also the first person to use the term God/Man when referring to Jesus Christ.

(23) St. Paul is considered an apostle of Jesus, although he was not one of the 12 apostles. He was also a persecutor of the early followers of Jesus. But he was knocked off his horse and Jesus appeared to him in a bright light. He was then struck blind. But his vision was restored three days later by a disciple of Jesus. He became a believer and spent the rest of his life proclaiming the values now known as Christianity. He is also purported to be the author of about half of the Acts of the Apostles.

(24) Justinian, Eastern Roman Emperor (527–565) - Known as Justinian the Great, he sought to rebuild the greatness of the Roman Empire. Historically he was not a nice person. Procopius (500 – 565) in his *Secret History* (chapter 8) describes Justinian as "deceitful, false, hypocritical, never moved to tears by joy or pain, and a liar always, not only offhanded but when he swore sacred oaths to his subjects." In 532, when having serious dissension with his rule,

Justinian invited his detractors to the Hippodrome on the pretense of discussion. When they were assembled, he had the doors locked and the detractors killed. Although likely exaggerated, the number is said to have been as many as 30,000. Justinian, besides writing his own edict condemning Origen in 543, was paranoid enough to outlaw the teaching of philosophy in Athens in 529. Justinian had a personal reason to outlaw anything that would promote a belief in reincarnation, as people who so believed had no fear of opposing him. This was a man instrumental in determining doctrine in the early Christian Church.

(25) The controversy about the Council involves more than almost all the bishops attending being from the Eastern Roman Empire. The bishops of the Eastern Empire were appointed by the Patriarch of Constantinople, who was appointed by the Emperor, which in this case was Justinian, who had ruled for 24 years at the time of the Council. Additionally, the Second Council of Constantinople was specifically called to reverse some of what the previous council had approved, which the Justinian and Eastern Empire bishops did not like. Pope Vigilius, who was from the Western Empire, actually boycotted the Second Council of Constantinople. He did not give his immediate approval to the Council even after being imprisoned by Justinian. Eventually he did give his approval and was released.

A possible reason for the pope's approval and release may be associated with the Germanic tribes (Goths) that were threating to overrun Rome. Rome at that time was being protected by Justinian's troops. Did Justinian threaten to withdraw his troops unless Vigilius approved the Council? It is interesting that within months after Vigilius's approval, Justinian's troops defeated the Franks in the battle of Volturnus and Rome was saved. Another concern is that if one council can reverse a previous council, what is to be believed?

(26) Dr. Morse - Graduate of John Hopkins University. Medical degree from George Washington University in Washington D.C. Practicing pediatrician involved with the study of near-death experiences of children. He has written numerous books on the subject.

(27) Dr. Ken Ring - Professor Emeritus of Psychology at the University of Connecticut.

(28) H.F. Puthoff: PhD from Stanford; University American physicist with patents in the laser, communications, and energy field; co-author of the text book, *Fundamentals of Quantum Electronics* (Wiley 1969); director of a program for remote viewing at Stanford Research Institute 1972–1985.

(29) Dr. Andrew Newberg - Director of Research Myrna Brind Center of Integrative Medicine at Thomas Jefferson University Hospital. Dr. Newberg is particularly involved in the study of religious and spiritual experiences and the relationship among the brain, religion, and health. He is a coauthor of a number of books based upon his research. For his book, *The Mystical Mind: Probing the Biology of Religious Experience*, he received the 2000 award for Outstanding Books in Theology and the Natural Sciences.

(30) Dr. Brian Wiess - Graduate of Yale University of Medicine and Chairperson Emeritus of the Dept. of Psychiatry at Mount Sinai Medical Center, Miami, FL. In his book "Many Masters," Dr. Weiss, who originally did not believe in any life after death, found that by regressing people with phobias back to a previous life that was responsible for the phobia, the phobias could be overcome.

(31) Edgar Cayce (1877- 1945) - Known as "The Sleeping Prophet," Cayce would give cures and speak on other subjects while in a trance. At one point when in a trance, he spoke of reincarnation which conflicted with his Christian belief. He became confused with what he had related in the trance and refused to give more readings. Eventually he gave more readings and came to accept what he said in the trance state.

Cayce provided a description of the mental journey he would take in finding cures for various unknown ailments. A shortened version of his journey is as follows. As entered the dreamlike state he was at first enveloped in darkness from which came a light he followed. Along the path he followed he became aware of movement. At the first level he saw grotesque, nightmare like shapes. As he went further he saw misshapen human forms and forms with dark hooded robes. He noticed other forms moving downward. As he went further he saw forms moving upward and the color of the robes became lighter and more colorful. Then there appeared a vague outline of what could be described a physical, earthly reality, but it was completely empty. He went further the light grew brighter and he heard beautiful music along with laughter and singing. The further he went the more beautiful the music and colors. Eventually he reached the Hall of Records, which had no walls, and in which he received the information about the person whose illness he was to cure and what was to be done.

Something interesting to contemplate: Because of his insight into the unknown, Cayce was asked a number of questions on religion. One particular question is if Jesus was immaculately incarnated. Cayce replied yes and that so was his mother Mary, and that the two were actually one entity. Could this be so? Who knows what is possible beyond normal physical reality.

(32) Incorruptible bodies are bodies that do not decay as is normal for humans. There are various articles available to look at. Among others on the internet is one by Jim Dunning, who was on the team that researched the Shroud of Turin, and who published *The Incorruptibility of Saints*.

(33) St. Thomas Aquinas (1225–1274) - An Italian Dominican priest considered by many people to be history's greatest theologian and philosopher.

(34) *Summa Theological*, authored by Thomas Aquinas. Intended as a manual for beginners as a compilation of all the main theological teachings of that time. It is famous for its five arguments for the existence of God. Throughout his work Aquinas cites Augustine, Aristotle, and other Christian, Jewish, Muslim, and ancient pagan scholars.

(35) The calculation of odds is not difficult. An example is the Irish lottery, which requires picking numbers out of a pool of 42 numbers. The numbers do not have to be in sequence and no number can be used more than once. The odds are calculated as 42/6 x 41/5 x 40/4 x 39/3 x 38/2 x 37 or 5,245,786 to 1.

The odds of a monkey typing correctly 11 consecutive characters and spaces on a 42-key typewriter at one key per second would vary somewhat with other factors (such as proximity of keys to be incorporated in a sentence). However, ignoring that fact, the odds would be 42 to the 11th power, or 7.173682×10^{17}. The number of seconds in the universe (assuming 13.5 billion years) is 4.32×10^{17}. The odds of getting 14 letters and spaces correct would be 1 in 5.314×10^{22} or about 168 trillion years.

(36) Sir Fred Hoyle (1915-2001) - Noted English astrophysicist. Hoyle was the founder of Institute of Astronomy and Experimental Philosophy at Cambridge University, at which he was a professor. At one time he was considered the world's top astrophysics theorist.

(37) Mark Waldman is considered one of the world's leading experts on communication, spirituality, and the brain. He has worked with Dr. Newberg and authored and coauthored numerous books on these subjects. He has a number of shorts on the subject on the internet. He recently received the Distinguished Speaker of the Year from the Mind Science Foundation.

(38) Zoroaster was a prophet believed to be from what is now Iran. Specifics of his place of birth, when he was born, and even his life, are not known. He is said to have had a revelation from a spirit at the age of thirty and other revelations later. Much of Islam is based upon his revelations.

(39) *The Great World Religions: Hinduism* is a book published by The Great Courses. The author of this book is professor Mark Muesse, Ph.D. Dr. Muesse
earned a masters of theological studies (1981), a Masters of Arts (1983) and a
Ph.D. in the Study of Religion (1987). In 1988, he became Assistant Professor
of Religious Studies at Rhodes College in Memphis Tennessee.

(40) Guatama Buddha (563 B.C 483 B.C) was originally a prince named Siddhar-
tha Guatama. Seeking a life of holiness, he gave up his possessions and went
to live as a hermit and escape the pain of the world. Eventually he gave
up that life for meditation and realization and reached the state of enlightenment. He is considered the Great Buddha. Information from the book
Great World Religions: Buddhism with Professor Malcolm David Eckel and
published by The Great Courses.

(41) This statement is condensed version of the words used by professor Bart D.
Ehrman in "The Diversity of Early Christianity" found in *Lost Christianities:
Christian Scriptures and the Battles over Authentication* (published by The Great
Courses.) Written by Bart Ehrman, Ph.D. - Professor and Chair of the Dept.
of Religious Studies, University of North Carolina at Chapel Hill.

(42) For those people wanting an overview of why scholars do not think the
Gospels were written by the apostles, the *Oxford Annotated Bible* would
be a good place to start, although there is much information as to why on
the internet.

(43) According to the book *Lost Christianities: The Battle for Scripture and Faiths We
Never Knew* by Bart D. Ehrman (Oxford University Press), authors of early
Christian writings used the names of the followers of Jesus to give credibility
to what they wrote.

(44) According to Tibetan writings, first made know to the Western World in1894,
Christ (known in India and Tibet as St. Issa) left Israel the age of twelve,
partly to avoid a religious requirement for Jewish boys to get married. He
supposedly went to India where he studied the Vedas and preached against
the caste system. He eventually fled to Tibet to avoid being killed for his
teachings. In Tibet, he studied Buddhism and worked miracles, including
raising people from the dead, before He went back to Israel, where he was
crucified by the Romans. He was not labeled a Buddha only because he was
not a teacher with a following while in Tibet. At the time the writings were
labeled a hoax, without being examined, and pretty much forgotten about.

The existence of the ancient manuscript and famous people who
authenticated its existence and what it said was well documented by

Elizabeth Clare Prophet in the book, *The Lost Years of Jesus: Documentary Evidence of Jesus' 17- Year Journey to the East*. The main authenticators were Nicholas Roerich and Swami Abhedananada, who could read the Sanskrit manuscript. Roerich's son, who was trained at Harvard in Oriental languages, accompanied Nicholas. Roerich himself was nominated for the Nobel Peace Prize three times and led the US and 20 other Pan-American Nations into signing the Roerich Pact of 1935. He was also instrumental in having the great seal placed on the dollar bill.

Swami Abhedananada lectured on the Hindu Veda in the US and Canada from 1897 to 1921. In 1922, he visited the Hemis Monastery and authenticated the manuscript. A most interesting fact is that Swami Abhedananada was a close friend of Mueller's, who was the most ardent voice in declaring the manuscript a hoax, even though he never saw it. The last manuscript authenticated viewing was by Madame Elizabeth Caspari. Dr Caspari was for years considered the world's foremost authority on the Montessori Method of education.

You can think what you like about this story, but as an inquisitive person, I have always wondered why Christ spoke in parables, which were traditionally Eastern; why someone who amazed his teachers at the age of twelve and told his mother that he needed to be in the place that belonged to his Father (Luke 2:49), was not heard of again for 18 years; why John, a cousin of Jesus' did not recognize him, when extended families were traditionally close; and why the Magi from the East are called "wise men." It could be that Jesus was off about his father's business somewhere else.

It is interesting how this story inadvertently combines Judaism, Hinduism, Buddhism, and Christianity. It is a controversy interesting to contemplate. It is more interesting when it is realized that the beginning of the gospel of St. John appears to have been taken from the Hindu Vedas and the fact Jesus (called Issa) was recognized as a saint by the Hindus.

(45) Sana'a Manuscript is the oldest Quranic manuscript known to exist. Found in 1972 during the restoration of the Great Mosque of Sana'a, it has been dated to 671 A.D. with 99 percent accuracy.

(46) After the death of Muhammad, Abu Bakr became the first Caliph, which created a disagreement that eventually led to the Sunni Shai split. The contention is that Abu Bakr and Umar ibn Al-Khattab conspired to have Abu Baker named Caliph rather than Ali, the young cousin of Muhammad who was raised by Muhammad. Umar became the second caliph as directed by Abu Bakr before he died. The Sunni claim that Umar was a usurper whose legacy was created by the next caliph 'Uthman ibn Affan.

Umar appointed 'Uthman to be the next caliph upon his death bed. The governing rulers agreed to appoint 'Uthman as they had lived well under Abu Bakr and Umar. 'Uthman (644–656) was known for lavishly bestowing rich presents and estates and high ranks to family members. The integrity of 'Uthman is questionable. The excesses eventually led to a revolt in which 'Uthman was assassinated. The revolt led to Ali being appointed the 4th caliph. However, that did not sit well with the greater family of 'Uthman and a civil war ensued, which led to the Sunni Shia split.

(47) Documented plans for mosques in both Iraq and Egypt as late as the 8th century had sanctuaries that did not point to Mecca, which conflicts with the direction of prayer (Qibla), supposedly required in the Quran as of 624AD. According to chronicler Jacob of Odessa, as late as 705 AD., Egyptians were not praying toward Mecca. Also, early quotations in the Dome on the Rock differ in detail from that which is found in the Quran today. Study of the early rock inscription in the Negev Desert suggests that Islam may not have been what is known today, but could have developed into it. The strangest thing is that is spite of numerous old inscriptions, the name of Muhammad is not found on any inscriptions until almost 60 years after his death in 690.

(48) Richard Bushman is an American historian and Gouverneur Morris Professor of History at Columbia University. He was the Howard W. Hunter Visiting Professor in Mormon Studies at Claremont Graduate University 2008-2011. He serves as one of three editors of the Joseph Smith Papers.

(49) Taken from the blog of Ronald L. Conte Jr., Roman Catholic theologian and bible translator. See http://roconte.wordpress.com/2011/07/10/salvation-for muslims

(50) Synopsized from the Old Testament Book of Wisdom
a. 7:8 - This I valued more than kingdom or throne; I thought of my riches in comparison.
b. 7:10 - I treasured wisdom more than health or beauty, preferred her to the light of day; Hers is a flame that never dies down.

(51) The Holocene Temperature Conundrum. Z. Liu, J. Zhu, Y. Rosenthal, X. Zhang, B. Otto-Bliesner, et al, in conjunction with numerous universities in the United States, United Kingdom, and China.

(52) Most models showing the climate is much warmer at present than any time in thousands of years, and that the rise in the earth's temperature is unprecedented, are based upon a limited amount of data collected and interpreted in the latter half of the 20th century. Because of the unknowns, more

recent and more sophisticated investigations have been undertaken as related to the northern hemisphere above 30° north. The results were put together in a paper entitled "The extra-tropical Northern hemisphere in the last
two millennia: reconstructions of low-frequency variability" by B. Christian,
Danish Meteorological Institute Copenhagen, Denmark and F. C. Ljungq-
vist, Department of History, Stockholm, University Stockholm, Sweden. The
analysis of this more recent data shows the variability of the climate is much
more radical than previously thought. It also shows a very rapid increase in
temperature between 950 and 1000 that brought temperatures as high as or
higher than they are at present.

(53) An example of the headlines declaring a new ice age was the April 13, 1973
headline of the *Chicago Tribune.* "The Ice Age Cometh: The System That
Controls Our Weather."

(54) According to the "Windows to the Universe" presented by the National
Earth Science Teachers Association, space weather affects earth's weather.
Also, a growing number of scientists are beginning to accept the contention
of Danish astrophysicist Henrik Svensmark that climate is highly influenced
by galactic cosmos rays (GCR), the intensity of which can change. The decrease of the earth's magnetic field by 15% in the past 200 years has had an
effect the radiation reaching the earth.

(55) Jonathan Schooler Ph.D. (Born 1959) - Psychologist and professor of
Psychological and Brain Research at the Univ. of Calif. Santa Barbara.

(56) Andre Papineau SDS, is a priest and also professor of homiletics at Sacred Heart
School of Theology in Hales Corners Wisconsin.

(57) From *Daily Mail*, e-publication March 29, 2016.

(58) Salvatore Maddi, is a psychologist at the University of California, Irvine.
Salavtore followed 430 employees when the company they worked for fell
apart. A third of them did well. It would be easy to assume these were the
workers who'd grown up in peaceful, privileged circumstances. It would
also be wrong. Many of those who did best had had fairly tough childhoods.
Childhood stress, then, had been good for them; it had given them something
to transcend.

(59) Thomas Merton, OCSO (1913 – 1968) was a Trappist monk of the Abby of
Gethsemani, Kentucky. He was also American Catholic writer and mystic, as
well as a social activist and student of comparative religion.

(60) Locust plague of 1873-1877 in Nebraska, Kansas, and Western Iowa, Missouri, and Minnesota. Aptly recorded in *The History of Henry and St. Clair County, Missouri 1883*, National Historical Company, St. Joseph Missouri, the locusts visited from the first week of May until the first of June and during that time, "every spear of wheat, oats, flax, and corn was eaten and all the vegetables received the same treatment." On April 26, 1877, Governor Pillsbury of Minnesota declared a Day of Prayer for the plague to end.

(61) Scientific study by Boguslaw Lipinski, PhD, Sc.

(62) From June 7 to July 31, 1993, up to 4000 participants of Maharishi Mahesh Yogi's Transcendental Meditation and TM-Sidhi programs gathered in Washington DC for a Government Global Demonstration project. The study presenting the findings was published in the *Journal of Social Indicator Research*. A report on the project was given by its director Dr. John Hagelin and is available to on the internet Found under John Hagelin, Institute of Science, Technology, and Public Policy, "The Power of the Collective."

(63) Article published in Journal of General Internal Medicine, Vol.30(4) Dec. 2014.

(64) "The Hidden Dangers of Soy Allergens" by Kaayla T Daniels, in *Nexus Magazine* Aug. - Sept. 2004.

(65) Irving Stone is a noted American writer who received an honorary Doctorate of Letters from the University of California – Berkeley. Prolific writer of fiction and nonfiction mostly based upon historical figures, many of which have been made into movies, such as *The Agony and the Ecstasy*. Quote from article on www.scott.net Dec. 9, 2012, "High-Dose IV Vitamin C Kills Cancer Cells."

(66) Dr Frederick Klenner (1907–1984) was a pioneer in the usage of high dosage intravenous vitamin C. Dr. Klenner was a Fellow of the American Collage of Chest Physicians, the American Association of the Advancement of Science, and one of the founders of the American Geriatrics Society. He was initiated into the Orthomolecular Medicine Hall of Fame. Dr Frederick Klenner writes about the significance of high daily intake of ascorbic acid in preventative medicine. *Journal of the International Academy of Preventative Medicine* 1:45-69.

(67) M. Zurieck (1950) writes about the treatment of shingles and herpes with intravenous vitamin C. *Journal des Practiciens 1950* 64:586 PMID: 14908970.

(68) Study by researchers from Boston University School of Medicine published by the American Academy of Neurology found a link between physical fitness and brain size.

(69) Dr. Al Sears is a graduate of Univ. of South Florida's College of Medicine; graduated with honors in Internal Medicine, Neurology, Psychiatry, and Physical Medicine. President of American Academy of Anti-Aging Medicine. *P.A.C.E.—The 12-Minute Fitness Revolution*, published by Wellness Research & Consulting Inc. ,2010.

(70) John Hagelin, PhD is a quantum physicist, science and public policy expert, educator, author, and president of the David Lynch Foundation. Recipient of the Kilby Award, which recognized Dr. Hagelin as a scientist in the traditio of Einstein, Jeans, Bohr, and Eddington.

ABOUT THE AUTHOR

Robert J. Brust is a respected structural engineer known for his ability to quickly and accurately analyze problems and arrive at creative, workable solutions. He grew up learning to use logic and to forgo emotions. His mother, although she had eleven children, never got angry. Instead, when problems arose, she would address them rationally and calmly. She instilled the concept of using reason and logic, not emotions, in all aspects of life. This upbringing helped the author to approach life and problems rationally rather than emotionally, but made him rather stoic. After the death of a son and a subsequent divorce, the author was troubled with his understanding of life. His solution to the dilemma was to find a rational understanding of life. What he discovered is that life is not all that rational.

The author's life experiences have been diverse: playing sports, running a trap line, riding the ice flows on the spring floods, raising bees, gardening, raising and butchering animals for food, hunting, golfing, coaching youth basketball and baseball, collegiate swimming, competitive sailing, college student counsel, honorary fraternity president, professional society president, refereeing college intramural sports, cub master, scout master, church lector and cantor, and volunteer.

He started a successful engineering business and has spoken nationally on engineering subjects. The author has worked on engineering projects from Florida to Oregon and from Massachusetts to Arizona. In Chicago, he worked on many noted projects, including the exterior of the Mercantile Exchange Center as well as renovations at of the Hancock and Sears building plazas.

He has been a guest speaker to the Chicago High Rise Committee. In New York City, his last projects were as a peer review engineer for the Central Park Police Station (completed in 2013) and a designer of unusual concrete shoring for an extension of the subway system. He is also a two-time cancer survivor.

In volunteer work, family, friends, extended family, and self-examination, the author observed or has been directly or indirectly involved with people suffering from depression, alcoholism, drug addiction, emotional issues, illness, and Alzheimer's, as well as anger, anxiety, and fear. In the process of searching, the author spent years of weekends helping and praying with the physically and mentally disabled, as well as with the dying. He has also studied the basics and histories of the major religions and a few others. All these experiences, and years of analysis, have led to good understanding of how people, including himself, try to attain the elusive feeling of self-worth and happiness. They have also led him to make spirituality an important part of his life.